Will Guy, Zdenek Uherek, Renata Weinerova (eds.)

Roma Migration in Europe: Case studies

Institute of Ethnology
of the Academy of Sciences
of the Czech Republic
(Prague)

LIT

Will Guy, Zdenek Uherek, Renata Weinerova (eds.)

Roma Migration in Europe: Case studies

LIT

Bibliographic information published by Die Deutsche Bibliothek
Die Deutsche Bibliothek lists this publication in the Deutsche
Nationalbibliografie; detailed bibliographic data are available in the
Internet at http://dnb.ddb.de.

ISBN 3-8258-6995-4

© LIT VERLAG Münster   2004
Grevener Str./Fresnostr. 2   48159 Münster
Tel. 0251-23 50 91   Fax 0251-23 19 72
e-Mail: lit@lit-verlag.de   http://www.lit-verlag.de

Distributed in North America by:

Transaction Publishers
New Brunswick (U.S.A.) and London (U.K.)

Transaction Publishers   Tel.: (732) 445 - 2280
Rutgers University   Fax: (732) 445 - 3138
35 Berrue Circle   for orders (U. S. only):
Piscataway, NJ 08854   toll free (888) 999 - 6778

Contents

Foreword

In recent decades the theme of Roma migrations has become the subject of many meetings at all kinds of level in both national and international contexts. In 2000 the Institute of Ethnology of the Academy of Sciences of the Czech Republic joined discussions on the theme by holding an international round table in Prague under the title "The Roma Migration in Central Europe; trends"[1]. The impulse for the organisation of the event was the one-year RB 22/8/00 grant allocated to the Department of Ethnic Studies of the IE AS CR by the Grant Agency of the Czech Ministry of Foreign Affairs.

The main aim of the academic meeting was to map the current migration activity of Roma in the countries of post-communist Europe and its connections with the situation in European Union countries. Experts from Hungary, Romania, Bulgaria, Yugoslavia, the Czech Republic and Great Britain accepted invitations to the round table. The meeting was also attended by representatives of governmental and non-governmental organisations based in the Czech Republic.

The round table provided the basis for the setting up of a research network of leading experts which then monitored the migration situation of Roma in selected areas of Central, Eastern and Western Europe on a running basis. The specialist studies presented at the Prague meeting were updated[2] in the course of the next two years, and edited for publication by the organisers of the round table together with the British expert on Roma studies Will Guy, who did much to ensure the linguistic standard of the book.

We offer readers a set of articles that are attempts to identify the current situation and trends in migration on the territories of Central, Eastern and Western Europe, as these have been affected since 1989 by the fall

---

[1] The round table was held on the 24th-25th of November 2000 in Prague at the Lanna Villa, which belongs to the Academy of Sciences of the Czech Republic.
[2] Continuing co-operation with members of the research network focused on Roma migration took place in the framework of the Programme for the Support of Targeted Research and Development project S9058101.

of communist regimes and consequently more precarious social situation of Roma communities.

Zdeněk Uherek
Renata Weinerová   Prague, March 23rd 2003

Brief notes on contributors

Dragoljub Acković PhD is a prominent campaigner for Romani human rights in Yugoslavia and throughout the world. Being a Roma, his interest and commitment in this field is natural. As the author of several books dealing with the life and problems of Roma worldwide, he was invited in 1997 to join the Romani and Yugoslav PEN club. Since 1997 he has also been a member of the Association of Writers and has participated in many international conferences on the Romani people, including the last three World Romani Congresses held in Göttingen, Warsaw and Prague. From the second to the third Congress, he served as President of the Romani World Organisation's Commission for War Reparations and at the fifth World Romani Congress in 2000 was elected as member of the Romani Parliament for Yugoslavia. Dragoljub Acković has published his work through the Commission for the Study of Romani Life and Customs (SANU), of which he has been an active member since its foundation.

Míťa Castle-Kaněrová was Senior Lecturer in Social Policy at the University of North London until 1999, when she left to work with Roma refugees returning to the Czech Republic as project manager with the International Organisation for Migration (IOM) in Prague. Since 1998 she has been a Visiting Professor at Charles University in Prague. She is currently working as a consultant for the Romani project RRAJE in Slovakia, sponsored by the UK Department for International Development (DFID).

Eva Davidová PhD is an ethnologist and ethno-sociologist, researcher on folkore and gypsiologist. She lectures in Romani studies at the South Bohemian University in České Budějovice while also working at the Museum of Romani Culture in Brno, which she helped to found at the beginning of the 1990s. In her research and publications she focuses on the traditional and changing life and culture of Roma in the Czech lands and Slovakia, and their folk music and song. She has published widely and has created an extensive archive of Romani songs and photographs.

Will Guy PhD lectures in sociology and is a member of the Centre for the Study of Ethnicity and Citizenship at the University of Bristol, where he is also a member of the editorial board of the international journal Ethnicities. In the early 1970s he carried out doctoral research on the Czechoslovak Communist assimilation policy for Roma, followed by further research among itinerant Travellers/Gypsies in Scotland. At the first World Romani Congress in 1971 he interpreted for the Czech Roma delegation and was an observer at the fifth Congress in Prague in 2000. He makes regular research trips to Central and Eastern Europe and lectures on structural changes in the region since 1989 and on Romani issues. In recent years he has carried out evaluations for the European Commission of Roma integration programmes in the Czech Republic, Slovakia and Hungary and has also worked for the Council of Europe. His writings include an edited survey of post-communist Romani experience – *Between Past and Future: the Roma of Central and Eastern Europe*, (University of Hertfordshire Press, 2001).

Ilona Klímová studied for her PhD in International Relations at the University of Cambridge, specialising in the Romani voice in world politics. She has published several articles on Romani issues, co-authored a chapter analysing the fifth World Romani Congress in the book edited by Will Guy, *Between Past and Future: the Roma of Central and Eastern Europe*. Ilona Klímová has also co-edited a special journal section on Romani migrations for the *Cambridge Review of International Affairs* (Centre of International Studies, University of Cambridge, spring/summer 2000, vol.XIII, no. 2) and a special issue of the *Nationalities Papers* (vol. 31, no.1, 2003) on the same topic. Since 2000 she has been co-operating as a rapporteur and analyst with the Contact Point for Roma and Sinti Issues at the Organisation for Security and Co-operation in Europe (OSCE).

Roman Krištof is currently director of the Office of the Council for Roma Community Affairs at The Office of the Government of the Czech Republic. In 2001/2002, he served as a member of the Specialist Group on Roma/Gypsies at the Council of Europe. Previously, in 1999, he was editor of *Romano hangos*, the bi-weekly journal of the

Association of Roma in Moravia and during 1997 and 1998 worked as manager of the Roma Section of the Helsinki Citizens' Assembly.

Elena Marushiakova and Vesselin Popov work at the Institute of Ethnology of the University of Leipzig and also at the Institute of Ethnography and Museum of the Bulgarian Academy of Sciences. They have written extensively on Gypsies in Bulgaria, the Balkans and Eastern Europe, including the recent book – *Gypsies in the Ottoman Empire* (University of Hertfordshire Press, 2001) and are also involved in publishing collections of Romani folklore. Currently they are conducting extended field research in the former Soviet Union. In 1998/1999 they organised an exhibition in Budapest on Roma in Central and Eastern Europe and in 1995 created the Roma Heritage Museum Fund at the National Ethnographic Museum in Sofia, establishing the first museum-based exhibition on Gypsies in Bulgaria. They founded the Society for Minority Studies/Studii Romani in 1991.

Csaba Prónai PhD, is a lecturer in the Department of Cultural Anthropology at the Eötvös Loránd University, Budapest and a researcher at the Minority Research Institute of the Hungarian Academy of Sciences, holding an MA in history, cultural anthropology, Hungarian language and literature, and aesthetics. His interests include the history of anthropology and the development of anthropological theory, especially in relation to Gypsy studies. Recently he edited a series in Hungarian translation *Cigányok Európában – Kulturalis Antropolóiai Tanulmáyok* (Gypsies in Europe – Cultural Anthropological Studies) (Új Mandátum, 2002). He is also author of the Hungarian textbook *Cigánykutatás és kulturális antropológia* (Gypsy Studies and Cultural Anthropology) (1995).

Zdeněk Uherek PhD is Deputy Director and Head of the Department of Ethnic Studies at the Institute of Ethnology of the Academy of Sciences of the Czech Republic. He specialises in the study of migration and ethnic processes, and lectures on the theory of ethnicity and ethnology at the Faculty of Arts of Charles University and on migration theory and urban anthropology at the Faculty of Humanities of the University of West Bohemia in Plzeň. He is a member of the research boards of the Faculty of Arts at Charles University, the

Institute of Ethnology of the Academy of Sciences of the Czech Republic and the Institute of Ethnology of the Slovak Academy of Sciences. He also sits on the editorial boards of the journals *Český lid* and *Slovenský národopis*, as well as serving as a member of the Czech Ministry of the Interior's Commission for the Integration of Foreigners and Relations between Communities. He has carried out research in Central and Eastern Europe, the Balkans and Central Asia.

Renata Weinerová was awarded a PhD for her study of Romani sustenance and nutrition in former Czechoslovakia. After completing her studies in ethnology at the Faculty of Arts of Charles University she was employed in Prague from 1985 to 1987 as a social welfare advisor for Roma. Since then she has worked as a member of the Department of Ethnic Studies at the Institute of Ethnology of the Academy of Sciences of the Czech Republic and from 1995 to1999 lived in Pakistan. In 2000 she was involved in organising a roundtable on Romani migration in Central Europe for the Academy of Sciences and currently specialises in Romani migration and ethnic processes in Central Europe. Meanwhile she also works as an external consultant for the *Socioklub* association and the UNHCR in Prague. She is a member of the research board of the Institute of Ethnology of the Academy of Sciences of the Czech Republic and is a member of the Academy of Sciences' Grant Agency subject committee for social and economic sciences.

The current academic debate on the political aspects of Romani migrations and asylum seeking[1]

Ilona Klímová

Roma migration in context

Although Prussia had concluded bilateral agreements with nine[2] other countries aimed at stopping Romani nomadism as early as 1906 and Switzerland had unsuccessfully proposed arrangements to its four neighbouring countries for exchanging information on Roma to regulate their movement in 1909 (Fraser 1992: 250, 253), Romani migrations have not been of much concern at international level until very recently. While states have been devising various measures and laws to deal with the movement of Roma since their arrival in Central and Western Europe from 1430 onwards (Fraser 1992: 85), it is only during the last decade of the twentieth century that this issue has appeared on the agenda of international organisations. Westward surges have been a recurrent trait of the European history of Roma, but since the Second World War international Romani migrations involved greater numbers than before. Nevertheless, they were not unique and mirrored the movement of other people. These started with war-time displacements and their reversal and transfers of people and territory between states, and continued with movement of *gastarbeiter*, mostly from the countries of former Yugoslavia (Fraser 2000: 17), and of asylum seekers from the rest of the Eastern bloc to Western Europe (Matras 2000: 34).

It was only with the ending of the Cold War in Europe that international Romani migration attracted attention as a specific phenomenon.[3] The resurgence of racially motivated attacks alongside

---

[1] Article written in 2000: see Postscript above.

[2] Austro-Hungary, Belgium, Denmark, France, Italy, Luxembourg, the Netherlands, Russia and Switzerland.

[3] For example, since 1993 the Romani issue has been at the heart of the work of the Council of Europe's European Committee on Migration (CDMG) within which the Committee of Ministers set up a Specialist Group on Roma/Gypsies in 1995. For

the rapidly worsening socio-economic situation of Roma in Eastern and especially Central Europe prompted new waves of westward migration at a time when the previous straightforward option of requesting asylum as refugees fleeing oppressive Communist regimes was no longer available (Lee 2000: 53). Between 1990 and 1993 (as earlier during the 1970s and 80s), Romani requests for asylum still did not differ much from those of other citizens of the former Eastern bloc, who attempted to gain permission to stay in the West by requesting asylum on the basis of generalised human rights violations and political crisis in their countries of origin. This first post-Cold War wave consisted mostly of Roma from Romania and the Balkans and was gradually stopped through the German-Romanian and other repatriation agreements signed throughout the 1990s and by changes in the asylum law in Germany and other countries (Gheorghe and Klímová 2000).

It was only the second post-Cold War wave of Romani asylum seekers that put the issue of Romani migration at the top of the agenda of many international organisations as well as states. This wave started in mid-1997 and is still continuing at the start of the twenty-first century. These Romani asylum seekers come mostly from the Czech Republic, Slovakia, Poland, Romania and Bulgaria and a very small number also from Hungary (Pluim 2000b: 13, 14). Roma fleeing the Kosovo conflict are often considered to be a somewhat separate category. In contrast to earlier arrivals, Romani asylum seekers in this last wave cite fear of persecution simply because they are Roma as the main reason for their asylum requests. This fact puts their asylum claims into a special class and has prompted a political debate at international level, particularly within the Organisation for Security and Co-operation in Europe (OSCE).

The need for academic debate

The aim of this paper is to identify the parameters of the current academic debate on the international political aspects of Romani migration and asylum seeking. Unfortunately, it has to be stated at the

more details see *Roma/Gypsies – Social Cohesion and Quality of Life*. Available World Wide Web, URL: http://www.coe.fr/dase/en/cohesion/action/roma.htm.

outset that academic debate on this topic in both countries of origin of Romani refugees and host countries is very limited and in some places virtually non-existent.[4] Although serious academic debate on Romani refugees and asylum seekers, that would generate and try to reconcile different perspectives and ideas, is urgently needed if informed policy-making is to take place, academic interest in Romani issues remains marginal. In addition, even in the developing field of Romani studies political issues are only of peripheral interest, while conversely no more than a handful of political scientists or international relations scholars have any awareness or knowledge of Romani issues. While anthropological, ethnographic and sociological studies are extremely important as a source for political analysis, they cannot become a substitute. The methodology and aims of such studies are not directly applicable in formulating policy papers, especially those pitched at the international level, and thus their findings need further reinterpretation by political scientists or international relations scholars for the purposes of policy prescription.[5]

This paper illustrates the handful of published views on various aspects of the Romani asylum debate put forward by those activists as well as scholars who attempt to address this topic as an international issue.

---

[4] For example, in both Czech and Slovak Republics which are currently among the main sources of Romani outmigration and where Romani issues are widely reported in the media as well as debated in political circles, the academic community has not yet taken a great interest in the issues of Romani migration and asylum. This is not just the opinion of the author of this paper but was also confirmed in a telephone conversation (4 August 2000) with Viktor Sekyt from the Interdepartmental Commission for Romani Community Affairs in the Czech Republic and a Slovak analyst of Romani issues, Michal Vašečka, from the Bratislava-based Institute for Public Affairs. However, both Michal and Imrich Vašečka and the Czech sociologist Ivan Gabal have recently made important contributions in this area.

[5] For example, anthropological, ethnographic and sociological studies often emphasise very localised and group-specific details and conclude that differences between groups render comparisons across borders fruitless. However, for the purposes of legal and political argument a certain amount of generalisation is necessary and can still provide a valuable framework for analysis. Especially for the purposes of policy analysis at the international level, strategic similarities across borders have to be emphasised over less significant group and national differences in order to identify comparable problems faced by various actors in different states who call for common solutions.

These views, where they exist, represent opinions of Roma and non-Roma and from both home and host countries of Romani refugees. Governmental perspectives are presented only as seen by activists or scholars as policy analysis is not one of the aims of this paper. Opinions of activists and scholars are intentionally presented separately because the author of this paper believes that for proper analysis it is important to understand these views in the light of the standpoint and ideology of those articulating them. Activist views tend to be based more on the ideology of human, minority or Romani rights organisations, following the logic that the right to asylum is a basic human right which needs to be granted in a non-discriminatory manner to all people in need of it, rather than in the belief that the provision of just asylum procedures is the answer to the current Romani asylum 'crisis' and to the problems that Roma experience. It is therefore essentially normative. Consequently, while the critical statements of activists offer states and organisations some kind of mirror, showing how their actions compare to the normative ideals of a democratic world fully respecting the equality of all citizens in the enjoyment of their human rights, activists do not often suggest workable solutions or strategies to deal with the problematic co-existence between Roma and other populations that is the root cause of all related difficulties such as the current asylum situation. This deficiency stems from the failure by activists to take into account the political constraints and interests of all parties to the conflict. After all, this is not their task. Their function is to advance human rights and not to seek political compromises. Therefore activists advocating the rights of Roma generally do not aim to offer an objective portrayal of the situation in their articles. Instead, they try to provide a counter-balance to governmental and media reports which are usually biased against the Roma.[6] The resulting bias, or at least selective focus of attention, limits (but by no means completely negates) the usefulness for policy-making of views presented by human rights activists.

Because of the inherent limitations of the activist approach, it is necessary for scholars to intervene and critically evaluate the data and

---

[6] In this context, officials need to recognise that as long as their reports remain biased and they continue to allow biased media reporting, they are unlikely to get information of a more objective kind from human rights activists.

views of both activists and officials, taking into account the existing state of affairs[7] and relevant theories. By means of such objective analysis they might succeed in reconciling these contrasting perspectives, leading to realistic suggestions for policy prescription that acknowledge actual political constraints. Although even scholarly writing can be biased, and often is, one can reasonably expect a higher degree of impartiality. Regrettably, as stated above, when it comes to Romani political issues objective and well-informed scholarship is so far extremely limited and it is only to be hoped that it will develop in future for the sake of better-informed policy-making. In the meantime, although it is impossible to present a well-balanced, academic debate on various aspects of and solutions to the current asylum 'crisis' due to the limited sources available, the intention is that the analysis provided in this paper might serve as a useful guide to recent thinking and debates and stimulate further discussion and study.

The extent of the current asylum 'crisis'

Although it is impossible to present definite statements about the extent of present-day Romani migration, scholars and activists agree that it is generally exaggerated and that the numbers involved are not sufficient to constitute a crisis. As Yaron Matras points out, '[t]he real volume of recent Romani migration westwards appears to be distorted by a superficial impression of a strong Romani presence throughout western Europe' (Matras 2000: 47).[8] Most activists and scholars ascribe this impression to 'traditional anti-Roma prejudices in western societies… creating irrational fears of a "tidal wave of Gypsies"' (ibid.) promoted by scandalous media reporting and unscrupulous anti-Romani speeches by populist politicians.[9] Matras further points out that the actual dimensions of Romani migration are in popular perception also distorted 'by Romani migrants engagement in a certain pattern of activities in western European cities, such as playing music or begging,

---

[7] Although here it could also be argued that detachment from reality is sometimes the major limitation of scholarly analysis and that this interface is where co-operation between grassroots activists and scholars needs to take place.

[8] However, this view is voiced in the majority of articles discussed in this paper.

[9] See e.g. Mark Braham (1993: 10), Lee (2000), generally and Colin Clark and Elaine Campbell (2000: 23–47).

as well as by the fact that Romani migration is usually a migration of families or extended families rather than individuals' (ibid.).

Before European countries themselves made available some statistical estimates of the number of Romani asylum seekers,[10] scholars and activists agreed that the recent Romani migration from Central and Eastern Europe (CEE) is proportionally certainly not higher than average migration from CEE[11] and that Roma do not represent an alarming proportion of all Convention-refugee claimants.[12] At the end of the year 2000, official estimates were published of the percentage of Roma among asylum seekers submitting their claims between 1997 and 2000 in various Western European countries. Several EU Member states, plus Norway and Switzerland, estimated that Romani claims represent between 85-99 per cent of all asylum applications made by Czech, Slovak and Polish citizens and between 30-60 per cent of applications by Romanian citizens.[13] Such numbers, if substantiated, are 'far from trivial considering that their countries of origin are [often] classified as "safe"' (Braham and Braham 2000: 98). The fluctuation of the number of asylum requests made allegedly by Roma from the same country within a short period of time also merits attention. For example, according to the statistics of the United Nations High Commissioner for Refugees (UNHCR), between 1998 and 1999 there was a 1000 per cent increase (from 467 to 4,836) in asylum requests made by Slovak citizens (Gheorghe 2000), virtually all believed to be Roma.

---

[10] Most scholars as well as activists reported that it is impossible to estimate the numbers of Romani asylum seekers because countries register asylum claims only on the basis of nationality, not on basis of belonging to an ethnic group or minority.

[11] See e.g. Matras (2000: 35, 47) citing two other recent reports arriving at this conclusion.

[12] See e.g. Lee (2000: 55).

[13] For example Belgium estimates that almost 100 per cent of the 3,970 Slovak, 987 Czech and 146 Polish asylum claims submitted between 1997 and 2000 are made by Roma, while for the 4,575 Romanian claims the figure is 50 per cent (2,288) and for the 2,958 Bulgarian it is 70 per cent (2,071). Norway estimates that during this time all of the 55 Polish and 466 Slovak applications were made by Roma, and some 80-90 per cent of the 631 Romanian (505-568), 20 Czech (16-18) and 10 Bulgarian (8-9) claims were also by Roma. (Pluim 2000b: 17–19).

Causes and stimuli of the current asylum 'crisis'

Until very recently activists and scholars almost unanimously challenged the portrayal of Roma as economic migrants by government officials and media. However, during the year 2000 opinions began to polarise. While some activists and scholars still maintain that Romani asylum seekers leave their home countries solely because of racism and discrimination, others acknowledge that Romani requests for asylum also have an economic motive. In some cases claims can be seen as a strategy of Romani individuals who view Western societies as more tolerant and hope to achieve personal development in less discriminatory surroundings (Gheorghe and Klímová 2000). Recent research suggests that both views are correct because a) Romani asylum claims are often motivated by multiple reasons and b) various groups of Roma migrate for different reasons.[14] Consequently, the current asylum 'crisis' must be seen as arising from a combination of factors (increased violence and discrimination as well as the rise of unemployment and lack of economic opportunities in transition countries). However, there is an underlying common denominator – the more disadvantaged situation of Roma in CEE combined with restrictions on legal migration (ERRC 1999). At the moment Roma from CEE have virtually no chance of long-term labour migration to the West and in practice their only hope of leaving CEE since 1989 has been to apply for political asylum in the West (Matras 2000: 39).

When giving a more detailed account, activists cite mostly external triggers for recent Romani migration such as organised and repeated hostilities, human rights violations, economic disadvantages, single acts of violence, particular vulnerability in war zones or former war zones, and change of status due to the emergence of new states or new citizenship provisions.[15] Scholars go deeper in their analysis and further identify intra-communal features that promote migration by Roma such

---

[14] This is the conclusion of the research carried out by the International Organisation for Migration in various countries and by the International Centre for Migration Policy Development (ICMPD), as reported at the *International Consultation on Roma Refugees and Asylum Seekers*, Warsaw, 23 October 2000.

[15] See also Červeňák (2000: 52) for a detailed list of causes related to racial discrimination, social and economic situation and other factors.

as deeply rooted attitudes like lack of confidence in and non-identification with the majority population and its institutions and specific measures taken in their respective countries of origin. These attitudes spring from their history of exclusion, expulsion, disadvantage, and persecution, and lack of territorial claims.[16] Matras explains that because Roma feel vulnerable and are reluctant to trust the representatives and institutions of wider society, they tend to seek individual solutions in response to personal insecurity and social and economic hardships rather than aim at participating in collective processes to bring about change in their individual home countries (Matras 2000: 36). Matras believes that this collective perception and lack of confidence is what drives most Roma out of their countries. He points out that He points out that '[a]lthough a direct link between migration and hostilities can only be documented in some cases, [this] collective awareness and non-confidence often give rise to a feeling of vulnerability among Roma who have not necessarily experienced violence directly' and so lead to mass outmigration (2000: 46).

However, the mass outmigration is presented in a slightly different light by scholars in CEE. For example, Michal Vašečka describes the dynamics of departure as starting with 'several Romani families with quite serious reasons for applying for asylum ... followed by Roma looking for improvement in their standard of living' (Vašečka, M. 2000: 5). This is where the so-called 'pull factors' come into play alongside the 'push factors' described above. While Roma themselves state their main pull factor to be their vision of multicultural western society where 'people of colour' also have equal opportunities and are treated with respect, majority populations believe that the main pull factor is the provision of generous social benefits in Western countries (Vašečka, I. 2000). Imrich Vašečka furthermore concludes in his study of Slovak asylum seekers that Roma do not come from places where most discrimination occurs. In his survey, all respondents apparently spoke about discrimination and racism but were not able to give specific examples. In his opinion, asylum seeking is only one of the strategies that Slovak Roma use to 'escape humiliating Romness [sic], deal with discrimination and distrust of society and emancipate

---

[16] All of these factors are listed in Matras (2000: 46).

[themselves]' because they do not see the possibility of 'the general application of other development strategies' (ibid.). However this migration strategy is restricted to certain areas of Slovakia and is specific to the unemployed Romani middle class. Based on this analysis, Imrich Vašečka identifies as one of the main reasons for Romani outmigration from Slovakia 'the partial blockage of emancipation opportunities of the so-called Romany middle class after 1989'. This consists of 'their restricted access to the labour market and arrangements "diverting" them to the discriminatory conditions of shadow labour' or unemployment, the 'feeling of the Romany entrepreneurs of their restricted access to business opportunities' and the feeling of Romani NGO representatives that they fail to find long-term support from donors, including the state (ibid.).

Mark and Matthew Braham take a different angle and in their analysis of the recent asylum 'crisis' reach the conclusion that the main force behind current outmigration from CEE is the same force that has stimulated Romani migrations throughout European history – the problem of coexistence of Roma and the rest of the population. In the latest asylum 'crisis', which originated mainly in the Czech and Slovak Republics, this problem of coexistence was manifested in an increasing, systematic discrimination by local authorities against Roma. According to the Brahams, Roma were leaving their home countries because of two fears – ghettoisation and expulsion, as opposed to physical violence. However, while the Brahams reach the same conclusion as Matras, that the readiness of Roma to leave their home countries when problems arise is due to their non-identification with majority societies, they stipulate that Romani non-identification with majority societies is not just an effect but also a cause of their marginalization and by implication a reason for outmigration. The Brahams believe that the 'Romani sense of integrity, belief in their racial purity, and the importance they attach to their social system has meant that the Roma have also chosen not to integrate and identify with their countries of residence' (Braham and Braham 2000: 101). The Brahams suggest that a Romani cultural style, which largely rejects the basic criteria for entering mainstream society such as better education and training as well as technical and professional competence, serves as an 'attractor' for victimisation and is as much a source of Romani marginalisation as is prejudice against them among majority populations. The Brahams, therefore, maintain that if the marginalisation of Roma – which is one of the main push factors for migration – is to disappear, their cultural incompatibility with European societies has to disappear first and Roma have to adopt certain fundamental values and rules of operation of the EU (2000: 111).

The Brahams' position deserves consideration because it stands out from all other views. While they do not deny the occurrence of persecution and discrimination against Roma, they conclude that Roma are partially responsible for their predicament. The authors' motives are undoubtedly well intentioned when they argue that there is no point in Roma making their own situation worse than it needs to be. They go on to point out that campaigns promoting tolerance and multicultural education are not likely to bring about a fundamental change in attitude of the majority of Europeans towards Roma in the near future. Nevertheless, their viewpoint is highly controversial for several reasons. Firstly, according to current rhetoric if not actual European practice, it is no longer politically correct or acceptable to demand that minorities change their cultural identity and expect that they will adjust to the standards of the majority. In addition, this view can be interpreted as portraying an 'implausibly static concept' of Romani culture (see Kovats 2000: 16, Trehan 2000: 117–8) or even as adopting the approach of 'blaming the victim' to justify moral exclusion.[17] However, we might also regard this view as simply pragmatic and solution-oriented. In fact, prominent Romani leaders have previously adopted this stance (see Mirga and Gheorghe 1997). On the other hand, it can be said that willingness to integrate by Roma in Kosovo did little to spare them from serious problems. Before the recent crisis in Kosovo Roma appeared to be well-adapted, loyal citizens, with reasonable educational qualifications and proper jobs. They had followed the recommended path for all Roma and had managed to integrate. Yet, when disaster struck, they were once again those who suffered most (Gheorghe and Klímová 2000). Whether one accepts or rejects the

---

[17] For more on this theory see Franke Wilmer's analysis of Opotow's theory of moral exclusion in Franke Wilmer (1993) *The Indigenous Voice in World Politics*, London: Sage, 58–93.

Brahams' standpoint, their work represents a unique[18] attempt to look at the problem without blaming one side alone and as such deserves further consideration and discussion.

Besides the causes described above, several authors also refer to certain specific stimuli that triggered the outmigration of the late 1990s. Most authors mention the documentaries screened by the Czech private TV station *Nova*, which were widely criticised for giving 'an overly optimistic picture of the carefree life led by Romani asylum seekers' (Lee 2000: 54) in Canada and Great Britain. In addition, Imrich Vašečka points to the existence of 'role-models' in general, referring to either successful Romani asylum seekers or what he calls successful returnees, who managed to return home with more savings than they had started with. In some countries, for example in Slovakia, the government and general public also believe that much recent migration is organised. In his study Imrich Vašečka agrees this is true to a certain extent in some areas. Some Romani usurers encourage their debtors to migrate to the West in the belief that opportunities of making money to repay the debt are more favourable. However, such an allegation is difficult to prove (Vašečka, I. 2000). Furthermore, legal changes can also generate outmigration by putting Roma at a disadvantage in their home countries or, on the other hand, by providing increases in benefits for asylum seekers in host countries (ibid.).

When analysing the causes and stimuli of Romani outmigration in pursuit of constructive solutions, a further point needs to be taken into account. It is significant that the most fundamental difference of opinion on this matter is not to be found among activists and scholars, whether in home or host countries. Instead, the greatest divergence in perspectives is plainly that between majority societies and Roma, whether asylum seekers or Romani representatives. Roma mention personal security concerns, anxiety about the future of their children, mutual distrust between Roma and state officials and institutions, as well as direct discrimination and racism as the main reasons for leaving home. In contrast, majority societies generally believe this migration is

---

[18] The attempt truly is unique because most contributions to any discussion on Romani issues are usually either completely for-Roma or completely anti-Roma.

prompted by shrewd, economic calculations and opportunities for speculative trading, in addition to the unwillingness of Roma to integrate or take responsibility for their lives.[19] It is vital for these opposing views to be acknowledged and clarified at the outset, because it is impossible for both sides to co-operate in seeking constructive solutions if their views on the causes of the problem are so fundamentally different.

Validity of Romani claims to asylum

Presence of a well-founded fear of persecution

Activists argue forcefully that most Romani claimants are extremely likely to have a well-founded fear of persecution. To support their case they cite numerous, well-authenticated reports which conclude CEE Roma are the victims of 'unremedied police violence, skinhead attacks and racially motivated pogroms, as well as pervasive discrimination in all spheres of social life' (ERRC 2000a). These reports have been published not only by human rights organisations but also by governmental and inter-governmental agencies. Some of the claims have been acknowledged by international organisations. For example, the UNHCR 1998 *Guidelines Relating to the Eligibility of Slovak Roma Asylum Seekers* stated clearly that 'Slovak Roma may well be able to substantiate refugee claims based on severe discrimination on ethnic grounds' (ERRC 1999).

Scholars are more cautious before jumping to conclusions and most do not openly argue that Roma have a well-founded fear of persecution. Law lecturer Helen O'Nions is an exception stating that a significant number of the 'new Europeans' (meaning CEE Roma) may have evidence of a well-founded fear of persecution (O'Nions 1999: 14). Others wonder why there is even a debate about whether Roma have a well-founded fear of persecution. Matras concludes that this is due to '[t]he complexity of personal motivations for migration [which] does not always allow for a clear-cut distinction between a well-founded fear

---

[19] This view was voiced e.g. by Imrich Vašečka and also by Míťa Castle-Kaněrová in their presentations at the international conference *Minorities in a Pluralist Society at the Turn of Millenium*, Brno, 2 September 2000.

of persecution and so-called "voluntary" reasons to migrate' (Matras 2000: 46–7). Angus Bancroft speculates that a well-founded fear of persecution might be often denied to Roma in the existing asylum system because they flee generalised violence, rather than individual human rights abuses. In his opinion, it is precisely cases of generalised violence 'which fall ... through the net of the asylum hearing' (Bancroft 1999: 14–15).

Another reason why a well-founded fear of persecution might be denied to Roma is because the persecution is not seen as political but 'only' social (Kuder 2000: 32) and is not carried out by governments. Mark Braham had already suggested in 1993 that an examination of Romani cases might lead to extending the protection offered by the Geneva Convention to cover cases of non-governmental persecution because Romani cases have demonstrated all four types of failure by the state to provide necessary protection, as identified by the Canadian Immigration Appeal Board (Braham 1993: 77). Such an extension, however, remains more the exception than the rule. Some scholars, while not openly arguing that most Roma have a well-founded fear of persecution under existing asylum law, do however call for a re-evaluation of the definition of a 'well-founded fear of persecution', so that it includes group or generalised persecution as a basis for asylum claims. This response is prompted by recognition of the need to devise new approaches when dealing with complex asylum cases such as those of the Roma.

Migration as an expression of nomadic tradition

In some cases, reference to a traditional Romani nomadic lifestyle has been used as a justification for claims that Roma are not 'authentic refugees' (see Peric and Demirovski 2000: 92). Activists as well as scholars reject the view that Roma migrate simply out of tradition and point out that most Romani asylum seekers have long been sedentary. In addition, scholars have provided more detailed explanations supporting their argument. In comparing specific features of Romani migration with migrations of other groups, Matras concludes that 'the extraordinary feature of Romani migration is that so many Roma are prepared to take the risks of migrating *despite their lack of nomadic traditions*' [original emphasis] (Matras 2000: 32). In his view, the readiness of Roma to move when problems arise, that is so often ascribed to their nomadic legacy, can be better explained by their non-identification with their countries of residence and a consequent loose attachment to those countries, as mentioned above. Matras contends that the contemporary debate on asylum seekers needs to be differentiated from the debate about nomadism or itinerant or semi-itinerant Romani lifestyles. He insists this is an entirely different issue that has already received significant attention from European bodies (ibid.). Jean-Pierre Liégeois and Nicolae Gheorghe, on the other hand, do not deny the link between Romani migration and nomadism, which they believe to be a factor in the lifestyle of many Roma. However, they point out that often this is not nomadism by choice but rather 'reactive nomadism', brought about by outside factors which generate migration (Liégeois and Gheorghe 1995: 16–17). In this context, some types of 'reactive nomadism' can be seen as equivalent to forced migration or involuntary nomadism.

Roma as economic migrants

Many Western scholars, like activists, challenge government and public opinion that Roma migrate *mostly* for economic reasons. British scholar Mít'a Castle-Kaněrová, formerly employed by the International Organization for Migration (IOM), describes the current Romani attempt to seek asylum as an expression of collective despair rather than an economic calculation (Castle-Kaněrová 2000). Matras argues convincingly that:

> [a]lthough citizens of EU Member states enjoy basic freedom of travel and employment throughout the EU, there has so far been no noteworthy migration of Roma from economically less advantaged member states such as Spain or Greece northwards, despite the large numbers of Roma living in these countries and the economic hardships they often endure.
>
> (Matras 2000: 36)

He believes that Spanish and Greek Roma are more willing to endure economic difficulties as a disadvantaged minority because they share a sense of general stability, as well as of historical attachment and belonging with the majority non-Romani (*gadje*) population. Imrich Vašečka similarly points out that in Slovakia outmigration does not occur from those municipalities where Roma feel relatively integrated with the rest of the population (Vašečka, I. 2000). Some researchers turn this debate into a critique of the current categories of motives. Bancroft believes that the experience of Romani asylum seekers has revealed the distinction between economic and non-economic migrants to be a bureaucratic construct that fails to encapsulate the complex and contradictory motives of migrants (Bancroft 1999: 17).

Nevertheless, researchers and politicians in the countries of origin do believe that economic considerations are a strong factor in determining reasons for Romani outmigration. In their opinion, the problem of Romani migrations is in large part due to the general decline in the standard of living in CEE and the substantial income gap between the European Union and CEE countries. Slovak researcher Michal Vašečka puts it bluntly, 'the problem will last until the average income in Slovakia will be equal to social benefits for asylum seekers in Finland' (Vašečka, M. 2000: 6). This view is supported by research conducted by the International Centre for Migration Policy Development (ICMPD). The findings reveal that one type of Romani migrants consists of a relatively large number of mostly middle class Roma using the asylum system as a means of entering the EU to improve their economic situation. The ICMPD voices the concern that some of these people are travelling in an organised way, more or less 'testing' the asylum systems in several EU member states as well as in other countries. They suddenly appear in relatively large numbers, perhaps 20 to 40 people a day for several weeks or months, apply for asylum and wait for decisions. After some claims have been refused, the remaining applications are withdrawn and the migrants disappear only to reappear, as if following a regular pattern, in the asylum system of another country (e.g. Belgium, Finland, the UK and the Netherlands). The ICMPD sees such migration as purely economic and therefore an abuse of the asylum system which furthermore tends to stigmatise all Romani asylum seekers and provokes host countries into taking measures that tend to discriminate against genuine Romani asylum-seekers and reduce the likelihood of successful claims (Pluim 2000a).

Evaluation of responses to the current asylum 'crisis'

Representation by politicians and media of the validity of Romani claims

Activists as well as scholars strongly criticise the way in which media and politicians have discredited the validity of Romani asylum claims. They believe that once again, as many times before in history, popular stereotypes of Roma as criminals and parasites have been used as a powerful tool to justify repressive measures against these people. Within the context of the current asylum 'crisis', these popular stereotypes have been further reinforced by scandal-mongering press reports, accusing Roma of creating a burden for taxpayers, being a drain on the economy and of 'sponging' off the welfare system.[20] The situation has been further inflamed by offensive, anti-Romani statements by politicians, 'in some countries caving in to a perceived electoral threat posed by racist and xenophobic right wing parties' (Cahn and Vermeersch 2000: 71).[21] Deborah Winterbourne, a former advocate for appeals of asylum seekers at the Refugee Legal Centre in London, believes that this rhetoric is all part of a larger plot. Although the Geneva Convention does clearly guarantee protection from persecution on account of race, in reality claims made on account of race, as in case of the Roma, no longer have much chance of success.[22] Interpretation of the Geneva Convention becomes most restrictive when 'an asylum seeker claims refugee status on the basis of the Convention reason of "race"' because granting asylum in such a case could set a precedent for all other persons of the same race claiming asylum. Since 'Western European governments are simply terrified of the economic and political consequences of allowing groups of people to settle in their countries', whether or not the group really is persecuted becomes irrelevant in the asylum-determination procedure.

---

[20] For examples see Lee (2000) generally.

[21] Peter Vermeersch is a Research Assistant at the Fund for Scientific Research in Flanders (Belgium), therefore the views put forth in this article are not solely those held by activists.

[22] See for example Lee's argument that throughout history Romani immigrants have faced opposition only when they have been publicly identified as Roma (Lee 2000: 51–4).

However, since these governments cannot be seen to reject genuine refugees, 'more legitimate' reasons for the denial have to be fabricated. Thus states declare that the particular group does not face persecution and its members are therefore not genuine refugees but rather 'bogus asylum seekers' or economic migrants (Winterbourne 1999: 70). This view is supported by Castle-Kaněrová who believes that Western governments are pretending that Romani persecution does not exist with the sole intention of maintaining a zero-level of immigration. In order to sustain this, they have to convey the message that Roma are 'bogus asylum seekers' and consequently emphasise that responsibility for handling the current asylum 'crisis' lies with each country of origin (Castle-Kaněrová 2000). In the opinion of activists, this response by Western governments to Romani asylum claims exacerbates tensions in their home countries by confirming the regrettable popular conviction that the mere presence of Roma is in itself the problem (Winterbourne 1999: 75).

Activists also believe that the asylum 'crisis' has once more revealed the depth of prejudice against Roma. In their opinion, '[t]hroughout Europe, Romani victims of systematic discrimination and racially motivated violence are denied effective domestic remedies, then summarily rejected when, in fear for their lives, they seek sanctuary in a foreign country'. After being 'relegated to "second class" status at home, Roma are treated as second class refugees when forced to flee' (ERRC 1999: 63). The asylum 'crisis' demonstrates that the adoption of the language of universal human rights by European states is an empty formality, since they do not hesitate to deny refugees entry if their 'national' interest is at stake (Cahn and Vermeersch: 78–9, Castle-Kaněrová 2000).

Scholars also criticise Western politicians and media for incorrectly labelling Roma as illegal immigrants. Matras points out that there have been no reports of illegal entry by the asylum seekers in question and no criminal charges have been brought against them for illegal entry. In this light, Matras believes that such naming was simply 'a rhetoric deliberately aimed at discrediting the group of refugees on a wholesale basis' (Matras 1998b: 9, 7). This view is supported by Cahn and Vermeersch (2000: 73).

Measures taken in response: Denial of Romani asylum claims and discrimination in access to asylum, border controls and other protectionist measures

As suggested in the above paragraph, activists and some scholars believe that, due to the contemporary trend in the European Union 'to apply highly restrictive interpretations of the 1951 Geneva Refugee Convention in order to reduce the number of asylum-seekers', the right to asylum for Roma was reduced to a formality. Since Roma are in any case perceived as unwelcome visitors and rarely as refugees, in practice this right is unavailable to them (Cahn and Vermeersch 2000: 71). Activists maintain that the fact that the vast majority of asylum applications filed by Roma are rejected, despite the evidence of widespread violence and discrimination against Roma in CEE, can be seen as a violation by states of their obligation to grant asylum under the Convention (ERRC 2000a).

According to activists, Western governments further violate international law by manipulating asylum determination procedures in order to justify rejection of Romani claims. Although determination procedures should be consistent, some applications are rejected because the individual claimants cannot prove that they personally have been, or could be, targeted for abuse while other applications have been rejected *en masse* as undesirable without considering the merits of individual cases (in violation of the Geneva Convention) (UNHCR 1999).[23] Activists also see the following as violations of the right of Romani applicants to fair determination procedures: an arbitrary application of 'the third safe country' concept (Gheorghe and Klímová 2000) and 'safe country-of-origin' lists, imposition of visas to prevent the arrival of potential asylum seekers, efforts to delineate areas of border facilities as 'international territory' to preclude applications for refugee status and the so-called 'manifestly unfounded claims procedures' (ERRC 2000b).

---

[23] Quoted in O'Nions (1999).

The discriminatory application of asylum procedures in the case of Romani applicants can be perhaps best illustrated in the case of Romani refugees from Kosovo. Activists maintain that 'Roma as a group had been targeted for violent attacks by ethnic Albanians' and, as such, 'all Roma from Kosovo have a well-founded fear of persecution in that province' and should be considered refugees in the sense of the Geneva Convention (ERRC 1999: 63). In their opinion it is beyond doubt that Roma in Kosovo face immense danger in terms of wholesale persecution and violence, yet cases of Kosovo Roma granted asylum in any country are extremely rare (Peric and Demirovski 2000: 92). However, allegations of discrimination in asylum procedures for Roma are strongly rejected by UNHCR representatives who believe that if there is discrimination in determining status, then it is against everyone and not just Roma. In support of their case they point out that between 1990 and 1999 only a tiny proportion (slightly more than 1.2 per cent) of all applicants seeking asylum in Europe were recognised as refugees (Gheorghe and Klímová 2000).

While scholars are not so explicit about whether Roma are unfairly denied the right to asylum, they do pay attention to the asylum determination procedures and some find them discriminatory. Matras does not characterise the procedures as deliberately discriminatory but explains how the structure of asylum procedures works against Romani applicants. They are disadvantaged by extremely bureaucratic procedures unfamiliar to them, by the use of prejudiced interpreters and by demands for proof of individual political persecution, even though it is well known that 'anti-Roma hostility is directed by its very nature at the group as a whole, rather than at individuals'.[24] However, some scholars do believe that in practice there is open discrimination against Romani applicants by asylum officers.[25] This discrimination is made easier by new trends in EU asylum policies that leave major decisions up to individual governments and legal officials and in this way reduce the legal right to an asylum hearing to a random act of mercy (Kuder 2000: 78). Other scholars take a more pragmatic view and argue that

---

[24] For details see Matras (2000: 39–40). See also Bancroft (1999: 16–17) for similar arguments.
[25] See e.g. Winterbourne (1999: 70) for an account of anti-Romani discrimination in British asylum procedures.

the success of Romani claims simply depends on getting a good lawyer. Arthur Helton believes that Roma have a fair chance of being granted asylum provided they can present highly individualised claims based on well-founded fear of persecution. In order to be found credible by adjudicators, their claims need to be internally consistent and supported by detailed evidence and relevant legal documentation. In his opinion, all that it takes is convincing proof and logical argument (Helton 1999: 46).

Instead of condemning denial of asylum on moral grounds as activists do, scholars rather explain its impracticality. In the opinion of Castle-Kaněrová, the existing asylum laws offer no solution to the Romani migration problem and are being abused by the recent migration of Roma which 'can be characterized not as searching for [a] permanent new home somewhere else, but as [a] temporary, often transitory stay of the Roma middle strata in the countries of the EU where their asylum applications are being refused' (Castle-Kaněrová 2000). Matras maintains that rejecting Romani asylum claims will not solve current asylum or migration problems. In his view, Roma differ from other migrants in their willingness to incur the risks of repeated expulsion and clandestine, self-sufficient existence on the fringes of Western societies. Accordingly, denial of asylum will only force Roma to revert to long-term, clandestine existence and from the outset encourage attitudes of non-co-operation with majority society (Matras 2000: 41). Castle-Kaněrová also asserts that denial of asylum and repatriation will not stop migration. To the contrary, as she observed in the Czech Republic, tendency to migrate increases after repatriation. In this way a re-emigration and repatriation cycle is repeated, producing refugees in orbit (Castle-Kaněrová 2000). This view is supported by recent interviews with repatriated, unsuccessful Czech Romani asylum seekers, the majority of whom are planning to migrate again.[26] Such a situation was predicted as early as 1994 by British researcher Donald Kenrick who warned that if social and economic conditions of Roma in CEE were not improved, neither visa controls nor frontiers would prevent their renewed migration (Kenrick 1994). The Brahams,

---

[26] Telephone conversation (4 August 2000) with Ivan Gabal, the author of a recent post-repatriation study for the International Organization for Migration.

condemn active encouragement and support of large-scale, westward Romani migration as misconceived, because of the inevitably hostile reaction (Braham and Braham 2000: 105) and since it would not 'resolve the socio-economic consequences of the problem, either for the migrants, or for that larger majority who will remain behind' (2000: 111). They also identify further problems in restricting the possibility of Roma seeking asylum.

> While introducing measures ... to limit asylum claims may well prevent large-scale influxes of Roma legitimately or illegitimately seeking refugee status, these same measures are also likely to increase illegal cross-border trafficking of Roma migrants. While welfare expenditure on asylum applicants may be saved, there will be direct costs involved in the strengthening of border regimes, and the search for and dismantling of the trafficking networks and the illegal entrants they bring. There will also be indirect costs for the countries involved and for immigrants who successfully enter illegally, as the immigrants will be forced to survive as 'undocumented' workers, thus further criminalising and marginalising them.
>
> (Braham and Braham 2000: 104)

Overall, the exclusion of Roma from the asylum process is seen by activists as a violation of their human rights. This contributes to their increased marginalisation and is a further denial of their basic rights such as access to an adequate standard of living, education and medical facilities. Roma who are summarily rejected by Western authorities are reluctant to return to their home countries but are unable to gain access to even a basic level of support in host countries (Pickup 1999: 60). Those who return often face conditions worse than prior to their departure.[27]

Activists also strongly criticise border controls and other protectionist measures taken by Western governments such as 'conducting more extensive border patrols, establishing more rigorous migration and political asylum procedures, and promulgating stricter visa requirements' (ERRC 1999: 62) because in this way Western

---

[27] This view has been put forth in various presentations and documents of the International Organization for Migration.

governments effectively deny protection to Roma fleeing ethnic persecution in CEE (Cahn and Vermeersch 2000: 79).

Legality of responses

Activists are concerned that Western governments dealing with Romani refugees show disregard for international commitments they have already adopted as domestic law, breaching such important legal instruments as the Geneva Convention, the Convention for the Elimination of All Forms of Racial Discrimination (CERD) and the European Convention on Human Rights (ECHR) (Cahn and Vermeersch 2000: 75). By adopting anti-refugee measures, Western European states also break their own recent commitment to apply 'the full and inclusive application of the Geneva Convention' and 'the principle of non-refoulement' to ensure 'that nobody is sent back to persecution'.[28] This commitment is violated by forced deportations such as those from Belgium described by Cahn and Vermeersch.[29] In addition, some scholars maintain that the agreement between Romania and Germany to repatriate Roma is a violation of the Geneva Convention because the repatriated Roma continue to face persecution on ethnic grounds in their home countries (Kuder 2000: 80). Activists also believe that European plans for synchronising the asylum process and recognising CEE countries as safe seriously undermine the spirit of the Geneva Convention (Cahn and Vermeersch 2000: 78). This view is supported by O'Nions, who questions whether the 'present restrictive approach can be seen to satisfy the provisions of the Geneva Convention' (1999: 14).

Impact of asylum measures on the situation of Roma in their home countries

While scholars do not advocate asylum seeking by Roma as a preferred solution to their problems, they do not denounce it as a tactic. Indeed, they believe that the current asylum 'crisis' has brought about some

---

[28] 'Presidency Conclusions, Tampere European Council 15 and 16 October 1999', Pt. 13, cited in Cahn and Vermeersch (2000: 78).
29 See Cahn and Vermeersch generally.

positive changes. Castle-Kaněrová believes that through their recent migration Roma finally succeeded in attracting world interest to their account of persecution, segregation and racial violence (2000). According to Matras, migration aroused the interest of governments and multilateral organisations in preventing the causes of migration and forced them to examine more closely the human rights and economic situation of CEE Romani communities. In other words, the current emigration and international responses to it have helped confront national governments with their responsibilities towards their Romani populations and have stimulated recent political and legal gestures, which can be interpreted as acknowledgement of these responsibilities (Matras 2000: 47). At the Warsaw migration consultation in 2000 a representative of the Czech government openly acknowledged that the impetus for a positive change in Czech policy towards Roma was the introduction of visa requirements for Czech citizens to enter Canada after the 1997 Romani exodus (Kryštof 2000).

Michal Vašečka also appreciates that Romani migration helped raise awareness of the need to improve the conditions of Roma and revealed 'the level of ignorance about the Romani issues on the side of representatives of EU state-members [sic], the need to change asylum policies of particular member states, and the necessity to understand the Roma problem as a European issue' (2000: 6). In comparison with the incomprehension surrounding previous Romani movement westwards in the early 1990s, Matras points to the positive aspects of later migration. 'In the case of the most recent migrations, despite the overall attempt by the authorities to stop further arrivals and to convince public opinion that the case of asylum is not justified, there is appreciation of the motivations for emigration and their connection to the human rights situation in the countries of origin'. He also believes that there is 'more sensitivity to the causes of migration and to international public opinion [and] [d]irect pressure from international organisations and western institutions is discernable, along with gestures of immediate action and short-term changes in policy and in some cases even in legislation concerning the Roma' (Matras 2000: 47).

Matras believes that, for Roma, focusing attention on emigration can be a powerful political tool for initiating processes of domestic change because of the kind of responses this provokes. Between 1990 and 1993 emigration aroused mostly negative responses in both host and home countries. In the former the impossibility of accommodating emigrants' needs and demands was emphasised and negative stereotypes were evoked in moral justification of what amounted to inadequate state action, while in the latter emigration was linked to the alleged unreliability and disloyalty of Roma. In contrast, recent emigration from the Czech and Slovak Republics stimulated more positive reactions, which showed that both host and home countries are now more ready to acknowledge the objective circumstances that motivate emigration. Although on its own such a shift has not yet led to models for a long-term solution, at least it draws attention to the feeling of insecurity and vulnerability of Roma, highlights the need for administrative flexibility in accommodating the needs of Romani asylum seekers and helps avoid scapegoating emigrants (Matras 1998b: 10–11).

At the same time, scholars are well aware of setbacks in improving the situation of Roma brought about by the current asylum 'crisis' as a result of both its occurrence and responses to it. Michal Vašečka explains that '[m]isunderstandings and the inability to handle "waves of Romani migration" from Slovakia to the EU member states directly resulted in increasing popular hostility toward Roma in Slovakia' (2000: 5) because their action is perceived as a threat to the majority population's right of freedom of movement and opportunities to exercise it. Matras similarly acknowledges that 'an integrationist view of Romani activities may have suffered a setback in the public image owing to the impression of Roma turning their backs on ... Czech society and the prospects of integration and coexistence there' (Matras 1998b: 11). He also points out that the way Western governments are handling present-day Romani asylum attempts is leading formerly integrationist Western Romani leaders, who became actively engaged in helping CEE Romani asylum seekers, to adopt attitudes of non-co-operation with the majority and its institutions. This response stems from their experience of growing political isolation in majority society and alienation from the mainstream political establishment. Matras warns that these attitudes might soon spread eastwards (2000: 46).

The asylum debate as a part of the EU enlargement debate

Some scholars[30] have also looked at how recent Romani East-West migration has influenced the EU enlargement debate and process. In this context they identified two types of response. As a short-term response, EU representatives decided to emphasise the significance of successful integration of Romani minorities in applicant countries by making this one of the criteria for accession to the EU. This step was taken in the hope it would bring about improvements in the situation of Roma in applicant countries that would, in turn, lead to a significant decrease in Romani East-West migration. At the same time, however, the current asylum 'crisis' arising from the closure of other migration possibilities made EU representatives realise that some degree of Romani migration westwards is inevitable (Amato and Batt 1998),[31] both during and after the enlargement process, and that a long-term response is also required.

When it comes to the short-term response, governments of the applicant states are less hopeful. They often feel that too much is demanded of them, since the integration of Roma has so far not been successful in any European country. Partly for this reason, they believe Romani migration should not be regarded as the concern of CEE alone but instead treated as a problem of Europe-wide dimensions. Consequently, solutions should be sought through the co-operation of all European countries and should be implemented with European resources. Michal Vašečka believes that the EU needs a common strategic programme in order 'to secure the human and minority rights of Roma, their equal social and economic opportunities, and their integration into society on the basis of toleration [sic] and respect for diversity'. He also thinks that the EU should commit substantial resources for this purpose. Although he agrees that EU pressure should be maintained, for example on the Slovak government, he adds that such pressure has to be set in the context of partnership and has to be accompanied by financial and other support from the EU (Vašečka, M. 2000: 13–14). Castle-Kaněrová also emphasises that solving the problems of Romani

---

[30] This topic has so far not been of much interest to activists.
[31] Cited in Michal Vašečka (2000: 6).

migration should not be the responsibility solely of the countries of origin as this is a modern, Europe-wide phenomenon touching upon many important European issues, such as the question of European citizenship in an enlarged Europe and associated privileges like freedom of movement (Castle-Kaněrová 2000).

Moreover, researchers doubt the effectiveness of the short-term response that is supposed to improve the situation of Roma in applicant countries. While the Copenhagen Criteria for EU membership require 'democracy, the rule of law, human rights and respect for and protection of minorities', they also demand 'the existence of a functioning market economy, as well as the capacity to cope with competitive pressures and market forces'. The Brahams argue that fulfilling the second market economy criterion might make it impossible to satisfy the first political criterion of minority rights provisions in relation to Roma. As market reforms usually disenfranchise under-privileged groups like Roma and increase their marginalisation, any improvement in their situation is improbable. Similarly, their integration into society is unlikely to be successful because it would require substantial investments, which would need to increase as marginalisation increases. Since present national budgets of candidate countries are inadequate for investment on this scale, it would be necessary to divert funds from the remainder of the socially-disadvantaged, creating even more animosity towards Roma and resulting in further social exclusion. Therefore, while *de jure* compliance with the political criterion is possible, *de facto* fulfilment is unlikely. However, *de jure* compliance would not be sufficient to remove all causes of present outmigration (Braham and Braham 2000: 107–9).

When it comes to the long-term response to Romani determination to move westwards, as indicated by the current 'crisis', researchers suggest that this will need to include educating Western public opinion about Roma and improved implementation of minority rights commitment in all member states (Amato and Batt 1998).[32] Researchers in both member and applicant countries agree that existing

---

[32] Cited in Michal Vašečka (2000: 6) and Braham and Braham (2000: 105–10).

EU legislation is inadequate in addressing the needs and rights of Roma who, after enlargement, will become internal migrants. Michal Vašečka notes that EU documents mention Roma only sporadically and devote far less attention to their issues than to those of autochthonous national minorities in applicant countries (2000: 7). The main instrument devised to improve the situation of minorities in Europe is the Council of Europe's *Framework Convention for the Protection of National Minorities*. There is the expectation that this should be ratified as a condition of accession. The Brahams point out, however, that this convention does little to help the Roma because many of the rights it establishes are diminished by a clause relieving governments from any financial obligation to assist minorities assert these rights (2000: 109). Some authors therefore hope that westward Romani migration will serve as a catalyst for the long overdue debate about whether international documents and treaties reflect the specific problems of Roma (Vašečka, M. 2000: 6). So far this topic has not received much attention at the international level, although for some years certain Romani activists have argued the need for a legally-binding European Charter on Romani Rights. This idea was first proposed by the Roma National Congress (RNC) in 1994. Such a Charter is intended to define the legal position of the Roma in Europe and safeguard their political and cultural rights and would aim 'to prevent the legal gaps which in the past have led to the displacement of Romani persons across Europe' (Kawczynski 2000). According to the RNC the Charter should include, among others,[33] two points relevant to the migration and asylum debate – freedom of movement within communities, states and member states of the European Community and immediate protection for refugees threatened by anti-gypsyism (ibid.).

Recommendations of activists and scholars arising from the asylum debate

Human rights activists recommend that Roma must be granted impartial, non-discriminatory treatment in consideration of claims for asylum and all their human rights have to be respected in every country without discrimination. In particular they urge states, when applying

---

[33] For details see Kawczynski (2000).

the Geneva Convention, to recognise 'that the character of persecution often entails non-violent measures by non-state state actors' and that in Romani cases this is manifested by 'sustained or systemic violation of basic human rights demonstrative of a failure of state protection' (ERRC 2000b). They also lobby for granting refugees and asylum seekers more substantive rights (such as for work, residence, etc.) rather than a mere temporary ban on expulsion. A further demand is that authorities as well as the media in countries of refugee exile must refrain from irresponsible or inflammatory comments, liable to incite hatred of Romani refugees (ibid.). A more radical suggestion for solving the asylum 'crisis' is that those CEE countries, which are at present persecuting their Romani minorities with impunity, should be condemned by the UN and have sanctions imposed on them (Lee 2000: 64).

In 2000 the two leading Romani international organisations, the International Romani Union (IRU) and RNC,[34] issued a joint statement concerning migration (IRU and RNC 2000) including the following three demands which urged:

- establishing a Roma-led assessment group to evaluate the effectiveness of existing national and international Romani programmes
- granting refugee status to Roma from Kosovo
- ensuring fair asylum procedures in compliance with the Geneva Convention for Romani applicants

Besides these three points in common, each organisation also put forward additional recommendations. The IRU (IRU 2000) urged democratic states to assist CEE countries to develop basic democratic principles that would ensure the safety of Roma from racism and discrimination and called for:

---

[34] These views are presented as activist views, although they could, to a certain extent, also be considered as political or even 'governmental' since the former organisation, in particular, claims to speak on behalf of the Romani nation. Nevertheless, for the moment, representatives of both organisations are viewed by governments as activists.

- accepting Roma as quota refugees in the EU, USA, Canada and Australia
- granting citizenship rights for Romani refugees in Western Europe
- developing co-operative projects between the OSCE and IRU
- convening an international UN conference on Romani refugee issues
- negotiating between CEE governments and an IRU mediator group, with OSCE support
- providing social and economic help to Romani communities in CEE

The RNC (Kawczynski 2000) further recommended:

- adopting a binding charter on the rights and safety of Roma in Europe (as mentioned above)
- strengthening the Romani civil rights movement
- accepting anti-gypsyism as special grounds for asylum
- putting into action previous European and international (UN) recommendations and decisions to enhance security of Roma
- requiring mandatory annual reports from OSCE states on equal treatment of citizens, including Roma
- securing decisive participation of elected Romani representatives in national decision-making processes
- recognising elected representatives of the Romani nation and permitting unrestricted freedom of travel for Romani officials
- ensuring continuous monitoring of the human rights situation of Roma by permanent co-operation between the OSCE and RNC
- preparing recommendations, strategies and aid programs for Roma by close co-operation between the RNC, EU and OSCE
- acknowledging Romanes as a recognised language, treated equally to others in Europe, including giving all Roma the right to use their language, orally and in writing, in dealings with courts and other authorities
- granting Roma the right to self-fulfilment (through their representatives) in the distribution of financial aid for projects to aid Roma
- promoting educational programs about the background of anti-gypsyism in Europe for politicians, civil servants and general public
- including Romani history in national curricula
- implementing confidence-building programs, such as employing Roma in the mainstream civil service instead of channelling them into alternative structures
- introducing a quota system for Roma in universities and the civil service

Interesting suggestions were also put forward by those Romani activists who acknowledge that economic factors play a significant role in the decision of Roma to leave their home countries. These activists advocate more economically-oriented solutions along with strategies aimed at re-opening legal opportunities for Romani migration. They envisage programmes aimed at achieving economic independence for Roma by improving work opportunities in their home countries, for example, through financial aid for Romani entrepreneurs and combating unemployment. In addition, they advocate normalising the movement of Romani workers by bilateral treaties to sanction the transfer of labour between countries that generate and receive refugees.[35]

Some scholars have also offered detailed recommendations. Matras (1998a: 22–3) calls for:

- adopting confidence-building measures and advisory measures aimed at different target groups of Romani migrants at present living in the West. These would seek to prevent clandestine existence and marginalisation by directing migrants to existing support networks in such areas as employment, vocational training, schooling, or medical care, as well as by helping clarify asylum claims and citizenship issues
- introducing confidence-building measures to promote active Romani involvement in community affairs and support the expansion of Romani networks
- encouraging Romani participation in decision-making processes in political fora, in setting social policies and within educational systems
- enhancing and institutionalising dialogue with Romani associations, elected Romani representatives and other delegated experts from Romani communities
- exploring possibilities of establishing a long-term scheme of constituency-based, directly elected or proportional representation of Roma in Europe
- conducting a survey of existing forms of representation in Romani communities throughout Europe.

The Brahams believe that anti-discrimination advocacy for all minority groups must be continued in order to change the hostile climate of public opinion both in host and home countries. However, at the same time, it is also necessary to alter the Romani cultural style through designing appropriate programmes with active Romani participation. Furthermore, there is a need to reconsider present initiatives, such as the Copenhagen Criteria and the *Framework Convention for the*

---

[35] For details see e.g. Rom-po-Drom (The Committee of Roma from Romania, refugees in Poland) and Romani CRISS (Roma Center for Social Intervention and Studies) (2000).

Protection of National Minorities, which appear to be inappropriate for the Roma. To counteract the socio-economic disadvantage of the Roma, which is one of the causes of their outmigration, massive long-term funding has to be set aside by the international community, particularly the EC, because such financial resources are unavailable at present within the EU candidate states. These should be targeted at whole communities, as opposed to Roma alone, in order to avoid resentment by the majority. Finally, they urge that:

> it is essential that policy makers, particularly at the EU level re-examine, on an inter-disciplinary basis, the whole question of ethnic identity and its economic, political, and social utility with regard to the Roma [because] [t]here is an urgent need to find a trade-off between maintenance of cultural identity and the adaptations to current economic and social demands that are required.
>
> (Braham and Braham 2000: 111–2)

Mark Braham previously advocated an increase in services for Romani refugees such as assistance at the borders of prospective asylum countries, when awaiting asylum procedures and in asylum centres. He also recommended that good practice should be observed at points of departure/expulsion and of return/repatriation as well as the establishment of national and international (European) Romani institutes (Braham 1993: 78-82). Michal Vašečka (2000: 13–14) recommends that EU member states should co-ordinate their asylum policies as this would prevent the Romani issue becoming an obstacle to enlargement. In his opinion such a development would sharpen hostility against Roma even further in their home countries. He also believes in:

- rewarding initiatives involving mutual co-operation of Roma and non-Romani communities
- providing better information to EU officials about existing CEE initiatives to improve the situation of Roma
- ensuring better collection and exchange of information about Roma at both public and official levels in both Western Europe and CEE
- expanding EU support for activities aimed at access to education for Romani children (such as pre-school education and Romani teaching assistant programmes) and providing the know-how for such programmes by EU social work experts in aiding children from disadvantaged environments
- assisting the formation of an effective Romani political elite through Europe-

wide affirmative action including scholarships for Romani higher education students, especially in law, education and business
- focusing on the role of Romani entrepreneurs in their communities by EU programmes to support the development of small businesses
- implementing development projects to improve the living conditions of Roma under the guidance of Western experts as in developing countries

Imrich Vašečka (2000) proposes:

- promoting extensive, nation-wide anti-racism and tolerance campaigns as well as information campaigns and communication training in the form of confidence-building measures to eradicate the sometimes unjustified Romani feeling of discrimination
- rethinking national approaches towards education and employment of Roma
- providing state aid to improve the socio-economic situation of Roma, especially in education, employment and entrepreneurial activity
- attempting to solve the social 'non-sovereignty' of a significant percentage of the Romani population by new approaches in social work
- assisting the development of Romani cultural identity and organisational networks, including the expansion of Romani civil society and political representation
- establishing networks of citizens' advice bureaux for minority and Romani issues and of Romani charitable organisations
- initiating dialogue between Romani representatives and international organisations as well as national bodies involved in migration issues
- supporting initiatives aimed at expanding the employment of Roma – especially the young and qualified, improving social work among Roma – particularly in segregated settlements and improving the housing and health situation of Roma
- offering financial, material and personnel aid to NGOs willing to co-operate with state and local administrations in devising integration programmes for Roma
- boosting educational initiatives, including help for Romani teachers and assistants in motivating talented pupils and their families and tutoring these pupils to prepare them for higher education

Several common threads are apparent in the recommendations of activists and scholars discussed here.

Firstly, there is a call for increasing active involvement of Roma in community affairs and in decision-making processes in political fora. This is not exactly a novel view, but nevertheless such engagement has never been properly and fully implemented anywhere. Scholars suggest that such initiatives could include establishing national and international (European) Romani institutes and introducing measures to promote the formation of an effective Romani political elite. Apart from building confidence and strengthening legitimacy in policy-making by broadening Romani representation, such a strategy might also exert a positive influence to modernise the Romani cultural style. On the other hand, Romani representatives believe that it is necessary to ensure that elected Romani representatives actively participate in national decision-making processes, instead of being sidelined into alternative structures. They also envisage strengthening the Romani civil rights movement and close co-operation between international Romani organisations and mainstream international organisations in the preparation of recommendations, strategies and aid programmes for Roma.

Secondly, the international community and particularly the EU is asked to commit massive, long-term funding for the integration of the Roma into majority societies. In the opinion of Romani representatives, such funding should go directly to Romani communities or, at the very least, their leaders should be involved in administering it.

Thirdly, changes in national and international legislation concerning asylum, but also wider issues, are required to be more compatible with the specific needs of the Romani community.

Fourthly, advocacy for anti-discrimination, tolerance and multiculturalism, as well as education, is needed in order to change the hostile climate of public opinion in both host and home countries.

Beyond these recommendations, activists agree that Roma have to be granted impartial and non-discriminatory treatment in consideration of claims for asylum and all their human rights have to be respected in every country without discrimination. The latter should be ensured through careful monitoring carried out by co-operation between Romani and mainstream international organisations. On the other hand, scholars frequently put forward three further proposals. In their view further academic research is needed to explore possibilities of helping establish a long-term scheme of constituency-based Romani representation in Europe. The question of ethnic identity and its applicability to Roma should be re-examined to find a trade-off between the maintenance of cultural identity and adaptation to contemporary economic and social demands. Finally, services for Romani refugees should be increased to prevent them reverting to a clandestine existence in host countries leading to further marginalisation.

All of these recommendations, except the very last one, reflect perspectives in both home and host countries, although these are possibly more individual than collective. However, home countries add several more requirements, mostly directed at host countries. These include co-ordination of asylum policies, better dissemination of information to and among EU officials about existing CEE initiatives to improve the situation of Roma, better collection and exchange of information about Roma in both Western Europe and CEE at public as well as official level. They also call for EU programmes to strengthen the role of Romani entrepreneurs in their communities by supporting the development of small businesses and implementing development projects similar to those in developing countries.

Identifying trends in perspective formation in the Romani asylum debate

The analysis in this paper shows that it is difficult to extrapolate clearly defined positions from existing, limited academic debate. While politicians and activists have a clear agenda and defined interests, scholars are freer to present different, often highly individualistic perspectives, and they do. Furthermore, since academic debate on this topic is just beginning, a real contest has yet to emerge where various standpoints are supported or challenged. Instead, contrasting approaches can be said to be in a formative stage and consequently even the views presented in this discussion need to be confirmed or challenged through further research and analysis. Similarly, for related reasons, it is impossible to distinguish yet between particular trends in perspective formation between scholars in the refugees' countries of origin and those in receiving countries. As a result, only a few meaningful generalisations can be made about this debate on Romani asylum seekers.

The activist view appears to be unequivocally pro-asylum and opposed to border controls and other protective measures.[36] On the other hand, scholars usually only criticise all protective measures, including restrictions on asylum and imposition of border controls, as failing to solve and sometimes even exacerbating the problems connected to recent Romani migration. However, they rarely adopt a clear stance for or against any particular measure.

The main difference in opinion between academics from home and host countries concerns the role of economic motives in present-day migration. Here scholars from home countries assign a more significant role to these motives than those from host countries.[37] The former are also more inclined to emphasise the need for a European approach towards Romani affairs, for co-operation in addressing related issues and financial burden-sharing and for co-ordination of asylum policies.[38] In contrast, those in host countries are more concerned with the need to provide assistance to Romani asylum seekers. Both agree in stressing that the public should be better educated on these matters, although academics in home countries tend to make the assumption – in some respects incorrectly – that their public is better informed. Interestingly, however, all of the authors analysed seemed to concentrate their attention and recommendations more on host countries than home countries.

Among other things, this paper aims to provide a detailed inventory of recommendations suggested until now in the on-going migration debate. These are overwhelmingly aimed at minimising outmigration of Roma and improving their overall situation. Several of these proposals

---

[36] It has to be noted, however, that although the views expressed here come from activists of different nationalities from both Western Europe and CEE, they all cooperate and adhere to a similar ideology. Therefore, it would be desirable to investigate other activist views that do not generally get published.

[37] This holds only for academic views; governmental views in both home and host countries emphasise the economic motives of Romani refugees.

[38] In this case in conformity with governmental views.

have already been presented to European policy-makers, but none have yet prompted an adequate response. In some cases no action at all has been taken. Nevertheless, it is to be hoped that the recent intensification of westward migration by Roma might lead at last to a more serious attempt to address their painful and highly problematic situation.

Postscript

This article was written in 2000 and reflects the state of the debate at that time. In 2000 academic consideration of Romani migration was very much in its early stages and the debate has in fact intensified in the last couple of years, perhaps due to efforts such as the Prague Roundtable which stimulated further discussion. However, the majority of the points addressed in this article remain extremely valid today. In addition, the article has a historical value because it presents the starting point of academic thinking about contemporary Romani migration. Some of the suggestions presented in this article are now actually being slowly implemented, showing that the debate has led to practical steps.

References

Amato, G. and Batt, J. (1998) *Mobility in an Enlarged European Union* (San Domenico di Fiesole: European University Institute.

Bancroft, A. (1999) *A Panic in Perspective: Czech and Slovak Roma Asylum Seekers in Western Europe and Canada*, Unpublished paper, British Sociological Association.

Braham, Mark (1993) *The Untouchables: A Survey of the Roma People of Central and Eastern Europe*, Geneva: UNHCR.

Braham, M. and Braham, M. (2000) 'Romani migrations and EU enlargement', *Cambridge Review of International Affairs* vol. XIII/2, spring/summer.

Cahn, C. and Vermeersch, P. 'The group expulsion of Slovak Roma by the Belgian government: A case study of the treatment of Romani refugees in Western countries', *Cambridge Review of International Affairs* vol. XIII/2, spring/summer.

Castle-Kaněrová, M. (2000) 'Roma as refugees in Europe', Presentation at *Conference 2000: New Directions in Romani Studies*, University of Greenwich, 29 June.

Clark, C. and Campbell, E. (2000) '"Gypsy invasion": A critical analysis of newspaper reaction to Czech and Slovak Romani asylum-seekers in Britain, 1997', *Romani Studies* 5, Vol. 10, 1.

Červeňák, J. (2000) 'The report on the reasons of the migration of the Roma in the Slovak Republic', Background paper for the Organisation for Security and Co-operation in Europe (OSCE)/Office for Democratic Institutions and Human Rights (ODIHR) *International Consultation on Roma Refugees and Asylum Seekers*, Warsaw, 23 October.

ERRC (1999) 'Forced migration of Roma and the current asylum "crisis"', Statement by the ERRC on the occasion of the OSCE Review Conference *Roma in the Kosovo Conflict*, Vienna, 22 September, Published materials.

ERRC (2000a) *Press Statement: International Roma Day,* 7 April, Budapest: ERRC. Available World Wide Web, URL: http://www.errc.org.

ERRC (2000b) 'Protecting Romani refugees around Europe: A position paper by the European Roma Rights Center', Prepared for the OSCE/ODIHR *International Consultation on Roma Refugees and Asylum Seekers*, Warsaw, 23 October.

Fraser, A. (1992) *The Gypsies*, Oxford: Blackwell.

Fraser, A. (2000) 'The present and the future of the Gypsy past', *Cambridge Review of International Affairs* vol. XIII/2, spring/summer.

Gheorghe, R. (2000) 'Asylum applications from Eastern European countries to Central European, EU member and other Western countries', Statistics prepared for the OSCE/ODIHR *International Consultation on Roma Refugees and Asylum Seekers*, Warsaw, 23 October.

Gheorghe, N. and Klímová, I. (2000) 'Consolidated summary and recommendations', OSCE/ODIHR *International Consultation on Romani Refugees and Asylum Seekers*, Warsaw, 23 October. Available World Wide Web, URL: http://www.osce.org/odihr/docs/m00-6-final.htm.

Helton, A. C. (1999) 'Roma and forced migration: lessons of recent Canadian cases', *Roma Rights* 1.

IRU (2000) *Statement on the Migration of Roma in East and Central Europe.* Available World Wide Web, URL: http://www.romnews.com.

IRU and RNC (2000), *Common Position Paper on Migration*, International Romani Union and Roma National Congress, 22 October. Available World Wide Web, URL: http://www.romnews.com.

Kawczynski, R. (2000) 'Report on the condition of the Roma in Europe', Background paper for OSCE/ODIHR *International Consultation on Roma Refugees and Asylum Seekers*, Warsaw, 23 October. Available World Wide Web, URL: http://www.romnews.com.

Kenrick, D. (1994) 'Romani: [sic] on the move', *Index on Censorship* 23.

Kovats, M. (2000) 'Academic introduction', *Cambridge Review of International Affairs* vol. XIII/2, spring/summer.

Kryštof, R. (2000) Presentation at the OSCE/ODIHR *International Consultation on Roma Refugees and Asylum Seekers*, Warsaw, 23 October.

Kuder, R. (2000) *Recent Trends in German Ethnic Politics: The Roma*, Unpublished MA thesis, International Studies and the Graduate School of the University of Oregon, June.

Lee, R. (2000) 'Post-Communist Romani migration to Canada', *Cambridge Review of International Affairs* vol. XIII/2, spring/summer.

Liégeois, J.-P. and Gheorghe, N. (1995) *Roma/Gypsies: A European Minority*, Minority Rights Group International Report, London: MRG.

Matras, Y. (1998a) *Problems Arising in Connection with the International Mobility of the Roma in Europe*, Report submitted to the European Committee on Migration (CDMG), 15 December 1996, CDMG (98) 14.

Matras, Y. (1998b) *The Recent Emigration of Roma from the Czech and Slovak Republics*, Report submitted to the Council of Europe Population and Migration Division, August 1998, MG-S-ROM (98) 9.

Matras, Y. (2000) 'Romani migrations in the post-Communist era: Their historical and political significance', *Cambridge Review of International Affairs* vol. XIII/2, spring/summer.

Mirga, A. and Gheorghe, N. (1997) *The Roma in the Twenty-First Century: A Policy Paper*, PER: Princeton.

O'Nions, H. (1999) 'Bonafide or bogus?: Roma asylum seekers from the Czech Republic', *Web Journal of Current Legal Issues* 3. Available World Wide Web, URL: http://webvcli.ncl.ac.uk/1999/issue3/onions3.html.

Peric, T. and Demirovski, M. (2000) 'Unwanted: The exodus of Kosova Roma (1998-2000)', *Cambridge Review of International Affairs* vol. XIII/2, spring/summer.

Pickup, A. (1999), 'Denial of basic rights: The marginalisation of Romani refugees in France', *Roma Rights* 1.

Pluim, M. (2000a) ICMPD, Presentation at the OSCE/ODIHR *International Consultation on Roma Refugees and Asylum Seekers*, Warsaw, 23 October.

Pluim, M. (2000b) *Current Roma Migration from the EU Candidate States*, Draft study prepared by International Centre for Migration Policy Development (ICMPD), November.

Rom-po-Drom and Romani CRISS (2000) 'Asylum seeking and its alternatives: The case of Roma from Romania asking asylum in Poland, during September 1999–October 2000', Research report on the immigration of the Romanian Roma people to Poland, Rom-po-Drom (The Committee of Roma from Romania, refugees in Poland) and Romani CRISS (Roma Center for Social Intervention and Studies), Working draft, 19 October, Background paper for the OSCE/ODIHR *International Consultation on Roma Refugees and Asylum Seekers*, Warsaw, 23 October.

Trehan, N. 'Romani migrations: Addressing continuing debates', *Cambridge Review of International Affairs* vol. XIII/2, spring/summer.

UNHCR (1999) 'Five centuries of discrimination ... and still counting', *Refugees Magazine* 1999b, New York: UNHCR.

Vašečka, I. (2000) 'Migration of Romany [sic] to the EU countries in reaction to unequal opportunitie*s*', Presentation at the international conference *Minorities in a Pluralist Society at the Turn of Millenium*, Brno, 2 September.

Vašečka, M. (2000) *Roma – the Greatest Challenge for Slovakia on its Way into the European Union*, Bratislava: Institute for Public Affairs, January.

Wilmer, F. (1993) *The Indigenous Voice in World Politics*, London: Sage.

Winterbourne, D. (1999), 'Love thy neighbour', *Roma Rights* 1.

Roma migration as an integral part of 'international Roma politics' in Europe

Roman Krištof

Roma migration in Europe from the end of World War II to the collapse of the communism in Eastern Europe (1945 – 1992)

Roma migration during the second half of the twentieth century was never really an important issue in terms of international relations. Nevertheless, it resulted in completely new situations and possibilities, which now play a decisive role in emerging, contemporary 'international Roma politics'. Most of the changes took place in East-Central Europe, where spontaneous migration as well as government-orchestrated transfer and dispersal policies and attempts to eradicate Roma settlements led to the wholesale departure of Roma communities or clans.

The most drastic case of the creation of completely new communities was exemplified by the policy of the Communist Party in Czechoslovak to eradicate (Serviko) Roma settlements in Slovakia during the period from 1966 to 1969[1]. The resulting mass movement of Roma from Slovakia to the Czech lands led to a situation where numerous Roma communities found themselves in an environment which was foreign or even hostile to their culture. Although not entirely reliable as hard data, the last realistic statistics produced by local authorities (national committees)[2] reported 145,700 Roma in the Czech lands in 1989 (Kalibová 2002: 32) in comparison with only around six hundred in 1945, who were the survivors of Nazi genocide from the original Czech and Moravian Roma and Sinti communities. Their numbers had been

---

[1] In April 1958 the Central Committee of the Czechoslovak Communist Party ordered the elimination of undesirable concentrations of Gypsy streets, quarters and settlements and in 1962 issued a directive to eradicate Roma settlements in Slovakia. A few years later, in 1966, Resolution 502/1966 of the Czechoslovak Government initiated a programme of 'controlled dispersal'.
[2] National committees (*národní výbory*) were the basic administrative unit in Communist Czechoslovakia.

estimated at approximately six thousand before the Second World War (Nečas 1995). Consequently, the migration of more than one hundred thousand Serviko (Rumungre) Roma from Slovakia to the Czech lands can be regarded as the largest post-war cross-border movement of Roma in European history.[3]

Meanwhile, during the 1960s, a wide variety of Roma groups also migrated from what was then Yugoslavia into Italy, Austria, Germany, France and the Netherlands, aided by a relaxation in travel restrictions by the idiosyncratic Tito regime (Fraser 2000: 17). However, no data is available about the numbers involved in this migratory wave.

At this point it is worth mentioning that during the post-war period many leading Roma personalities migrated from East-Central European countries to Germany, such as Rajko Djurić, ex-president of the International Romani Union (IRU), from Yugoslavia and Rudko Kawczynski, founder of the Roma National Congress (RNC), from Poland. Likewise Emil Ščuka, current IRU president, came from Slovakia to the Czech lands in the 1970s and Jan Cibula, one of the founders of the international Romani movement, migrated from what was formerly Czechoslovakia to Switzerland in the 1960s. In addition, many family clans of the Lovari and Kalderash group travelled from the Balkan 'second cradle'[4] via Poland and Czechoslovakia to Scandinavia, particularly to Sweden. This last migration is highly significant for the development of contemporary international Romani political activities.

Roma migration in Europe during the past decade (1992 – 2002)

The fall of the Iron Curtain started a great 'travel boom' among citizens of former Soviet bloc states, journeying towards the advanced economies of Western Europe – that is to say to Western Europe as

---

[3] Post-Second World War Czechoslovakia was at first a unitary and then a federal state, before finally being divided in 1993 into two independent states – the Czech and Slovak republics.

[4] The term 'second cradle' is used to refer to Balkan countries in the 'Frame statute (Moral Charter) of the Rromani people in the European Union', issued in Belgium by the Romani Activist Network in Legal and Political Issues (RANELPI), p.3, §4/c.

defined by forty-five years of post-war development, not culturally or geographically. This 'travel boom' consisted of trips to 'Western' countries with the aim of staying for a shorter or longer period in order to make a profit – whether by legal, semi-legal or illegal means. The point of the exercise was either to acquire goods to be exchanged advantageously at some later date or to earn money, usually through illicit employment. Some of these new migrants were successful in managing to legalise their temporary visits by degrees into extended stays, using their professional and other skills to obtain work permits, student visas or permanent residence through marriage. In practice, Western Europe has been able to absorb this kind and scale of migration without much difficulty and, in principle, there should have been no adverse foreign policy implications. In a handful of cases a few individuals had tried to demand asylum, which before the collapse of Communist rule was quite justifiable.

If we consider the underlying parameters of this stratagem, a necessary condition was either entry without visa requirements or easy access to various kinds of short or long-term visas. However, this device has not been adopted by Roma migrants from Central and Eastern Europe. Only exceptionally have Roma used the tactics employed by fellow citizens of their home countries. From the very beginning of the 1990s Roma have travelled to Western countries by making use of the possibility of claiming asylum under the 1951 Geneva Convention, turning their migration into a political case. As Yaron Matras correctly stated:

> Roma from eastern Europe have virtually no possibility of long-term labour migration to the West. Short-term labour migration is usually made impossible by the nature of Romani migration, which is one of nuclear or extended families rather than of individual skilled labourers. Thus the only possibility since 1989 to leave the East and seek an improvement in quality of life in the West has been to apply for political asylum. Typical post-1989 Romani migrants are therefore either asylum applicants from central and eastern Europe, or refugees from the war zones in former Yugoslavia.
>
> (Matras 2000: 39)

The goal of Roma migrants from East-Central Europe has often seemed to become nothing more than 'asylum seekers', in the knowledge of the practical improbability of making a successful claim. This kind of economically rational choice is based on hearing the positive evaluation of their experience abroad made by other members of their community after their return home. As recent field research conducted by the Czech Ministry of the Interior indicated, the 'positive migratory experience', i.e. experience of simply being an asylum seeker, leads to repeated asylum claims in various Western European countries (Ministry of the Interior 2002).

The countries of origin of Roma migrants can be divided into two groups:

- The Balkan 'second cradle' – specifically Romania, Bulgaria, Albania, Macedonia, Serbia, Bosnia and Herzegovina. These countries all have substantial, impoverished Romani populations that suffer extreme social exclusion from majority societies. In addition, many of these Roma have been severely afflicted by the civil wars erupting from the break-up of the Yugoslav federation and some are also victims of ethnic cleansing in Kosovo. On the whole, the West imposed strict visa requirements for the Balkans (now lifted for Romania and Bulgaria as a consequence of strict migration controls).

- Central European countries – Poland, the Czech Republic, Slovakia and Hungary. Generally speaking, Western Europe has relatively liberal visa requirements for Central European states, penalising only Slovakia for migration by Roma asylum seekers by sporadically imposing and revoking visa requirement (e.g. Great Britain, Belgium, Finland, Denmark, Norway, Ireland)[5].

---

[5]'[I]n many cases EU governments used *ad hoc* measures to stem the number of Slovak asylum seekers. For example, in October 1999 Belgium carried out a very controversial collective repatriation clearly aimed at specifically discouraging this group from seeking asylum (Cahn and Vermeersch 2000). Later, Belgium – like the UK, Finland, Ireland, Denmark and Norway – introduced visa requirements for Slovak citizens. This latter measure obviously gave rise to additional pressure on the diplomatic relations between Slovakia and the EU countries. Particularly symbolic for many Slovaks was the consequence that they had to possess a visa for travelling to the European institutions in Brussels, this in spite of Slovakia's recent admission to the first group of candidate states to hold detailed negotiations on EU membership. Not

However, the mere threat of the imposition of visa requirements has had an adverse effect on the relationship of the Czech Republic with Great Britain and Belgium. (In fact, Canada re-imposed visa requirements for the Czech Republic in 1997 and more recently for Hungary in 2001. In response, both countries also re-introduced visa requirements for Canadian citizens).

The situation of Roma communities in Balkan countries is highly complex and the region as a whole is so unstable that any attempt at discussing the issue of Romani migration from the Balkans would exceed the scope of this article. There is no comparison between victims of ethnic cleansing in Kosovo and Bosnia and those migrants engaged in the sort of travel stratagems described above. Therefore the following remarks will be entirely confined to the Roma of Central Europe.

In the second half of the 1990s Central European countries were more successful than their Balkan counterparts in their attempts to join European and Atlantic political structures. Nevertheless, during the same period the Czech and Slovak republics in particular were severely criticised by a range of international bodies for mistreatment of their Roma populations. Yet, in spite of this condemnation, European funding was meanwhile made available through PHARE programmes as part of the EU accession process, supporting projects to improve the situation of Roma communities. Additional financial and other assistance was also provided for the same purpose by various international initiatives. Nevertheless, it appears that international assistance has had minimal influence on improving the situation of Roma in EU candidate countries. Instead, it has given rise to an international 'Roma industry' (i.e. NGO activities comparable to those of commercial businesses, which although linked to Roma issues have no discernible effect at community level). This complaint has been made frequently and quite justifiably by many Roma representatives (e.g. constantly by the Roma National Congress).

---

surprisingly, the blame for spoiling Slovakia's relations with Europe was again put on the Roma' (Vermeersch 2002: 97).

In recent years numbers of Czech, Slovak, Polish and Hungarian Roma have claimed political asylum in the West, especially in those countries with liberal asylum procedures such as Canada, Great Britain, Ireland, Sweden, Norway and Finland. However, it is apparent that many of these Roma asylum seekers have been extremely confused about exactly what they are applying for. There are documented cases of Roma from the Czech Republic asking the Czech embassy in Brussels for assistance in completing forms to apply for asylum in Belgium and for help in sorting out their social welfare claims in their home country. Likewise, the office of the Inter-Ministerial Commission for Romani Community Affairs (attached to the Government Office of the Czech Republic) has received a number of phone-calls and letters asking for guidance and advice about leaving the country to seek a better life. Some of these enquiries were orchestrated by NGOs with close links to the Roma National Congress, an international Romani organisation based in Germany. Studies commissioned by the Office for Democratic Institutions and Human Rights (ODIHR) and the International Organisation for Migration (IOM) (e.g. Gabal 2000), as well as by government bodies (e.g. People in Need 2000), have indicated that most Roma asylum seekers from Central Europe do not come from the poorest and most deprived strata of Roma communities but, instead, from relatively advantaged urban and educational backgrounds, though these may have experienced a decrease in living standards in the 1990s.

The puzzle remains – why is it that Roma migrants have not adopted the travel stratagem but, almost exclusively, have used asylum claims in their search for a better life? Probably there can never be a satisfactory answer to this question. However, I should like to put forward several relevant factors:

- being victims of misinformation and manipulation, combined with generally different perceptions and expectations of Roma;
- marginalisation of and discrimination against Roma and the widening gap between rich and poor in post-communist societies;
- inconsistent and counter-productive initiatives or policies of governmental and non-governmental bodies.

It is totally comprehensible that international Romani organisations, seeking to represent the Romani cause at international level, have seized upon and championed the issue of the migrants' demand for political asylum. However, the dynamics of the underlying political processes are best explained by Pavel Barša in 'Romanies at the crossroads: The dilemma of contemporary Romany politics' (Barša 2000).

> ... [T]he new deficiencies and new opportunities of the 1990s have started to change the identity of Romanies. A significantly ethno-culturally ... [varied] population has started to be represented by its elite as an ethnic or national collective 'subject', which raises a claim for representation both on the national and the international political scene. Migration also contributes, at least potentially, to the unification and homogenisation of Romany identity.

> A good example of the consequences of migration for the reformulation of group identity is given by events in Germany in the 1990s. In the course of the 1970s a self-governing organisation, both recognised and materially supported by the state, was formed. Up until the arrival of Romanies in Germany this was based on the position that Sinti and Romanies living in Germany represent ethnic groups which belong to the German national state.[6] Following the Jewish model this organisation called itself *Zentralrat deutscher Sinti und Roma*. The name itself by using the word 'German' emphasises the appurtenance to the German nation. This becomes clear in comparison with the name *Zentralrat der Juden in Deutschland*, which unambiguously speaks of Jews living in Germany rather than of German Jews. The specific inclusion of two ethnic groups – Sinti and Romani – also gives an expression of distance towards the unifying, Pan-Romani and Pan-European nation-forming project, represented by the International Romani Union.

> More nationalist streams at that time did not have great weight in the case of German Romani[es] and Sinti. However, this changed with the arrival of Balkan Romani[es] in the first half of the 1990s. A section of Romani activists led by Rudko Kawczynski started to organise a movement of solidarity with them. This group declared itself against the aims of the German government to refuse the

---

[6] The following description of the German situation draws on Matras, Y. (1998) 'The development of the Romani civil rights movement in Germany 1945 – 1996', in S. Tebbutt (ed.) *Sinti and Roma: Gypsies in German-Speaking Society and Literature*, New York, Oxford: Berghahn, 49–63.

Balkan Romani[es] their right to exile and return them to their countries of origin, and asked the German government to grant them special status. Immigration thus poured new energy into disputes within the German Romani community over whether Romani[es] and Sinti are simply one German *Volksgruppe*, that is a German ethnic minority, or whether they should join together with other Romanies in a Pan-European national movement and attempt to achieve the recognition of all Romanies as a subject of international law. At least in Germany this dispute remains unresolved.

(Barša 2000)

The contentious debate described above is now taking place all over the ex-Soviet bloc in Europe and is fuelled by the phenomenon of Romani 'political migration'. This accelerates the need for swift decisions at governmental level, that is, to implement effective policies leading to Roma integration as well as zero tolerance of both discrimination and social exclusion. Unless such decisions are taken promptly, unpreventable migration by Roma will lead to nationalist segregation and bury all hope of multicultural integration.

A recent Joint Declaration by Rromani NGOs of France and Romania stated:

...we deplore that some political movements should use this painful issue (i.e. migration and repatriation) for partisan ends, demanding either a blind regularisation or a blind repatriation of all the persons concerned, which is neither in their interest nor in the interest of justice. Both these positions, which are equally demagogic, are moreover unworkable.

...In a number of countries, there exists simultaneously a strong pressure in order to 'de-tsiganise the area' and networks which are sometimes well-established and which offer an idyllic exile to gullible candidates. Emissaries of western NGOs also sometimes hang around, needing 'fresh refugees' in order to justify their existence and above all their subsidies, even if it means dictating to refugees what attitude or behaviour they should adopt, or even if it means making up cases of discrimination from start to finish. The persons concerned unanimously agree to these observations.

(Romani NGOs of France and Romania 2002)

Roma migration from the perspective of Roma nationalism

According to Yaron Matras, '[m]igration forms a repetitive pattern throughout Romani history. It is part of the collective memory and cultural and historical legacy of the Roma as a nation' (Matras 2000: 34). However, the view of the international Romani movement, based on the assumption that migration embodies a 'right' of Roma people, a 'right' which is both individual and collective, has been seriously challenged by recent developments in the European theatre. Reactions of destination countries have been largely negative and in Great Britain led to the introduction of a new asylum law in November 2002, under which all candidate countries were regarded as 'safe'. Other destination countries have adopted similar restrictive measures. Some of those making use of the migration issue to bring pressure to bear on their own governments have probably realised by now that their states are determined to stop migration that abuses the 1951 Geneva Convention. Understandably the reactions of their political counterparts in the home countries of Roma migrants were also unfavourable,[7] since their negotiating position was weakened. European Union states have had mixed feelings about raising issues that are sensitive in their own back-yard, such as the recognition of national and ethnic minorities. Peter Vermeersch rightly concluded in his study of the case of Slovakia:

---

[7] 'Roma activists, supported in this by human rights organisations, emphasised that growing numbers of Roma asylum seekers were fundamentally the result of a general discriminatory climate in Slovakia, which had over the years deeply affected the economic position of many Roma. The Slovak Roma tried to translate international scrutiny into a complaint against their government. The idea of building a protest movement this way seemed a logical strategy, since Slovakia's treatment of the Roma more than ever evoked comment and reporting in domestic and international mass media. ....

The widespread conception of an essential 'Roma culture' understood as characterised by a number of very negative traits produces a difficult position for those activists who want to contest government policy from a 'Roma' perspective. The Western reaction to the refugee wave seems to have stimulated this negative conception. Hence, it is likely that as long as international attention is not aimed at changing this image, the pressures exerted on Slovakia will not lead to significantly better opportunities for Roma activists and politicians, but, on the contrary, to more negative pressure on the Roma' (Vermeersch 2002: 96–7).

As an empirical exploration indicates, Roma political activists in Slovakia have to contend with a number of difficulties when they want to utilise the minority protection requirements of the EU to buttress their political mobilisation. The first reason is that the Union has been hesitant in embracing a clear minority rights policy for itself and therefore has not developed a consistent vision on minority rights in its enlargement policy.

(Vermeersch 2002: 97)

The current quest in international Romani circles for recognition at national as well as international level will be pursued by different means and thoughts have already been voiced anticipating a fresh approach. A new opportunity presented to Roma nationalism is not just migration within the territory of Europe but arises from the process of unification itself. Ivan Veselý, IRU commissioner for media, outlined present-day perspectives at a recent seminar, *Roma and the Question of Self-Determination: Fiction and Reality*, hosted in Warsaw in April 2002 by the Project on Ethnic Relations NGO (PER):

The diminishing role of the state and emergence of supra-national structures, above all the European Union, tear down barriers between particular national states and offers a chance for the creation of non-traditional forms of national existence, represented for instance by the idea of an a-territorial nation. At first sight even what appear as negative phenomena – continuing segregation or the threat posed by Nazi skinhead groups – might be used for positive ends. A need to defend ourselves against external threats may increase feelings of belonging and of the necessity for co-operation. Larger settlements and more numerous communities will enable us to assume a stronger position in relation to the majority and its institutions. In this way conditions are created for establishing a system of self-government, which is capable of solving internal problems and thus defending the interests of the community against others. Demands to the central state administration for greater autonomy are unlikely to succeed unless they are supported by working examples. ... [We should] not just demand more care from state and local authority officials and representatives but firstly more rights, for example the right to make independent decisions about a specific part of budgets, whether a municipal, regional or even state budgets.[8]

(Veselý 2001)

---

[8] Extract translated from the Czech by R. Krištof.

In his own contribution to the Warsaw seminar, Andrzej Mirga, the Polish Roma scholar, reflected on the growing involvement of non-Roma actors in the Romani self-identification process.[9] In his view, the fascination of European and American intellectual and activist circles with the 'Roma question' has currently become a major concern of many genuine Roma actors. They feel the intervention of these outsiders to be a threat at international level and an influence at national level, where they experience the 'internationalisation' of their local struggles and stability pacts deteriorating under the poisonous attention of the media to the 'Roma problem'.

Roma integration into the societies of European states or into the European Union?

If we interpret recent Roma migration, i.e. the migration of the mainly sedentary Roma population of CEE countries, as a move to better their socio-economic conditions and to achieve a certain kind of upward social mobility, then we should not be surprised that the emerging international Romani elite, whose main actors have themselves migrated for such reasons, make use of migration as a tool for pressing demands for their own recognition at international level. Consequently,

---

[9] 'The ERRC conference from December 2000 introduced additional references to the Roma's self-determination question. Non-Romani participants were more forthcoming in suggesting models of self-determination for the Roma to follow. In J. Goldstone's 'fantasy' vision: "Surely Roma, who number anywhere from 8 to 12 million, enjoy at least as much entitlement to a full fledged State as the Palestinians do. [...] Since 1990, numerous people – Macedonians, Bosnians, Croats, Slovenes – have demanded and secured by violence, by fiat or by other means their own states. Why not Roma? " (Roma Rights, No 4, 2001).

C. Cahn on the other hand invites Roma to learn from the Zionist movement that led to the establishment of the Jewish state – Israel. According to Cahn there are a number of similarities between the Zionism of the first half of the nineteenth century and the current Romani movement. As he claims " [...] it is not only on this strict organisational/mechanistic front that Zionism has ideas of potential use for a Romani movement – the core challenges of Zionism, such as breaking the primary allegiance of Jews to the national states of other people and building the Jewish patriot and the Jewish body politics, were nearly identical to challenges facing Romani activists today" (Roma Rights, No. 4, 2001)' (Andrzej Mirga 2002, quoted from website http://www.dzeno.cz).

a change in attitude is unlikely, due to the origins of the present-day international Romani elite. Therefore, the emphasis on a pan-European approach is simply a logical outcome of the position and expectations of its main actors.

Should the international Romani elite renew itself and its main actors become genuine leaders of specific Roma national or ethnic minorities of individual states, then it could be also expected that the instrument of migration would no longer be used to blackmail weaker actors in the sphere of international organisations or to seek an institutional framework for the elite's pan-European aspirations. Such a new Romani political class would naturally prefer first of all to emphasise integration and recognition at national and local level and see mutually beneficial co-operation with Roma representatives established on a territorial basis.

References

Barša, P. (2000) 'Romanies at the crossroads: The dilemma of contemporary Romany politics', *Central European Political Studies - Review*, no. 1, II, winter, International Institute for Political Studies, Masaryk University, Brno. Available at: http://www.iips.cz/cisla/texty/clanky/romanies100.html

Cahn, C. and Vermeersch, P. (2000) 'The group expulsion of Slovak Roma by the Belgian government: A case study of the treatment of Romani refugees in Western countries', *Cambridge Review of International Affairs*, vol. XIII/2 spring/summer, 71–82.

Fraser, A. (2000) 'The present and future of the Gypsy past', *Cambridge Review of International Affairs*, vol. XIII/2 spring/summer, 17–31.

Gabal (2000) *Analysis of the Migration Climate and Migration Tendencies to Western European Countries in Romany Communities in Selected Cities in the Czech Republic*, research report for IOM Praha, Praha: Gabal Analysis and Consulting.

Kalibová, K. (2002) *Analysis of the Socio-economic Situation of the Roma Population in the Czech Republic*, Praha: Ministry of Labour and Social Affairs.

Matras, Y. (2000) 'Romani migrations in the post Communist era: Their historical and political significance', *Cambridge Review of International Affairs*, vol. XIII/2 spring/summer, 32–50.

Ministry of the Interior (2002) *Analysis of Reasons of Roma Community Members for Emigrating from the Czech Republic*, submitted to the Czech Government on 13 November 2002.

Nečas, C. (1995) *Romové v České republice včera a dnes*, Olomouc: Univerzita Palackého.

People in Need (2000) *Report on the Situation of Roma Re-emigres in the Czech Republic*, commissioned by the Government Office of the Czech Republic, Praha: People in Need.

Rromani NGOs of France and Romania (2002) *Joint Declaration by Rromani NGOs of France and Romania*, drafted in co-operation with the Contact Point for Roma and Sinti of OSCE/ODIHR, Warsaw: OSCE, 9 September 2002.

Vermeersch, P. (2002): 'Minority rights for the Roma and the political conditionality of European Union accession: the case of Slovakia', *Journal of Ethnic and Migration Studies*, vol. 28, 1:83–101.

Veselý, I. (2001) 'Contribution to the discussion on Roma emancipation', *Roma and the Question of Self-Determination: Fiction and Reality*, Warsaw seminar held by the Project on Ethnic Relations (PER), Princeton: PER. Veselý's paper is available in Czech at www.dzeno.cz on the *Amaro Gendalos* website.

Contemporary Roma Migration from Central and Eastern Europe: In Comparison with Post-Second World War Mobility

Eva Davidová

This paper seeks to examine aspects of contemporary Roma migration in and from Central and Eastern Europe by comparing this phenomenon with Roma mobility after the Second World War during the communist period, particularly with reference to the former Czechoslovakia as regards motivation and the development process after migration.

Introduction

Roma migration during the 1990s is a modern phenomenon as regards its extent, impact and motivation. This migration is motivated not only by socio-economic reasons, that is solving the problem of adequate living standards for Roma and their families, but at the same time by socio-political considerations. These include not only an attempt to improve migrants' social standing but often genuine fears for the lives of their family members and groups as a consequence of racial discrimination or even attacks. Even though only a small percentage are actually victims of racist attacks, nevertheless many give this as a reason for seeking, at first, support and, then later, asylum. Indeed, in reality the motivation for migration always involves such expressions of the xenophobia and intolerance of majority groups.

This great migratory movement of Roma from Central and especially South-Eastern Europe to a range of western European lands is quite different from the traditional nomadism of part of the Roma population and also from the migratory flow of Roma and Sinti from their Indian lands of origin. Moreover it is only partly comparable to the post-war migration from Slovakia to the Czech lands, as will be discussed.

Contemporary Roma migration was initially precipitated and made possible by the disintegration after 1989 of the former 'socialist bloc', which included not only the Soviet Union but Hungary, Poland,

Romania, Bulgaria and Albania. Other member states, former Yugoslavia and Czechoslovakia, divided even further – the latter into the Czech and Slovak Republics.

Recent migration from the Czech and Slovak republics

From the beginning of the 1990s latent problems began to emerge in society, concerning mutual relations between people and their behaviour towards each other. At the same time the so-called 'Roma problem' became more evident and complicated.

On the one hand gaining freedom brought Roma acknowledgement of their independence and the possibility to develop their language and culture, including the publication of books and other materials in the Romani language. It also provided the opportunity for them to found their own political party – *Romská Občanská Initiativa* (Romani Civic Initiative) – and other Roma organisations, as well as the chance to have their own freely elected representatives for the first time. Some even served as deputies in the Czech and Slovak National Councils and in the Federal Assembly, although this only lasted for the initial electoral period. Roma were also recognised as a nationality and gained other advantages, which only the more educated were able to utilise.

On the other hand this new period brought sudden unemployment to the Roma of the Czech and Slovak Republics. The vast majority of Roma in these lands (around 70 per cent or more) lost their jobs and became predominantly or wholly dependent on state support. Their descent into unemployment was far more abrupt than for others in the population and the reasons for this are well known. These include the low level of qualifications of the great majority of Roma and, in some cases, less reliable work morale and tendency to change jobs. For reasons like these, Roma were among the first to be made redundant and also were unlikely to be offered the possibility of other work. But these were by no means the only grounds, for often the most significant and hidden reason was that 'they are Roma'. During the first half of the 1990s notices appeared in several employment offices: 'Roma-Gypsies are not accepted'. Even today it is still common that when Roma job seekers arrive in person they are told: 'the vacancy is already filled'.

These basically racist practices and similar ones, such as the exclusion of Roma from certain wine bars and restaurants, are sometimes hard to prove but they also play their part in the decision of some Roma to emigrate.

The more or less hidden animosity of *gadje* (non-Roma) towards 'Gypsies' quickly surfaced after the November revolution and exposed the roots of a problem which had been neglected for years. Meanwhile Czech and Slovak politicians basically reconciled themselves to the situation on the grounds that the legal position of the Roma minority was protected both by the Charter of Basic Rights and Freedoms and article six of the Constitution. Likewise, the unproblematic co-existence of majority and Roma ethnicities was not helped by the Czech Citizenship Law on the break-up of the Czecho-Slovak Federation.

This law turned tens of thousands of Roma, who had lived for years in the Czech lands but who formally retained Slovak citizenship, into second class citizens and became the target of repeated criticism from international organisations.

The fuse of Roma dissatisfaction, which led to the mass departure from both republics in 1997 and 1998 was, above all, the continuing, brutal 'ethnic cleansing' perpetrated by skinheads. If these criminals were sentenced at all for such attacks, they received unbelievably light penalties. Undoubtedly certain politicians bear their share of the blame for the whole climate in society, where Roma were automatically judged as 'members of an inferior race' and yet, at the same time, it was denied that this behaviour was racist.

The problem of the situation of Roma and of mutual relations between communities grew worse between the years of 1993 and 1997. Indeed, this was demonstrated in 1997 when these pressures culminated in the autumn exodus of Roma, first to Canada and then to Britain. In 1997 this was the result of an irresponsible TV Nova documentary, 'Na vlastní oči' (See for Yourself), made by Josef Klíma, which presented Canada as the 'promised land' for Roma emigrants. The same cause led to the slightly later wave of emigration in the altered direction of Britain.

One of the many disturbing elements of this contemporary emigration is that those likely to migrate are drawn from the most educated, skilled and politically active among the Roma population. For example, in recent years several influential figures have left Prague and north Bohemia for Germany, Belgium, Holland, Sweden, England and Canada. This has the effect of depleting the number of skilled personnel remaining to continue organising to better the situation of Roma in their homelands.

The growth in contemporary Roma emigration from a whole range of countries in from central and eastern Europe was a matter of great concern to the fifth World Romani Congress, held in Prague in July 2000. Although a commission of the International Romani Union, which continues the work of the Congress, has been assigned to the problem of Roma migration, this whole problem remains as yet unsolved in every state that has been affected.

Roma migration in post-war Czechoslovakia

Roma migration in Czechoslovakia after the end of the Second World War happened for the most part in a spontaneous and unorganised way. This consisted of a large-scale migration of Roma from Slovakia, from where Roma families moved westwards, mostly to improve their living standards by taking advantage of work opportunities and flats to house their large families. The post-war migratory process from Slovakia 'to Czech', as Roma termed it, was really a process of urbanisation - of voluntary movement from poorer agricultural districts, mainly in eastern Slovakia, to largely industrial and border towns in the Czech lands in search of better jobs and accommodation.

Incoming migrant families tended to concentrate in these destinations, which were particularly attractive to them, and still do so today, although to a lesser extent. Consequently these industrial and border areas became relatively heavily populated by Roma, as opposed to other more rural areas of less interest. In the immediate post-war years the migratory flow gathered pace. In the Czech lands these migrants compensated for the decrease in the original population, such as Sudeten Germans expelled in 1945 and part of the younger generation of Czechs from border areas, who migrated internally and to industrial areas for higher earnings and better opportunities.

There are many factors in the post-war Roma migration which can be compared with that of several other migrant groups. Their migration also had specific characteristics in that the deliberate intention of Roma migrants was to move with their families, preferably to town centres or larger villages in border areas. This had a decisive significance for their family and group structure and social bonds and often led to chain migration. Here families related to each other would leave, either together in groups or in succession, from a single location in Slovakia for a destination in the Czech lands where their relatives were already established.

The reserve of potential emigration included many 'social outsiders' – Roma who had been unsuccessful in the new Czech surroundings, partly through difficulties of adapting to a new environment and problems in fitting in with different work and living patterns. Another major change which had confronted migrants in the Czech lands was living among the majority population rather than dwelling apart from them, often in segregated Roma settlements deep in the Slovak countryside. Some Roma migrants, often numerous in the initial stages, moved on to further border areas such as the surroundings of Cheb, Most and Ostrava, where they found similar conditions, or returned back to Slovakia. Some remained there but others set off again once more on further migrations to the Czech lands.

This post-war migration by Roma has been characterised as modern urbanisation, with rural-to-urban movement from impoverished areas to industrial areas offering jobs and accommodation, but at the same time it also represents an attempt to break out of the social isolation suffered by Roma in their segregated settlements in Slovakia. Indeed some of these settlements still remain to this day. This type of migration is a special kind of territorial movement quite distinct from nomadism, which emerged in another period and was generated by fundamentally different social factors. Therefore migration was undertaken not only by originally nomadic Olach Roma but also by traditionally settled Roma groups and families. This rural-to-urban migration is an entirely modern phenomenon and is comparable, to a certain extent, to contemporary migration.

The Czech Republic and Roma Migration after 1989

Zdeněk Uherek

The Czech Republic has now become simultaneously a country of destination, origin and transit for Roma migration. Typically it is a destination for Roma mainly from Slovakia and to a lesser extent from other countries of Central and Eastern Europe as well. At the same time it is traversed by Roma from Romania, who are just one of the various groups attempting to cross the Czech border to reach other European Union (EU) countries. Finally, the Czech Republic is also a source of migration for its Roma citizens travelling mainly to EU states, North America, Australia and other parts of Oceania in search of better living conditions. In this paper, I will mainly discuss illegal migration to the Czech Republic and Romani asylum seekers in this state but will also mention different forms of migration to the Czech Republic. However, in view of the character of other contributions to this volume, I will only focus on a few of the reasons motivating Roma to leave and return to the Czech Republic in my treatment of Roma emigration from this state.

The Czech Republic as a migratory destination

Roma immigration in historical perspective

The role of a destination country for Roma migration is not new for the Czech lands, since Roma from Slovakia have been migrating there continuously since 1945. Approximately 100,000 new Romani arrivals were absorbed, mainly by Czech industrial cities, and these migrants have now been established in the Czech Republic for up to four generations. In the meantime, a high birth rate has led to at least a doubling of their numbers. This population movement on a mass scale between the 1960s and 1980s was partly spontaneous and partly the result of chain migration to specific destinations. According to Petr Víšek, the number of Roma living within the borders of the modern-day Czech Republic in 1998 represented an increase of 155 per cent from the 1967 figures (Víšek 1999: 208). This migration was prompted by job opportunities in Czech industrial cities, chances of obtaining better quality housing and social support benefits. At the same time pressures forcing Roma to leave their original homes included the policy of evicting Roma from their settlements and demolishing their dwellings in exchange for compensation. Consequently, the migration of Roma from Slovakia in the period from 1945 to 1989 can be seen partly as a spontaneous process but also as the result of state policy towards Roma.[1]

After the division of the Czechoslovak state in 1992, Roma immigration from Slovakia took place within a new political context and changed its character to some extent. At the beginning of the 1990s, this population movement represented a last wave of internal chain migration within a single state. As such, it was a continuation of the previous migration process that had lasted until 1989. The causes of this migration were almost always economic, even though it led to families being reunited.

The structure of this kind of migration is relatively straightforward. A family from Slovakia would seek information through family networks or acquaintances to check out living conditions and possibilities of accommodation and work in the Czech lands. Family members would compare the prospective benefits with the situation in their home area and calculate where conditions were more advantageous. If they could, they would take advantage of the fact that part of their family network lived in the Czech lands and would move in with relatives, either all together or in stages – first the man as provider, followed by his wife and children. Sometimes this migration was linked to job opportunities and offers of suitable accommodation but sometimes the search for work and a place to live only began after their arrival. Frequently this resulted in overcrowded flats, due to the long-term presence of extended family members who were not official residents. In the 1990s, however, Roma families experienced considerable economic insecurity because employment opportunities had shrunk.

---

[1] On the subject of state policy towards Roma, see Grulich and Haišman 1986, Haišman 1989, Jurová 1996, Haišman 1999 and Víšek 1999.

It is extremely difficult to demonstrate the exact course of this process by statistical data but qualitative research indicates that the flow of migration tended to slacken at the beginning of the 1990s. However, factors such as poor material conditions – especially in rural Roma settlements – which had driven Roma families from their original communities, continued to operate, while barriers against resettling elsewhere were constantly raised. These obstacles included not only a reduction in employment opportunities due to an over-saturated labour market, but also increased selectivity by employers in recruiting workers where Roma were not preferred. In addition, the question of finding somewhere to live became more difficult in the 1990s due to the privatisation of municipal flats, the transfer of state-controlled flats to municipal ownership and other restructuring measures.[2] At the same time, Roma who had already been living in the Czech Republic for longer periods were often unwilling to proved shelter for their relatives from Slovakia. This was especially true of Czech areas where Roma had been established for several generations and were relatively well integrated into the local majority population. In such situations Roma tended to distance themselves from their Slovak relatives and, in this way, had a dampening effect on the migratory flow to the Czech lands. This kind of behaviour was widespread but most evident in areas where Roma enjoyed a relatively high standard of living and more employment opportunities.[3]

Not much attention has been paid to Roma migration from 1989 to 1992. This was not felt to be a burning problem until 1 January 1993, when the two federated states separated and for the first time Romani migration from Slovakia became international migration. The dissolution of Czechoslovakia placed a large number of earlier immigrants in a serious predicament when, on 29 December 1992, the Czech National Council passed Law 40/1993 on the acquisition and termination of state citizenship of the Czech Republic. Since Roma in

---

[2] For more detailed information on this question, see Baršová 2001.
[3] Český Krumlov is a classic example (research carried out in 1993, 1995, 1998, 2000, 2002). Also, an investigation in Jablonec nad Nisou by Markéta Rybová convincingly demonstrated that Roma who had moved most recently were generally considered to be 'the worse type' and that Roma in this town regard long-term residence as having a certain value (Rybová 1996).

the Czech Republic mostly originate from Slovakia, the expectation was that the majority would be assigned Slovak citizenship rather than Czech. However, choice of state citizenship formed an integral part of the newly enacted legislation. The original deadline was 30 December 1993 but this was later extended to 30 June 1994. For various reasons, a number of Roma did not take the necessary steps to acquire Czech citizenship by this further deadline. Meanwhile the law was strongly criticised by Roma activists and even attracted international criticism because many Roma citizens of the former Czechoslovak state, who lived in the Czech Republic, were unable to satisfy the legal requirements for gaining Czech state citizenship.

Nowadays, it is evident that the precise formulation of this law and the debates about its amendment not only provoked the hostility of many Roma towards the new state but also promoted a view of Czech society as prone to racial discrimination, even though the law was discriminatory in entirely different aspects than race. Thereafter, the law was amended in 1994 and 1996 and made less stringent, in response to criticism from Romani politicians and also from the European Union and Council of Europe. Nevertheless, on field trips we still encounter Roma who migrated to the Czech lands before the division of Czechoslovakia and yet are still not legal residents of the Czech Republic.[4]

Illegal immigration

Roma migration from Slovakia to the Czech Republic is still continuing after the division of the former state and typically involves a long-term illegal stay with the following features. Such immigrants have no possibility of legal employment; they cannot to be registered as job seekers at employment agencies; nor can they claim any social security benefits such as social support and they are excluded from health and social insurance schemes. In addition, they are not even allowed to find their own private accommodation. According to the rules, illegal immigrants can be expelled from the Czech Republic to their home country – in this case to Slovakia – and their early return is forbidden.

---

[4] There are various reasons for this and they are often highly individualistic.

However, this procedure is rarely followed because long-term illegal residence by individuals, or entire families, from Slovakia is very difficult to prove. Roma, as Slovak citizens, can cross the border without a passport by showing only an identity card, where the entry date is not stamped. Away from checkpoints this frontier is relatively easy to cross and in practice it is possible to return the following day after having been expelled, once more illegally. This porous frontier has resulted in overcrowded Roma flats, people making a living in illegal ways and friction between Roma and non-Roma communities.

After the dissolution of Czechoslovakia, certain towns with large numbers of Roma tried to use their own initiative to solve the problem by making by-laws to regulate the coexistence of Roma and non-Roma inhabitants. However, these municipal by-laws discriminated against Roma, failed to comply with existing laws and consequently had to be rescinded. In 1992 the towns of Jirkov, Most, Ústí nad Labem and Duchcov resorted to such measures and, in 1993, they were joined by the towns of Krupka, Bílina and Kladno (see Baršová 2001: 14–15 for further details).

In 2001, research in the Sokolov district revealed problems in inter-communal relations, especially in blocks of flats where Roma and non-Roma live side-by-side. As well as protesting about noise and large numbers moving about the building, the non-Roma tenants of blocks with such overcrowded flats often complained about completely trivial problems. They objected to the number of rubbish bins and containers used by Roma neighbours and the inequitable charges for rubbish collection (each flat pays the same amount), the electricity consumption for lighting public areas of the building (once more the sum is divided equally between flats), the excessive use of common washing and drying facilities by overcrowded families, the high volume of water consumed (again equally divided), etc. Non-Roma tenants often admitted that some of these problems could easily be solved by measuring the consumption of individual flats (for example, separate water meters rather than just one for the entire building). However, non-Roma tenants in these blocks did not usually talk much with their Roma neighbours about matters relating to what happened in the building, often saying they were afraid to do so. In almost all the cases we came across there were noticeable communication barriers.

Our research also revealed that in small and medium-sized Czech cities the presence of illegal migrants or families did not go unnoticed by their neighbours, even where Roma lived in remote surroundings. If such families had children, then district government offices and advisors for ethnic and national minorities were informed about them shortly after their arrival. Nevertheless, the usual outcome is not persecution, but instead improvised, 'temporary' solutions, which over the years turn into prolonged anomalies, that neither local government officials nor immigrants know how to resolve and to which both sides gradually adapt. These improvised solutions, however, give rise to a whole range of intractable problems that affect both Roma and non-Roma alike.

One of these difficulties is the provision of medical care because illegal immigrants do not usually pay health insurance. Romani migrants from Slovakia do not accept that their actions in migrating illegally absolves the Czech Republic of any responsibility for their health care. While they are willing to buy medication, they are frequently surprised when payment is demanded for examinations. Because families are unable to pay, children are examined on a credit basis, even though there is no expectation that any payment will ever be made.

Compulsory education is also a problem area. In accordance with the Convention on Basic Rights and Freedoms, the UN Rights of the Child and other international agreements, every child in the Czech Republic has the right to education free of charge. In elementary schools providing compulsory education, children of migrants are accepted regardless of the legal status of their parents. This means that if immigrants without legal residence in the Czech Republic register their children for school, these children are enrolled. However, from a financial point of view where schools receive funds on a 'per capita' basis, such pupils in effect do not exist. Since they do not contribute to school budgets, they are therefore taught at a loss. Where there are larger numbers of these pupils, their presence puts a strain on the school budget and leads to a reduction in the quality of teaching.[5]

Their presence also poses a health problem for schools. For example, illegal migrants have not undergone the same series of compulsory medical examinations as asylum seekers. On the one hand, schools are required to accept the children of illegal immigrants but, on the other, they are responsible for the health of all their pupils. In such circumstances, schools cannot in practice avoid the risks threatening them.[6] Compulsory education is one institution that some Roma have accepted as part of their value system. Therefore, they often want their children to be educated, even though they are illegal residents and negotiate this on the basis of verbal agreements between advisors for ethnic (national) issues and school headteachers. In this way, the residential status of illegal migrant families is partially legalised at a local level and, provided that clearly troublesome individuals are not involved, local inhabitants become reconciled to their presence.

Although such practices serve to partly 'integrate' illegal immigrants into local communities, at the same time they often have the effect of luring away Roma from taking steps to legalise their residence. This is because Roma individuals or families realise that, even as illegal immigrants, they are permitted to remain where they are living for an extended period and to some extent can even integrate into local society. Roma who migrate illegally to the Czech Republic usually realise that their right to social security lapses in the place where they formerly lived and are still officially registered, but often only begin to take this seriously when they face economic problems like failing to find a job in the Czech Republic.

Asylum seekers

The number of Roma asylum seekers in the Czech Republic is hard to calculate, because asylum seekers are not recorded by ethnicity but by

---

[5] The financial burden for the school is mainly the expense of providing these pupils with teaching materials.
[6] Staff of an elementary school in Bílina drew attention to this problem during an interview in 2001.

state citizenship. Consequently, only an estimate of the extent of Roma migration can be made on the basis of information from the Ministry of the Interior of the Czech Republic. From fieldwork, however, we know that Romani asylum seekers come mainly from Romania and Slovakia, while a smaller number come from the former Yugoslavia and other countries. Above all, Roma from Slovakia are almost exclusively asylum seekers of Slovakian state citizenship.

The Czech state encountered the problem of foreign Roma seeking asylum in the Czech Republic for the first time in the 1990s. A mechanism for establishing an asylum process and an asylum policy complying with international conventions were only introduced after 1989. Applicants' ethnicity is rarely taken into account but rather their citizenship when decisions are made about individual cases and in compiling statistics. Therefore, the number of Roma from different countries claiming asylum in the Czech Republic can only be estimated and these approximations need to be confirmed by empirical investigation and interviews.

Available statistical data show that the strongest response to the altered circumstances after 1989 came from Romanian Roma. In 1990, 1,080 persons from Romania applied for asylum in the Czech Republic and although their numbers decreased slightly in the following years, they began increasing again after 1999 (see Table 1). However, not all of these asylum seekers were Roma.

Table 1: *Romanian citizens claiming asylum in Czech Republic: 1990–2002*

Year	Number of Claimants
1990	1,080
1991	656
1992	78
1993	60
1994	58
1995	490
1996	693
1997	159
1998	27
1999	124
2000	510
2001	1,848
2002	98
Total	**5,881**

Source: Ministry of the Interior, Czech Republic

Until 1997 some of these claims were upheld and applicants were granted the status of recognised refugees (*asylants*). After 1997, however, asylum claims by Romanian citizens were ruled unjustified and were therefore rejected with the exception of one sole individual in 1999 (see Table 2).

Table 2: Asylum claims by Romanian citizens granted in Czech Republic: 1990–2002

Year	Claims upheld
1990	23
1991	325
1992	26
1993	54
1994	11
1995	1
1996	28
1997	5
1998	0
1999	1
2000	0
2001	0
2002	0
Total	**474**

Source: Ministry of the Interior, Czech Republic

It is hard to understand why Romanian Roma chose the Czech Republic as a destination and even Ministry of the Interior employees at residential centres for asylum seekers were unable to provide a satisfactory answer. However, taking into consideration the fact that these claimants frequently attempt to make illegal border crossings to Germany or Austria, it can be assumed that many arrivals from Romania came to the Czech Republic with this goal in mind. Other Romanian Roma were motivated by the desire to improve their living conditions, by opportunities for petty trading and by possibilities for expanding their territory for begging. Workers at residential centres, located in the vicinity of large towns, discovered that Roma asylum seekers regularly travelled to town in order to beg.[7] In one interview the director of a residential centre gave his opinion about the motivation underlying the 1996 migratory wave of Roma from Romania: 'It was a kind of tourism. They stayed here for six months and then we paid their trip home.'[8]

---

[7] See, primarily, interviews with employees of the residential centre at Zastávka u Brna.

[8] Interview, 13 July 2000.

Another significant Roma group seeking asylum in the Czech Republic are Roma from Slovakia. Asylum seekers from Slovakia in the Czech Republic are exclusively Roma. Up until 1999, asylum claims from Slovak citizens were an exception but they increased sharply in 2000, only to decrease by approximately a half in 2001 (see Table 3). Most claims were made on behalf of entire families and only 48 were lodged by individuals.

Table 3: *Slovak citizens claiming asylum in Czech Republic: 1990–2002*

Year	Number of Claimants
1990	0
1991	0
1992	0
1993	2
1994	2
1995	4
1996	3
1997	19
1998	6
1999	13
2000	723
2001	389
2002	843
Total	**2,004**

Source: Ministry of the Interior, Czech Republic

The sharp increase in the number of Roma asylum seekers has raised a whole series of questions. Responses from Roma reveal that they have a particular perception of the asylum procedure and make use of it in an attempt to solve their problems in ways that the majority population had not originally anticipated. It appears that the asylum process offers Roma an entire range of attractive possibilities. Under Czech Law on Asylum no. 325/1999 Coll. as amended, an asylum seeker is admitted to a Ministry of the Interior reception centre after first making contact with Czech government officials.

The reception centre consists of secure premises which may not be left without good reason and permission having been granted. At the present time, the Ministry of the Interior operates two reception centres, one in Vyšní Lhoty in north Moravia and the other in Červený Újezd in north Bohemia. Asylum seekers refer in slang to time spent at these centres as 'quarantine'. In the reception centres, claimants undergo medical examinations and are interviewed by workers who prepare documentation relating to the asylum process. The administrative director of the Ministry of the Interior refugee facilities states that asylum seekers remain in reception centres for approximately one month but some of our respondents claimed to have been there for longer.[9] In the case of Roma asylum seekers, they are contacted by International Organization for Migration (IOM) employees at this stage and interviewed to try and discover what motivated them to migrate, so that solutions might be sought in their country of origin. If asylum seekers decide to return to their homeland, assistance is provided by paying the travel costs and making a grant to support them during the first fortnight after their return.

However, when asylum seekers decide to continue with their claim, they are issued with an identity card (known in slang as the 'green card') to show they have entered the asylum process. They are then transferred to an open residential centre, where their movements are not restricted. Indeed, they are able to travel freely throughout the Czech Republic, although as a rule travel documents are not issued for trips abroad. However, Roma asylum seekers from Slovakia were not prevented from making trips home by the lack of travel documents since it is possible to cross the Czecho-Slovak border with only an identity card.

In fact, asylum seekers admitted to residential centres were previously not discouraged from finding their own private accommodation but now the amended law, which came into effect on 1 February 2002 (No. 2/2002 Coll. as amended), makes it more advantageous for asylum seekers to live in residential centres rather than in private accommodation.

---

[9] The director of the refugee centre at Červený Újezd estimated that asylum seekers spend on average about 14 days in 'quarantine' at this centre.

In these residential centres, individuals either have their own room or share with others of the same gender, while families are generally given a separate room to themselves. Here, asylum seekers are supplied with food and are sometimes provided with clothing by humanitarian organisations. While their bedding is washed for them, they are responsible for cleaning their own rooms. While the rules permit asylum seekers to remain outside the centre for up to 24 hours without reason, residential centre staff has no authority to discipline claimants. Should any conflict or fights occur, these incidents are handled by police or the courts as with any other civil disturbance.

Even though the regime of the residential centres does not fundamentally restrict individuals' behaviour in any way, living in such an institution can be psychologically demanding for active persons of working age. Such pressures lead to arguments and conflicts and barely anyone lasts more than a year and a half there, even though there is no maximum time limit for the duration of stay. Until 1 February 2002 asylum seekers were able to find their own private accommodation, inform the centre of their new address and leave without any other formalities. However, the amended law on asylum limits this option and guards against asylum seekers giving false addresses.

Residential centre staff believe that a relatively large number of asylum seekers in the Czech Republic took advantage of this process to legalise their stay in the Czech Republic and, by this means, gain time to attempt legal or illegal border crossings to Germany or other more prosperous Western countries. In addition, a number of them also manipulated this process to obtain an asylum seeker's 'green card', which allowed them to find employment legally without needing to apply for a work permit.[10]

However, for Roma this is not generally the motive for seeking asylum in the Czech Republic. Roma from Slovakia, in particular, can look for work in the Czech Republic without restrictions and they can travel directly from Slovakia to countries in the West that have not imposed

---

[10] From 1 February 2002, as stated in the relevant paragraphs of the new employment law, asylum seekers are not permitted to work earlier than one year from the day of starting the asylum process.

visa restrictions on those holding a valid Slovak passport. Their motives in claiming asylum are quite different. During fieldwork we encountered the following:

Flight from persecution in their home country

In such circumstances the institution of asylum virtually serves the purpose for which it was originally established. However, in such cases the actual hostile incidents provoking flight are frequently described in vague terms. As a typical example of a description of this kind of persecution we selected the testimony of Mrs I. K. from Slovakia, who had been living in the Stráž pod Ralskem residential centre. She explained how she and her husband were attacked in the bar where her husband worked by unknown assailants who beat her brutally, striking her with chairs and leaving her with a bruised face, a sprained arm and temporarily impaired vision. In the same assault her husband suffered four broken ribs, lost consciousness and presumably almost died and the bar owner was also beaten up. On being asked about the identity of her attackers, the woman replied that many people took part but she did not recognise them as they were masked. They were not skinheads, as none exist in her home area, but were probably mafiosi and arrived by jeep. She and her husband and children fled to another district where a doctor examined them. Then, fearing a further assault, they left for the Czech Republic where, supposedly, they had never been before. On arrival, they were given shelter in Mladá Boleslav by an acquaintance of Russian descent. For a short while they lived in a hostel in Mladá Boleslav and then their acquaintance advised them to apply for asylum.

Accounts of this type show that some Roma seeking asylum really go in fear of their lives and that they are terrified of being pursued. Racially motivated violence, however, is only part of the story here. Frequently such incidents involve violence committed in connection with organised crime, extortion, debt recovery and settling scores among rival gangs, etc. and for people threatened in such ways, residential centres can serve as a temporary refuge. Of course, persecution by the state cannot be ruled out as a possibility, but we did not come across anyone who directly claimed that this had occurred.

From their testimonies it is evident that not all Roma seek asylum immediately after crossing the border. Sometimes, the possibility of claiming asylum is only considered at a later stage, after other possibilities of living abroad have been explored.

Economic security

In addition to Roma whose lives are endangered, asylum seekers also include those who use this process as a means of solving their economic problems. Some sell their property where they live and pay off their debts with the proceeds. Since the border is easy to cross, they can live in the residential centre, and at the same time collect social support payments where they are officially registered and in this way slightly improve their economic situation.

Social reasons

Some Roma families find it gratifying to receive constant care, regular meals or small payments for food, clothing from charity organisations, proper hygiene and other amenities which were either minimal or unaffordable in their former homes. In the residential centres for asylum seekers, we saw reasonably well equipped, comfortable living quarters that Roma families had transformed from temporary accommodation into relatively pleasant and acceptable homes. Evidence from fieldwork suggests that some families are playing for time and are in no hurry for a decision about their uncertain situation. The methods of processing asylum claims in the Czech Republic allow such a stratagem to be pursued.

The asylum process consists of several stages. After the initial claim, asylum is only granted in clearly grounded cases in accordance with the UN Geneva Convention Relating to the Status of Refugees of 28 July 1951.[11] In such cases asylum is granted by the Czech Ministry of the

---

[11] §12 of Law 325/1999 in the latest version states: Asylum will be granted to a foreigner if the foreigner
a) is being persecuted for exercising political rights and freedoms or
b) has a well-founded fear of persecution for reasons of race, religion, nationality, membership of certain social group or for holding certain political opinions in the

Interior following an administrative procedure. A period of 90 days is specified by law for completion of the entire process but this term is usually exceeded. If asylum is not granted, claimants can appeal against the decision of the ministry within 30 days of receiving the verdict. Because this essentially amounts to a second stage of claiming asylum, those who appeal are often referred to as 'second-timers'. However, even where claims are rejected by the highest court, claimants cannot be returned to their home countries if they are in fear of their lives. Such situations are often resolved by claimants being granted a 'termination' of the asylum procedure – where, in fact, their presence is tolerated. This allows them to remain in a residential centre and decide what to do next.

The experience of staff working with asylum seekers is that they do not last longer than two and a half years in residential centres. By that time, they have found work and a place to live and have the financial resources to satisfy the conditions of Law 326/1999 on Foreigners Residing in the Czech Republic. In the meantime they have acquired the status of long-term or permanent residents. However, during this period they often leave for other countries, mainly Western Europe, the USA, Canada or elsewhere.

Of course, asylum seekers can call a halt to the process and opt for repatriation, either to their homeland or to a safe third country. This actually happens in practice. Up until 1 February 2002, repatriated individuals could apply again at any time for asylum in the Czech Republic. The amended law now specifies that at least two years should elapse before a further asylum claim can be made. In fact Roma often make such repeated claims for asylum within two years. On the basis of past experience Roma from Slovakia in particular have no expectation of being granted asylum in the Czech Republic but instead take advantage of the situation while awaiting court decisions.

During fieldwork in 2001, we frequently encountered cases where Roma asylum seekers left the residential centres on one-month passes

---

state whose citizenship he holds, or, should he be a person without citizenship of any state, in the last state in which he had permanent residence.

to Prague or other towns in the republic. The usual practice was for Romani mothers to remain in the residential centres with their children while the men travelled around for several days to pursue various activities in Czech towns, returning only occasionally to the centres and their wives and children. Many found this kind of arrangement convenient. However, the amended asylum law has now placed new restrictions on leaving the centres. Moreover, living in 'quarantine' is now less attractive to Roma than formerly and, consequently, some Roma have been deterred from proceeding to this stage of the asylum process. In 2000, most claimants withdrew from the asylum process after the first weeks of 'quarantine' and opted for repatriation to their home country.

To sum up, our experience reveals that Roma from Slovakia used the Czech Republic's asylum process as a way of at least partly solving some of their problems of making a livelihood and of legalising their presence in the Czech Republic. By this stratagem Roma gained time, shelter, and were treated in a way they appreciated.

The Czech Republic as source of migration

It would certainly be inaccurate to claim that Roma did not migrate at all to foreign countries before 1989. However, the extent of this migration was considerably restricted.

Roma from the Czech Republic began to migrate abroad in larger numbers following the partition of the former Czechoslovak state. Roma crossing borders, other than that between the Czech and Slovak republics, became more noticeable in 1996, and even more so in 1997 when a wave of Roma migrants left for Canada, attracting the attention of the domestic and international media. In 1996, approximately 150 Roma travelled to Canada but the following year, in the two-month period between 7 August and 8 October, this number increased ten-fold to about 1,500 people. The migratory flow was terminated in October 1997 by the imposition of Canadian visa requirements for Czech citizens. Roma declared that they were not leaving for economic but political motives, claiming that the main reason driving them to such a course of action was racial discrimination. However, their motives for migrating were evidently mixed.

If we classify this migration in terms of the dichotomous categories of conservative and innovative migration, this was clearly the latter. Roma did not migrate to maintain their current living conditions, but, on the contrary, they desired change. They wanted to raise their social status, improve their economic situation and secure their personal safety.

As stated above, the size of the influx provoked countermeasures by the Canadian government – visa restrictions. At the same time it demonstrated the position that was later to be adopted by several prosperous Western states, that they had no intention of helping to solve the problems of Roma families from Central and Eastern Europe by accepting significant numbers of would-be Roma migrants. In 1998, some of the Roma asylum seekers were expelled from Canada back to the Czech Republic and, although Roma had represented only 7.5 per cent of all refugees to Canada in 1997, this swift defensive reaction clearly indicated that any further Roma immigrants would be unwelcome.

Following this initial migration, Czech Roma then travelled to Great Britain, the Netherlands, Belgium and to a lesser extent other Western states. As early as 1997 Great Britain was singled out as a preferred destination. The British press reacted to the flood of Roma immigrants in a series of hostile articles where the new arrivals were characterised unequivocally as economic migrants (Guy, 2000: 6). Since then, however, Great Britain has become a less popular destination for Czech Roma. The last substantial wave of asylum seekers to Great Britain occurred in 2001. The British government responded by establishing a checkpoint of their own to vet prospective travellers to Great Britain, actually located inside Prague's Ruzyně Airport – a move strongly criticised by Roma activists.[12]

Roma emigration from the Czech Republic to Canada initiated a wide-ranging discussion that progressed through several phases.

---

[12] See, for example, Bednář 2001.

At first, immediately after the Roma had left, commentators tended to look for obvious causes underlying their departure. One such cause was the television program *Na vlastní oči* (See for yourself), which screened images showing how Roma asylum seekers from the Czech Republic were living in Canada. It is undeniable that the number of asylum seekers increased as a result of this broadcast; nevertheless, the television programme in itself clearly did not constitute a motive for migrating. Racially motivated violence was seen as a further cause. This interpretation was widespread abroad and in the 1990s began to have a significant impact in the Czech Republic, polarising perceptions of the Roma question from the point of view of both Roma and non-Roma. The third cause can be summarised as the economic problems of the Roma population.

The mass emigration of Roma began in an atmosphere of strained relations between Roma and the majority population. Over time these relations gradually deteriorated, particularly after 1992 with the division of the federal republic. At this time, the debate focused on the previously mentioned Law 40/1993 on the acquisition and termination of state citizenship of the Czech Republic. During early exchanges about this law little state interest was expressed about the fact that Roma were frequently unable to fulfil the conditions specified for acquiring state citizenship. The main difficulty concerned §7 requiring applicants to have no criminal record during the previous five-year period. This law forced some Roma into the position of internal immigrants and led them to adopt an uncooperative attitude to the new state. The stance of international institutions, such as the Council of Europe, the Office of the United Nations High Commissioner for Refugees (UNHCR), the Organization for Security and Co-operation in Europe (OSCE), as well as the often inaccurate reporting by domestic media, fostered the belief among Roma that should they emigrate from the Czech Republic, Western states would support them unconditionally. Accordingly they began to believe they would be openly accepted as asylum seekers. Meanwhile many other related issues were widely discussed, such as the violent death of the young RomaTibor Danihel at the hands of non-Roma and the municipal by-law, termed the Jirkov declaration, etc. As early as 1995, an investigation by the Roma National Congress and the Soros Society revealed that 90 per cent of Czech Roma respondents were considering emigration and 10 per cent stated that they had already attempted to emigrate .

Nevertheless, doubts remain as to the extent to which questions about citizenship in the Czech Republic and racially motivated violence were actually sufficient incentives to emigrate because Roma migration to Western Europe began much earlier and in greater numbers from other post-communist countries, mainly from Romania and Bulgaria. As early as 1992, an agreement was signed between Germany and Romania on the repatriation of migrants whereby Germany would provide assistance to re-integrate them in their original home areas. In that year alone, 25 per cent of all asylum seekers in Germany came from Romania, and it is estimated that of these, approximately 100,000 were Roma (Matras 2000, Guy 2000). If, in 1995, Roma from the Czech Republic expressed their desire to emigrate to the West, it is not possible to infer too much from this isolated fact since no comparable data exists of opinions expressed before 1989.

Stung by criticism at home and abroad, the Czech government had already started to develop initiatives to find ways of improving relations between Roma and the non-Roma majority and to raise the social standing of Roma before the mass flight of Roma to Canada. On 8 January 1996, the relevant ministries and the chair of the Council for Nationalities entrusted government minister Pavel Bratinka with producing the Report on the Situation of the Roma Community in the Czech Republic. This report was not prompted by Roma emigration but since the initial migratory wave occurred while it was being prepared, greater attention was paid to it as a result. The Council for Nationality discussed the report at its meeting on 14 August 1997 and recommended its submission to the Czech government. On 10 September, in its debate on the report, the government decided to withhold its approval and required Bratinka to make revisions, mainly 'with regard to evaluation of government action on measures previously approved, formulation of basic problems and clear policy proposals'.[13] The report was modified as required and represents a landmark in renewed commitment to launch an active policy for solving the problems of the Roma minority.[14] In addition, the report puts forward arguments and proposals, which were mostly implemented in the following years and served as a guide for other measures aimed at improving relations between the Roma and the majority population.[15]

In 1997 there was an increase in Roma emigration from the Czech Republic. This was prompted not only by the problems already mentioned but also by the steadily deteriorating conditions for Roma in the job market. It is important to recognise that at this time the Czech Republic was on the verge of economic collapse, requiring emergency measures and other reform packages aimed at reviving economic growth. Romani migration, therefore, became a way of solving the economic problems of Roma, a means of providing a living for those who handled the sale of flats and organised journeys abroad, a tool for applying political pressure, an opportunity for gaining new experience and also a matter of social prestige. The following section discusses these particular aspects in more detail.

Inter-personal relations

Discussion of inter-personal relations raises the issue of racially motivated violence once more, since there is evidence that a number of asylum seekers in Western countries experienced unpleasant incidents of this kind. In 2000, employees of the association *Člověk v tísni* (People in need) carried out a sociological survey in Britain among asylum seekers from the Czech Republic. Interviews revealed that asylum claims were motivated by the following basic reasons: repeated racist attacks (physical and verbal); inability of the police to protect

---

[13] See the Report on the Situation in the Roma Community in the Czech Republic (Czech government 1997).
[14] For a broad attempt to define different periods as regards the development of the position of the state towards the Roma minority, see Frištenská et al. 1999: 496–500.
[15] On 14 July 2000, the *Conception of Government Policy towards Members of the Roma Community, Helping their Integration into Society* was accepted by the Government of the Czech Republic.

them; discrimination against children in school and poor prospects for the future (Člověk v tísni: 2000). In addition, inter-personal relations are involved in emigration because of extortion, debt collection, flight from the mafia, etc. These motives were encountered in fieldwork among asylum seekers from Slovakia. However, they cannot be ruled out entirely for Czech asylum seekers as well. In our research, however, we have not come across cases of Czech Roma who were motivated to emigrate by these types of coercion.[16]

Economic problems

As regards economic prospects for Roma, it has often been said that Roma workers are not popular in the job market. This is true not only at home but also abroad. In both cases they are only suited to manual labour in view of their deficiencies in professional training, education and language skills. It follows that the most direct way of improving their social position, leaving aside illegal activities, is to raise the level of social support payments. A natural consequence of this situation is that decisions must be made about which form of social security is preferable from a range of alternatives. Advisors for ethnic affairs at district government offices claim to know of cases where social support payments were being received both at home and abroad as asylum seekers. Further resources are obtained either from the sale of the emigrants' homes or flats or payments received for transferring to others the right to use their municipal flats. In the eyes of the majority population, such behaviour appears quite immoral. These practices can be viewed in another light, however, if it is recognised that some Roma saw this as the only possible way of improving their living conditions.

Victims of speculators

The emigration of large numbers of uneducated people always provides opportunities for speculators and middlemen to prey on the naivete of others and get rich on the proceeds. Even among the Roma themselves, some have been attracted by the potential of the current situation and

---

[16] I investigated the topic of 'usury' in the Czech Republic together with Renata Weinerová in 2001.

have exploited it. They took advantage of the increasing emigration and the critical economic situation by offering Roma trips abroad. This is another reason why Roma emigration was so heavy, for even families who had not originally intended to emigrate sometimes took this course of action.

A tool for applying political pressure

Roma emigration attracted extensive media coverage. However, in spite of the resulting threat of visa requirements for Czech citizens, these were actually imposed in only a few cases. Nevertheless, criticism by EU states was very evident and the Council of Europe clearly expressed its reservations about the coexistence of Roma and non-Roma in the context of preserving human rights. Consequently, in the latter half of the 1990s, Roma migration to Western Europe as asylum seekers became an effective way of exerting pressure to draw attention deservedly to Roma issues and press for solutions to their problems. In February 2001, a report by the International Centre for Migration Policy Development stated, without naming specific countries: 'In several instances, it was suggested that Roma are lured into giving up their residence and moving westward by opposition politicians, who try to profit politically from the unfavourable situation of the Roma in Central and Eastern Europe.' (Pluim 2001: 17).

Gaining new and experience and social prestige

The screening of documentaries, showing Roma migrants in Canada and Great Britain and interviews with them from Dover and Calais, were more than just portrayals of media images. They represented adventure and exciting new experience, as well as an element of risk and even a game or gamble. Seeing this, some Roma wanted similar experiences. People do not always act rationally; they also harbour deep psychological needs for retaliation, satisfaction and new experience. In recent years Roma periodicals have been providing information about Roma migration on a regular basis and have also published interviews with those who have been repatriated. It is clear that their impressions of travel abroad are mostly positive and they recall their experience of Western Europe with pleasure. They

93

remember the new cities they visited and the attractive accommodation, recollect that they were treated with respect and boast that their children can speak a foreign language, etc. Sometimes they declare that they will attempt to emigrate again. It seems that in the West they experience what approximates to the way of life of the majority population – something unachievable for them in the Czech Republic. For a limited period, they become the object of institutional attention and gain access to means of social advancement, unavailable to them in their home areas. Furthermore, their experiences are of interest to others after their return. The psychological satisfaction in demonstrating the courage to escape the stereotype of Roma and gain new experience is far from negligible as a stimulus for emigration. If groups or individuals are unable to satisfy their basic human needs in any other way, emigration and subsequent asylum claims appear a viable opportunity to realise these aims. We must remember that Roma, too, were previously trapped behind the Iron Curtain and, like others, their freedom of movement was limited.

Repatriation of asylum seekers to the Czech Republic

The current political pressures on the Czech government would appear to require the return of asylum seekers to the Czech Republic and the prevention of continued migration. However, fieldwork revealed that the interests of the state frequently diverge from those of local political representatives and community leaders, as well as the interests of local society. Roma usually finance their journeys abroad by selling their personal possessions and transferring the right to use their municipal flats to others for cash payments. When they return, they naturally need somewhere to live, social services, schooling for their children and other basis requirements. There is no work for them and as regards social and economic conditions, they frequently find themselves in a worse situation than before they left the country. Municipal and district offices would willingly provide repatriated Roma with the support they need but usually this is not possible, simply because there are insufficient resources. It is impossible to explain to non-Roma and Roma alike, who have been on the waiting list for basic flats for a long time, that immediate priority will be given to Roma returning from abroad, who previously sold their flats voluntarily. Social justice within a given society is only possible to the extent that it is prosperous. In spite of the assistance of the IOM and other agencies, the situation of repatriated people is often critical and this leads them to consider further migration. In the Czech Republic, for example, at least 30–40 per cent of those who have returned intend to emigrate again.[17]

Other forms of migration from the Czech Republic

In addition to the forms of Roma migration discussed above, our research has revealed cases of short-term migration for work from the Czech Republic. Such journeys abroad to earn money are made by non-Roma too. While the migration of asylum seekers only started to be significant after 1997, short-term trips abroad to help make a living began after the fall of the Iron Curtain. While asylum seekers made their choice of a destination based on the nature of the asylum process in particular states, Roma who travelled abroad for the single purpose of casual employment mainly targeted neighbouring countries such as Germany, Austria and Italy. However, it seems that the range of their destinations has greatly expanded. For example, the activities of Roma in New Zealand are an unexpected surprise. It would certainly be interesting to learn more about this situation. Other types of migration undertaken by Roma are migration for work between the Czech Republic and Slovakia and family migration where one partner follows the other. In limited cases, some Roma men in the Czech lands prefer women from Roma settlements in Slovakia, for whom the better-off Roma from the Czech Republic are regarded as a good match.

Conclusion

Roma migration and Roma asylum seekers not only exerted a negative influence on international relations and the process of European unification. Roma migration also prompted a closer examination by European institutions of the economic situation and human rights issues in post-communist states. It also led to the establishment of a whole series of regular control mechanisms and comparable programmes aimed at correcting unfavourable indicators.

---

[17] According to information from an IOM worker.

After the initial years of growing migration, when Western European states mostly criticised post-communist countries and imposed restrictive measures on them, there is now an increasing tendency to construct models of co-operation. These models seek to create acceptable conditions for Roma in their home countries as a positive means of preventing further migration. Western Europe states have made it clear they will not allow the problem to be solved by exporting it to their countries in the manner the Roma question in Slovakia was once solved by exporting it to the Czech lands.

At the present time the Czech Republic occupies a specific position as both a source and destination of Roma migration. However, if the migration process is viewed over a wider time-scale and differences between internal and external (foreign) migration are examined, the Czech Republic is revealed as primarily a destination, where migratory movement was beyond the reach of any kind of control or planning. A dynamic immigration policy cannot be based solely on available accommodation and employment opportunities, but also on the provision of effective integration programmes. All Western states where Roma seek asylum realise this and therefore seek to regulate levels of immigration. In contrast, the Czech Republic did not consider the implications of introducing a controlled immigration policy and consequently there are now groups of people living in that country without links to the region where they live, to the territory surrounding them or to the society of which they should form an integral part.

The Roma community in the Czech Republic is a migratory group and all migratory groups have an increased tendency to migrate again. This is a common pattern which is easily demonstrated, for example, by the behaviour of Czechs abroad. This greater propensity to migrate is derived from the situation where there are few factors attracting individuals or groups to a given place and, therefore, factors drawing them elsewhere are likely to exert an influence. After their first migration these groups often adapt to such journeys, adjusting to changes of location without disrupting their primary emotional links. The concept of home becomes confined to the family and close relatives who migrate with them and ceases to be bound up with a local community, region, house or other familiar locality.[18] Such groups appear to be relatively egotistical in being focused on achieving their own interests, because their own interests are not associated with those of wider social groups.

At the beginning of this century, William Isaac Thomas and later Robert Ezra Park and Roger Burgess in Chicago expressed the idea that individuals or social groups find themselves in a state of disorganisation after migrating to a new environment. It is a situation where individuals or groups are insufficiently anchored in extended family ties and where secondary institutional bonds in the local society now surrounding them seem alien. Especially in the case where formal, state-created institutional networks are weak or function poorly, migrating individuals display a tendency either to create structures within structures or enter existing structures, because they replace the abandoned primary groups. Such structures within structures can be various gangs and other groups on the fringes of the law. The implementation of Czech migration policy without including associated integration measures has until now allowed Roma groups to exploit the social network and state institutions but in no way to establish their own.

Previous research has shown that Roma migration takes various forms. Consequently, at issue is not just long-term migration, but also short-term migratory journeys linked to casual work and business opportunities. At the present time, this includes visiting family members, reuniting incomplete families, cross-border marriages, etc.

Czech Roma began their widespread international migration relatively late in comparison with their Romanian and Bulgarian neighbours and have migrated less than Roma from other post-communist states. Roma citizens of the Czech Republic did not imitate the migration of their original sub-ethnic groups. Instead, it appears that from time to time they intentionally created a kind of trade network. They migrated in family groups and gained notoriety as asylum seekers, that is to say,

---

[18] We verified these mechanisms during studies of resettled Czechs from the Ukraine and Kazakhstan.

people who did not make sufficient use of democratic structures but rather tried to take advantage of formal state procedures to legalise their presence as refugees. It was a peculiar road to Europe and an idiosyncratic way of realising their vision of an acceptable life style not possible in their homeland. However, migration of Roma from the Czech Republic cannot be considered as a continuation of the nomadic life style, as in the case of some other groups of Bulgarian or Yugoslav Roma.

Roma migration from the Czech Republic was not enough of a problem for neighbouring states to impose visa requirements as they did, for example, against Slovakia and other states. Pressure by European institutions for a dynamic integration policy towards Roma in the Czech Republic can be seen, therefore, primarily as a preventative attempt to bring the situation under control before the integration of the Czech state into the European Union.

References

Baršová, A. (2001) *Problémy bydlení etnických menšin a trendy k rezidenční segregaci v České republice*, Praha: Open Society Fund.

Bednář, J. (2001) 'Ohlédnutí za tvrdou realitou britských "dočasně" stažených kontrol v Ruzyni', *Romanu kurko* 11, no. 9: 4, 13 September.

Brochmann, G. and Hammar, T. (eds) (1999) *Mechanisms of Immigration Control: A Comparative Analysis of European Regulation Policies*, Oxford: Berg.

Člověk v tísni (2000) *Zpráva z Doveru* (Report from Dover), January and April, Praha: Člověk v tísni (People in Need).

Czech Government (1997) *Report on the Situation of the Romani Community in the Czech Republic and Government Measures assisting its Integration in society*, (known as the Bratinka Report), Praha: Office of Minister without Portfolio, accepted 29 October.

Fraser, A. (1992) *The Gypsies*, Oxford: Blackwell.

Frištenská, H., Haišman, T. and Víšek, P. (1999) 'Souhrnné závěry', in H. Lisá (ed.) 473–528.

Gheorghe, N. and Klímová, I. (2000) ODIHR International Consultation on Romani Refugees and Asylum Seekers: Consolidated Summary and Recommendations, Warsaw, 23 October, World Wide Web URL: http://www.osce.org/odihr/docs/m00-6-final.htm

Grulich, T. and Haišman, T. (1986) 'Institucionální zájem o cikánské obyvatelstvo v Československu v letech 1945–1958', *Český Lid*, 73, 2: 72–85.

Guy, W. (2000) 'Recent Roma Migration to the United Kingdom', paper delivered at international roundtable *Roma Migration in Europe: Trends*, Academy of Sciences of the Czech Republic, Institute of Ethnology, Praha, November 24–5 (see this volume).

Haišman, T. (1989) 'Snahy centrálních orgánů státní správy o řešení tzv. cikánské otázky v českých zemích v letech 1945–1947 ve světle tisku', *Český lid* 76, 1: 4–11.

Haišman, T. (1999) 'Romové v Československu v letech 1945–1967: Vývoj institucionálního zájmu a jeho dopady', in H. Lisá (ed.) 137–83.

Jurová, A. (1996) *Rómská problematika 1945–1967*, Praha: Ústav soudobých dějin.

Lisá, H. (ed.) (1999) *Romové v České republice* (Roma in the Czech Republic), Praha: Socioklub.

Matras, Y. (2000) 'Roma migrations in the post-Communist era: Their historical and political significance', *Cambridge Review of International Affairs*, vol. XIII, 2, spring/summer, 36–37.

Okely, J. (1983) *The Traveller Gypsies*, Cambridge: Cambridge University Press.

Pluim, M. (2001) *Current Roma Migration from the EU Candidate States*, Draft study prepared by International Centre for Migration Policy Development (ICMPD).

Rybová, M. (1996) 'Postoje a názory jabloneckých Romů', in B. Müller and Z. Uherek (eds) *Všední den v Jablonci roku 1994: Od novoosídleneckého pohraničí k euroregionu*, Wien: Internationales Forschungszentrum Kulturwissenschaften, 91–110.

Srb, V. (1993) 'Romové v Československu podle sčítání lidu 1991', *Demografie* 35, 4: 282–289.

Šatava, L. (1989) *Migrační procesy a české vystěhovalectví 19. století do USA*, Praha, Univerzita Karlova.

Vašečka, I. (2000) *Príčiny odchodov Rómov zo Slovenska do niektorých krajín Európskej únie*, Dokumentačné centrum pro výskum slovenskej společnosti, International Organization for Migration project, Bratislava: IOM.

Víšek, P. (1999) 'Program integrace – řešení problematiky romských obyvatel v období 1970 až 1989', in H. Lisá (ed.) 184–218.

Slovakia and Roma Migration after 1989

Renata Weinerová

Mass emigration of Roma from Slovakia to West European countries first became a serious political problem for Slovakia when it entered the EU accession process. At the turn of the new century discussions about what had formerly been a politically undesirable subject became more frank and bold – a shift that included breaking the taboo on the issue of what were termed Roma settlements. Up to the present, the problem of these rural shanty-towns has featured in many governmental and non-governmental studies by Slovak as well as other European social scientists, including reports by the Council of Europe, the Organization for Security and Co-operation in Europe (OSCE) and the World Bank. This article, is intended as a contribution to the discussion about Roma emigration from Slovakia. It is based on evidence gathered during fieldwork in the Czech Republic and also on my perspective on this issue. Understandably, it reflects this viewpoint to a certain extent. Bearing in mind that both countries shared a common history for decades and that the migration of Slovak and Czech Roma displays a number of similar characteristics, I hope that this contribution will bring new momentum to Slovak and Czech Romani studies.

Methodology

Our investigation of the migration of Slovak Roma, drew on information gained mainly from fieldwork that we carried out among asylum seekers in residential centres of the Czech Ministry of the Interior. We interviewed staff at these centres and also Slovak Roma who had been placed there. Together with members of the Interdepartmental Commission for Romani Community Affairs, attached to the Government Office of the Czech Republic, and especially with the help of officials in the Ministry for Regional Development, we identified locations with high concentrations of Roma arrivals from Slovakia and carried out research in selected districts (Prague 5, Prague West, Sokolov and Ústí nad Labem).[1] At the same time, we contacted non-governmental organisations (NGOs) involved with Romani migration (People in Need, International Organization for Migration (IOM) and United Nations High Commissioner for Refugees (UNHCR) in Prague), and with their assistance, we were able to analyse the data more fully.

To investigate the situation in Slovakia as a source country of migration, we drew first of all on previous experience in publications and other materials produced by governmental and non-governmental organisations and by social scientists in Slovakia and elsewhere. The Czech press was also an important source of information, while the Roma quarterly *Romano nevo l'il* provided telling testimony on the actual situation in Slovakia. In addition, we utilised our earlier experience from carrying out research in Slovak settlements during the 1980s and 1990s.

Migration of Slovak Roma after 1989

The first migratory wave of Slovak Roma in post-communist Europe had already taken place before 1993 within the territory of the Czechoslovak federation. Between 1990 and 1992, immigrants to the Czech lands came mainly from eastern Slovakia. Prompted by reports of the impending division of Czechoslovakia, they came to stay with relatives who were already long-term residents in the Czech lands. This movement represented the last wave of the internal chain migration that had been taking place within Czechoslovakia since 1945 and during which almost 100,000 people migrated to the Czech lands from Slovakia. The legal right of these new arrivals to remain in the Czech Republic was challenged in 1993 by a newly enacted law on state citizenship. Following strong criticism from abroad, this law has since been amended several times.[2] However, the law also had a severe

---

[1] Fieldwork carried out in the territory of the Czech Republic by Zdeněk Uherek and Renata Weinerová in 2001.

[2] For further details about reaction to the drafting of Law 40/1993 on acquisition and termination of state citizenship of the Czech Republic, both among the Czech and Romani public as well as internationally, see Zdeněk Uherek 'The Czech Republic and Roma Migration after 1989' in this volume.

impact on Roma with Slovak citizenship who had been living on a long term basis on Czech territory within the Czechoslovak federation. To this day, it is still debated where to apportion blame for the desperate situation of thousands of Slovak Roma who, following the break-up of the federation, continue to live illegally in the Czech Republic without residence permits or indeed any legal status whatsoever (Miklušáková 1999: 267–270).

The second migratory wave of Slovak Roma began in 1997 when large numbers emigrated to West European countries. The first surge of this wave flooded Great Britain and Roma migration from Slovakia soon became such a problem for other West European states that most considered it necessary to impose visa requirements. In August 1998 Great Britain introduced visa requirements for Slovakia, followed by Ireland, and then in July 1999 Finland and Norway imposed them as well, joined four months later by Denmark. In November 1999, the Finns and Norwegians lifted these restrictions but shortly after, in January 2000, the Finns reimposed them. In addition, the Belgian government reintroduced visa requirements in April 2000. Problems for the Slovak Republic arising from the emigration of their Roma attracted extensive press coverage. From reports appearing in the Czech press it was evident that the Slovak government was trying to discredit Roma accounts of their reasons for emigrating, which were stated to be primarily political, such as racism and neo-nazism. In response, the Slovak government accused Roma of abusing the right to political asylum.[3]

Demographic indicators of Roma in Slovakia

Slovakia traditionally contained the highest concentration of Romani inhabitants in Czechoslovakia. In the post-war years their numbers grew significantly, increasing from 97,000 in 1945 to 411,000 in 1991

---

[3] Cf.: 'The government will send a special aircraft for Roma returning from Finland (Slovakia)' (*Metro*, 9 July 1999), 'The government warns off Roma from ethno-tourism (Slovakia)' (*Metro*, 1 July 1999), 'Hundreds of Slovak Roma will have to leave Belgium' (*Metro*, 30 September 1999), 'Britain sends strong warning to Roma (The British Home Office does not rule out the reimposition of visa requirements)' (*Metro*, 21 October 1999).

(Srb 1993: 283). During the same period, there was an increase in the numbers of Roma migrating from Slovakia to the Czech lands. In some cases this migration was organised by officials and other non-Roma but also occurred spontaneously. This phenomenon began in the early post-war years and gathered pace in the 1960s, 1970s and especially the 1980s. This is why statistical data indicate a smaller increase in numbers for Roma in Slovakia than in the Czech lands. The following table shows an increasing trend for numbers of Roma in the Czech lands in comparison with Slovakia.[4]

---

[4] Migration intensified after government decree 502/65 was put into practice, thus implementing a policy of evenly-spread 'dispersal' of Roma from locations where they were highly concentrated. Consequently the plan to eliminate Romani settlements and disperse Roma had the effect of increasing levels of chain migration of Slovak Roma to the Czech lands. The main outcome was that Czech cities largely absorbed the demographic growth of the Romani population from East Slovakia. At the end of the seventies the continuation of such transfers led to conflict between Czech and Slovak authorities. Czech authorities claimed that progress in integrating Roma was being impeded by the arrival of the most backward Roma from Slovak settlements. Slovak authorities maintained, to the contrary, that it was the most advanced Roma who left the settlements – those who realised the need to improve their lives – and that after their departure, the settlements were reduced to those who were invalids, elderly and mothers with children. The migration assumed various dimensions. Roma considered leaving their settlements for the Czech lands, whether temporarily for work or permanently, as completely acceptable – viewing this as a positive way of improving their social and living conditions. Some left voluntarily and others under pressure as a result of the newly introduced dispersal policy. In practice these pressures still existed at the end of the 1980s and stemmed from the planned elimination of settlements, since although compensation was paid for demolished huts, there was no guarantee of alternative accommodation (Haišman 1999: 175). On the basis of all the evidence, it is possible to speak about 'exporting the Romani issue' to other parts of the republic, especially the industrial areas of Bohemia and Silesia. In this way the social pressures building up in eastern Slovakia, especially from a demographic boom in the Romani population, were alleviated. Both planned and spontaneous dispersal led to considerable mixing among Roma and disruption of their existing social structure. On the other hand, however, their horizons were extended and their mental passivity dispelled – features usually indicating positive signs of life in the desperate conditions of Romani settlements.

Table 1. Increase in numbers of Roma in the Czech lands and Slovakia: 1945 – 1991

Year	Czech lands	Slovakia
1945	1,000	96,000
1947	16,752	84,438
1966	56,519	165,006
1967	59,467	164,526
1968	61,085	165,382
1970	60,279	159,275
1980	101,193	203,405
1981	112,192	208,217
1982	115,877	213,026
1983	120,784	219,180
1984	124,899	224,694
1985	132,167	229,782
1986	136,812	235,169
1987	140,915	242,053
1988	143,071	247,755
1989	145,738	253,943
1991	151,000	260,000

Source: Srb 1993: 283

According to the most recent census in the Slovak Republic (26 May 2001), there were 89,920 Roma living in Slovakia, constituting 1.7 per cent of the entire population.[5] However, this data hardly corresponds to reality, and instead reflects the low social status of Roma citizens and

---

[5] According to the latest information published on the internet pages of the Statistical Office of the Slovak Republic. Compare:
http://www.statistics.sk/webdata/slov/scitanie/tab/zu
The ethnic mix of the population of the Slovak Republic in 1991 and 2001:

Date of census	Total Population	National/Ethnic Minorities					
		Slovak	Hungarian	Roma	Czech	Ruthenian	Ukrainian
3.3. 1991	5,274,335	4,519,328	567,296	75,802	52,884	17,197	13,281
26.5.2001	5,379,455	4,614,854	520,528	89,920	44,620	24,201	10,814

their problematic ethnic identification in Slovak society. Roma prefer to conceal themselves under a cloak of Slovak or Hungarian ethnic identity, which causes fewer problems in relations with the authorities than if they declare Roma ethnicity. The failure of the media campaign conducted by the Roma quarterly *Romano nevo l'il*,[6] which aimed to strengthen ethnic consciousness and Roma-ness (*romipen*) among the Slovak Roma, is very evident. Official estimates from 1995 speak of approximately 480,000 to 520,000 Roma living in Slovakia, which represents 9–10 per cent of the total population of the Slovak Republic (Pluim 2001: 6). Therefore, it can be said that the Slovak Republic has one of the largest Roma populations in Europe.

Politics and Slovak Roma

Under the previous communist regime several different policy models were employed to deal with Slovak or Czechoslovak Roma. There was the assimilation programme (which meant stripping Roma of their identity), the policy of integration (in which Romani identity was replaced by that of a 'citizen of the Romani origin'), the programme of enforced settlement for nomads and the attempt to limit population growth by sterilising Romani women, that was implemented mainly in Slovakia.

Meanwhile, new forms of social stratification emerged among Roma in Slovakia during the period of communist rule. In his IOM study, Imrich Vašečka (Vašečka I. 2000) explains how the Romani population started to integrate into the developing socialist structure in new ways when the previously isolated inhabitants of Romani settlements started to communicate with the outside world. Whether they had been coerced or had left their settlements voluntarily, Roma migrants ended their

---

[6] *Romano nevo l'il* (Romani New Paper) – an independent newspaper of Roma in Slovakia featuring cultural and social issues. Edition 468 in 2001 was devoted to issues related to the 2001 population census in Slovakia, including houses and flats. This edition contained articles aimed at dispelling Roma fears that if they affirmed Romani nationality they would lose their state citizenship of the Slovak Republic. The newspaper carried a number of interviews with popular Roma personalities and Romologists who voluntarily and proudly declared their Romani nationality. For example, in one of the articles the well-known Czech Romologist, Milena Hübschmannová, argued why she had adopted Romani nationality.

territorial and social isolation and new opportunities opened up to them in the world of institutions and organisations. In simple terms, growing social divisions began to create distinctions between urban Roma enjoying higher prestige and less esteemed rural Roma. New influences started to penetrate the internal structure of Roma society, which previously had been organised hierarchically on the basis of families and local rules. More and more the nuclear family began to form the basic organisational unit in place of the extended family and in this way the situation of Roma came to resemble that of the majority population.

This process of social differentiation affected the entire Romani population in various ways. A thin stratum of Romani intelligentsia came into existence, as well as a Romani middle class,[7] but by far the largest number consisted of those who were utterly destitute, living in the often inhuman conditions typical of Romani settlements. The terrible housing conditions of the many Roma still living in what are called osady – exclusively Romani communities resembling rural slums is a problem peculiar to Slovakia. An estimated one-quarter of all Roma in Slovakia live in such settlements, many of which are in the poorer eastern regions of the country.[8]

To a large extent the notion of a 'Romani middle class' has become a misleading concept, particularly in international discussion. In both governmental and non-governmental publications and reports, it has often been stated that the core of Romani emigration to Western Europe has been formed by what is called the Romani middle class. However,

---

[7] It was not a real 'middle' class. In relation to overall stratification in society, both Romani and non-Romani, this segment still formed part of the lower class. From this point of view, the only representatives of a real middle class under socialism were the small group of Romani intelligentsia. The lowest Romani class grouping, Romani settlement-dwellers, are located at the lowest depths of society, sometimes even lower.

[8] Settlements vary considerably depending on geographical location and level of ethnic segregation. Some settlements have their roots in policies adopted during the Second World War and early socialist period, requiring Roma to move out of towns. The numbers of Roma living in settlements has been growing during the past decade, since many Roma have returned to settlements because of the availability of cheaper housing. Within regions, the levels of poverty in Roma settlements seem to be closely linked to levels of ethnic integration and segregation.

what these documents do not adequately explain is that this term, in fact, refers to the former 'socialist' Romani middle class. Following post-1989 developments, this segment of the Romani population became de facto pauperised to the level of the poorest groups. Therefore, we are talking in this case of literate but unqualified people. Consequently, after 1989 almost the entire Romani population of Slovakia plummeted to the very bottom of the social scale. According to official sources, the level of unemployment among Slovak Roma is around 95 per cent but, according to unofficial estimates, this is nowadays virtually 100 per cent.

Various signs indicate that negative perceptions of Roma are strengthening and that relations between Roma and non-Roma have deteriorated over the past ten years. There are a number of possible explanations for this, including the declining social status of Roma and their growing unemployment and increasing dependency on social benefits. Negative stereotypes are also reinforced by geographical separation and the limited contact between Roma and non-Roma.[9] A British expert on Romani issues in Central Europe, Will Guy, compares the position of Slovak Roma to the former situation of black inhabitants of South Africa. He summarised his impressions from his most recent visit to Slovakia in 2001 as follows:

The same settlements – the same poverty and segregation that I saw when I was in these settlements in late sixties. In fact the only substantial thing that has changed is the fact that today they do not even have the jobs they used to have under communism.[10]

Likewise, the Canadian social anthropologist David Z. Scheffel, who has been undertaking applied field research in the east Slovak settlement of Svinia since 1993, described the social situation in the Romani settlement in similar terms:

---

[9] Cf. Thesis on segregation in eastern Slovakia: Hornák, R. 2000: *Porovnání segregace dvou romských osad na východním Slovensku*, Department of Social and Cultural Anthropology, University of Plzeň.
[10] Cf.: 'Expert: Roma "life is worse"' ('Expert: Romům se žije hůř'), (*MF Dnes*, 8 September 2001, p.1, 8).

I do not want to apply this to all Slovakia – circumstances are different – but the level of spite which exists at Svinia, that's something one cannot imagine. Roma at Svinia represent for the locals kind of a subjugated nation. It is a nation consisting of people they consider to be half animals. And what shocked me there the most is the everyday relationship of these communities. Really, I call it apartheid. I cannot imagine a bigger apartheid than what exists right there. There are total barriers built up between the two communities and there is almost no communication between them. The only communication which exists, is a negative communication when they call each other names or steal something from one another or do something equally harmful.

(Scheffel 2001: 71)

In addition to their oppressive unemployment, another burden Roma must bear is the loss of their homes. Because their rent is frequently in arrears they are often evicted from flats, where they had been dispersed among non-Roma, to basic accommodation for rent defaulters, graphically termed 'bare flats'. This happens mainly in eastern Slovak cities where Romani ghettos or 'colonies' are being created, isolated both territorially and socially. With the deterioration of social conditions in the 1990s it is even possible to see impoverished urban Roma returning to the settlements.

The frustrated Roma from the former Romani middle class began to perceive their desperate socio-economic situation as signifying the lack of any prospects whatsoever for them in Slovakia. Either spontaneously or by organised means, Slovak Roma started to emigrate to West European states and the Czech Republic.

Spontaneous emigration occurs mainly among urban Roma, who have lost their previous social status associated with what was called the Romani middle class. This type of emigration is increasingly interpreted in non-governmental spheres (Klímová 2002: 4) as a considered strategy of Romani individuals who are motivated primarily by economic concerns. In our research we also encountered people whose lives were threatened (most commonly by unspecified mafiosi or by usurers), who emigrate to seek a respite from persecution, if only temporarily.

Usury

Organised emigration of Slovak Roma is usually planned by Romani usurers, called úžerníci in Slovakia. These began to take advantage of the unbearable social situation of their Romani fellow citizens, mainly in the settlements but also in cities, and exploit them quite illegally.[11]

According to reports in the Slovak press[12], Romani usurers in Slovakia were lending money to impoverished Roma at a monthly interest rate of 50 per cent. Consequently, the debts grew exponentially, so that debtors found themselves unable to pay even interest on the interest. The most indebted Roma became victims of what is called ethno-business. The usual practice was for usurers to send Roma against their will to Prague or Budapest airport. There, they were given tickets to a West European country where they could obtain higher social benefits than in Slovakia, enabling them to make larger repayments to the usurers. Since asylum law does not permit applicants to leave the country where asylum is sought, Slovak Roma regularly claimed to have lost their passports when returning home, since they needed to avoid having their passports stamped on re-entry to Slovakia. Slovak Roma seeking asylum in the Czech Republic usually travelled home by taxi which, together with the fact that they were known to be receiving social benefits both where claiming asylum and in their original place of residence, aroused the antipathy of local authorities and local inhabitants alike.

Media accounts of Romani usurers condemn their practices in Slovakia as not only immoral but bordering on illegality, if not outside the law.

---

[11] According to reports in the Romani press, usury practices had been known about since 1995. At that time, only a priest, P. Pavel Procházka, made a public stand against them in Northern Bohemia and the Prešov region (without any response from government bodies). However, it was only in 2001 that cases of usury in Ústí nad Labem were referred to the prosecution service. ('It was known that usurers existed.', *Romano kurko*, 11 May 2001, 8).

For further details concerning usury issues, see articles below:

Lavička, Vojtěch (2001) 'Rom Romestar na čorla?' (A Rom won't rob a Rom?), *Amaro Gendalos*, 5/5, May, 14–16; Koláčková, Jana (2001) 'Loans and usury' (legal advice), *Amaro gendalos*, 5/5, May, 17; Kalejová, Soňa (2001) 'Fight against usury', *Amaro gendalos*, 5/4, April, 3; Krištof, Roman (2001) 'Usury' (commentary), *Amaro gendalos*, 5/4, April, 12.

[12] Cf.: 'Usury clan in the background', *Moment*, 14 April 2000.

However, Slovak journalists fail to discuss the real roots of the problem. A Czech anthropologist, Stanislav Kužel (2000: 151–153), made a thorough analysis of the problem of usury in Slovakia. Above all, he identified 'the hidden economy of Romani segregation as a communist legacy' from which evolved, after 1989, 'the hidden economy of Romani segregation as an economy of indifference'. In his study Kužel analyses in detail the origins of Romani impoverishment and the mechanism by which it develops. This impoverishment is always accompanied by a decrease in social support payments and indebtedness at pawnshops, leading to a greater dependency on the intra-ethnic clientism system (usury). Rent arrears of more than 5,000 crowns represent a disaster for many Romani families living in blocks of flats. Because they are practically illiterate, they are unable to save in order to pay off these arrears and fall into debt, either with Romani usurers or with pawnshops which charge monthly interest of at least 17 per cent. Consequently, they are plunged into a state of chronic dependency. Many Romani families solve the problem of this drop in income by selling their flats and retreating 'back to the rural settlements where they have relatives and can move into illegal shacks, which from a practical point of view are cheaper' (Kužel 2000: 152). If usury interest rates in Slovakia vary between 17 per cent and 50 per cent, in the Czech lands, specifically in Ústí nad Labem, they reach 100 per cent. Our research reveals that the anonymity of an urban milieu makes it possible for interest rates to soar to exorbitant levels.

At the start of the new millennium, the phenomenon of usury became a serious social problem, not only in Slovakia but in the Czech Republic too.[13] In 2002 it was reported for the first time in the Czech Republic that the problem of 'usury' was not solely an intra-community Romani

---

[13] An official of the Commission for the Prevention of Criminality of the Ministry of the Interior, Radek Jiránek, revealed that thousands, possibly tens of thousands, have been afflicted by the problem of usury in the Czech Republic. However, precise data is not available. In the 2001 report, the police listed only a small number of recorded and reported cases of usury. Nevertheless, estimates by social workers in the field, by Roma themselves and by Roma counsellors confirm that usury occurs in every community where there are suitable conditions (http://www.infoservis.net/tema.php3?cid=1015433326)

issue.[14] Non-Roma (*gadžo*) private money lenders were operating in several Czech districts (for example, the 'Past Finance' company in Hodonin), offering loans with interest rates as high as 130 per cent. The loan conditions were never transparent but Roma and non-Roma residents of temporary housing or asylum accommodation, living in a virtual information vacuum, were so unwitting that the terms of such loans did not appear suspicious. Consequently, they fell easy prey to Czech usurers. In this way the problem of usury in the Czech Republic lost its stamp of ethnic exclusivity and became instead a typical problem of ghettos and poverty.

The UNHCR has recorded cases of usury in different parts of the world among members of various ethnic groups. As UNHCR workers stated, the common factor in all communities afflicted by usury is extreme poverty.

In this context is necessary to point out that in the Czech Republic, specifically in Ústí nad Labem and Ostrava, the fight against usury is being waged successfully in the criminal courts despite the difficulty of securing testimony from eyewitnesses. The victims of usury, in particular, are terrified and naturally fear for their own safety and are concerned about the pace and outcome of the criminal proceedings. The NGO People in Need and the UNHCR in Prague have followed the problem of usury in the Czech Republic over an extended period and have supported the investigation of individual cases.[15] Meanwhile the UNHCR in Prague has developed an imaginative initiative to prevent the recurrence of usury and further victims. In June 2001 the Social Emergency Fund project was launched in the two towns most severely afflicted by usury, Ústí nad Labem and Ostrava. This project is based on the principle of solidarity and aims to provide financial support for endangered people and their families through interest-free loans. It is targeted at people on the edge of poverty, who, without help, could plunge to the bottom of the social scale and become easy prey for

---

[14] Information taken mainly from the Seminar of Roma Counsellors in Velké Karlovice in the Vsetin region, which took place on 28–30 April 2002. The event was organised by the Czech Government Council for Romani Community Affairs.

[15] The NGO People in Need regularly posts information on problems of poverty and usury on its web page: http://www.infoservis.net/tema

usurers. Unfortunately, the Czech state is unable at present to re-establish the Social Emergency Fund as a local self-administered system and consequently, this project is likely to terminate in the near future.[16] However, it would be beneficial to develop a similar project, supported primarily by national resources and structures, to eliminate usury and prevent subsequent Roma emigration from the Czech Republic and Slovakia.

Characteristics of Romani migration in Slovakia

Slovakia is first and foremost a source of Romani emigration. So far, it has not been a target country for immigration, but does constitute a transit country for Roma migrants. The territory of the Slovak state serves as a part of the migration bridge between Bulgaria and Poland as well as between Romania and the Czech Republic. While the first migration bridge primarily serves the interests of Bulgarian Romani 'entrepreneurs', the second forms part of the route for groups of Romanian Roma who unsuccessfully seek to gain asylum in Germany.[17] These Romanian Roma usually end up in Czech asylum centres from which they make attempts to cross the German border.

Migratory motives of Slovak Roma

We have not carried out any specific research in Slovakia aimed at establishing the migratory motives of Slovak Roma. However, the reasons for Slovak Roma to migrate listed most frequently in the literature include racial discrimination and socio-economic factors (Vašečka, I. 2000, Pluim 2001, World Bank et al. 2002). Our research in the Czech Republic among Roma asylum seekers from Slovakia corroborates the reasons given above. At the same time, however, we

---

[16] Discussion at UNHCR meeting, Prague, 13 May 2002.

[17] The migration of Roma to Germany started in the early 1990s, the first large group of asylum seekers coming from Romania. Approximately 60,000 Romanian Roma sought political asylum in Germany in the period 1990–1995. In 1993 Germany decided to make a number of amendments to its asylum legislation in response to general migratory movements. Furthermore, Germany concluded a repatriation agreement with Romania and has since established similar programmes in co-operation with various countries (Pluim 2001: 30).

recorded a much greater incidence occurrence of motives stemming from serious conflict in interpersonal relations. During fieldwork, we encountered migrants fleeing extortioners, debt collectors or more immediate threats by unspecified mafiosi. Even though respondents did not speak directly about usury, it was clearly evident from their reactions that they had fallen into the clutches of cruel extortioners who would not hesitate to use extreme physical violence against those failing to meet their financial demands. Usurers usually become wealthy by exploiting the igrorance and helplessness of their victims. When making decisions whether or not to migrate, our respondents were often threatened by such ruthless people.

The migratory motives of Slovak Roma to are generally mixed. Socio-economic factors and racial discrimination are accompanied by pressures from a variety of speculators, taking advantage of the unsatisfying social situations and unfulfilled lives of Slovak Roma. Nevertheless, Slovak Roma emigration has been characterised from the outside as 'ethno-tourism', as this phenomenon has been infamously dubbed by the Slovak media. However, the real causes of Slovak Roma emigration are more complicated and require more careful investigation. For example, studies carried out by Imrich and Michal Vašečka have yielded detailed analyses of the migratory motivation of Slovak Roma (Vašečka, I. 2000, Vašečka, M. 2000).

Emigration of Slovak Roma to the Czech Republic

The Czech Republic is one of the countries that can be classified both as a country of origin and as a migratory destination. In the period between 1 January 2000 and 15 December 2000, a total of 723 Slovak asylum seekers were registered in the Czech Republic (Pluim 2001: 28–29). Slovak asylum seekers started to arrive as early as 1994 but until 31 December 1999 these mostly involved claims by Slovak asylum seekers already living in the Czech Republic.

In the Czech lands the turning point in numbers of Roma refugees from Slovakia was 1999. The most likely explanation is that most West European countries (Great Britain, Ireland, Finland, Norway and Denmark) imposed visa requirements for Slovakia in the years 1998 –

1999. However, Czech asylum centres were relatively accessible and from 2000 residence procedures were made even simpler. Roma asylum seekers could move freely about the Czech Republic and were not prevented from travelling to and from Slovakia by their lack of passports since this border could be crossed by Slovak citizens with only an identity card. In 1999, according to an unnamed source, 650 Roma from Slovakia sought political asylum, affirming Slovak or Hungarian ethnicity, but none satisfied the conditions for asylum.[18]

The Czech government carried out in-depth research on arrivals in 2000, revealing the following details. Most of the 723 asylum seekers in that year came with their families and there were only 48 individual applications. A very high percentage of claimants (43 per cent) were children under 15, while, on the other hand, only 9 per cent were in the 41–60 age group. Males and female were roughly equal, not normally the case with other asylum seekers. Another remarkable feature was that only a few claimants (54 cases) affirmed Roma ethnicity whereas 72 per cent declared Slovak ethnicity. Most claimants came from towns in the Michalovce district in east Slovakia and intended to seek asylum. Some had previously made claims in other countries, such as Hungary, Switzerland and Germany.

During their first month in the reception centre at Vyšší Lhoty in northern Moravia, Romani asylum seekers are usually contacted by the IOM staff. These workers interview them and try to find answers to the problems that led them to migrate, so these might be tackled in their home countries. Should the political asylum seekers decide to go home, IOM tries to assist their homeward journey by covering travel expenses and making a payment to help them through the first two weeks after their return.[19] Nevertheless, since usually nothing has changed in their former home areas, Slovak Roma often decide (or are forced by usurers) to make further attempts to emigrate.

Even though regulations governing travel between the Czech and Slovak Republics have been tightened since 1 January 2002 so that

---

[18] In 1999, Slovak Roma formed the second most numerous group of claimants for political asylum in the Czech Republic, immediately after Afghans (unnamed source).
[19] Field research by Zdeněk Uherek and Renata Weinerová.

passports are now required, illegal border crossings continue. Although our fieldwork in the Czech Republic did not yield detailed information on this, it is evident that Slovak Roma continue to travel towards the Czech lands, ignoring the problems they will face as foreigners in the Czech Republic.[20] Illegal stays by Roma with Slovak state citizenship can end in legally sanctioned deportation back to their homeland, although in practice this does not happen because long-term illegal residence is difficult to prove.

Conclusion

The mass migration of Roma became a serious political problem for the Slovak Republic in view of its long-term foreign-policy goal of joining the EU. The Slovak government reacted to the emigration of its Romani citizens to EU countries by issuing statements and taking policy decisions. The statements mostly asserted that Romani emigration was organised rather than spontaneous but because they did not take account of internal principles regulating the life of Romani communities confronted by a 'white' environment, they simply denigrated the emigration by dubbing it ethno-tourism.[21] Roma have been repeatedly accused of behaving irresponsibly and having no regard for the good name of Slovakia.

As regards policy measures adopted and implemented, however, it is evident that the Slovak government pays considerable attention to the issue. A number of policy measures were approved and attempts have been made to ensure that even lower administrative levels adopt the same approach. With the ratification of the European Charter for Regional and Minority Languages in June 2001, Slovakia is now party

---

[20] For more information on the life style of Slovak Roma in the Czech lands, see Zdeněk Uherek 'The Czech Republic and Roma Migration after 1989' in this volume.
[21] Cf.: For example, a quotation from an article in the daily *Metro*, 1 July 1999: 2.
In connection with claims by hundreds of Roma for asylum in Finland, the Slovak government, through its vice-premier for minorities and human rights, appealed to Romani citizens not to yield to 'improper practices and offers of irresponsible individuals who see a business opportunity in this form of ethno-tourism'. In the government's opinion, no Slovak citizen has any reason to emigrate on political or nationality grounds. 'So far the Finnish authorities have not granted asylum in even a single case', the spokesperson of vice-premier Pal Csáky pointed out.

to all major international minority rights instruments. Indeed, the European Commission has recognised progress in the area of minority rights protection, although noting '"a gap between policy formulation and implementation on the ground"[22] and a lack of practical improvements in the daily life of minorities – notably Roma' (Open Society Institute 2001: 431).

Meanwhile, the activities of both Romani and non-Romani NGOs have expanded significantly and these now resemble each other more closely. However, as far as we can tell, these endeavours are more or less futile, especially in the setting of the Slovak countryside where they are challenged by the cultural and social barriers of local communities. The cliché of development programmes is repeated, usually based on the idea that problems of Romani settlements have to be addressed within the settlements themselves and separately from 'white' villages, by what is termed the ethnic emancipation of Romani settlement-dwellers. Development programmes based exclusively on ethnic principles do not usually achieve their aims and often lead to ethnic conflict. Instead, the strategy of development programmes should be focused on the parallel emancipation of citizens from ethnically different population groups (Kužel 2000: 144). The emancipation of citizens in the context of a Slovak village means the kind of emancipation capable of confronting rampant forms of paternalism and nepotism to which both governmental and non-governmental organisations often fall victim. In Slovakia, therefore, it seems that the co-existence of the Roma minority with the rest of the population has become a real challenge for society in its entirety.

References

Haišman, T. (1999) 'Romové v Československu v letech 1945–1967: Vývoj institucionálního zájmu a jeho dopady' (Roma in Czechoslovakia 1945–1967: Evolution of institutional interest and its outcomes), in H. Lisá (ed.) 137–83.

---

[22] European Commission (2000) *Regular Report on Slovakia's Progress Towards Accession*, 8 November, 21–22.

Klímová, I. (2000) 'Analysis of the current debate on the political aspects of Romani migration and asylum seeking', paper delivered at international roundtable *Roma Migration in Europe: Trends*, Academy of Sciences of the Czech Republic, Institute of Ethnology, Praha, November 24–5 (see this volume).

Kužel, S. (2000) *Terénní výzkum integrace a segregace* (Field research on integration and segregation), Praha: Cargo Publishers.

Lisá, H. (ed.) (1999) *Romové v České republice* (Roma in the Czech Republic), Praha: Socioklub.

Miklušáková, M. (1999) 'Stručný nástin důsledků zák. č. 40/1993 Sb., o nabývání a pozbývání státního občanství ČR' (A brief outline of consequences of Law 40/1993 on acquisition and termination of state citizenship of the Czech Republic, in H. Lisá (ed.) 267–70.

Open Society Institute (2001) *Monitoring the EU Accession Process: Minority Protection*, Budapest: Central European University Press, Website: www.eumap.org.

Pluim, M. (2001) *Current Roma Migration from the EU Candidate States*, Draft study prepared by International Centre for Migration Policy Development (ICMPD).

World Bank, *et al.* (2002) *Poverty and Welfare of Roma in the Slovak Republic*, joint report of the World Bank, The Open Society Institute, INEKO, Foundation S.P.A.C.E., Bratislava, April.

Scheffel, Z. D. (2001) 'Interview', *Český lid*, 88, 1: 63–76.

Srb, V. (1993) 'Romové v Československu podle sčítání lidu 1991', *Demografie* 35, 4: 282 – 289.

Vašečka, I. (2000) *Príčiny odchodov Rómov zo Slovenska do niektorých krajín Európskej únie* (Reasons for Roma leaving Slovakia for various countries of the European Union), Dokumentačné centrum pro výskum slovenskej spoločnosti (Documentation Centre for Research of Slovak Society), International Organization for Migration project, Bratislava: IOM.

Vašečka, M. (2000) *Roma: The Greatest Challenge for Slovakia on its Way into the European Union*, Bratislava: Institute for Public Affairs, January.

Gypsy Migration in Hungary

Csaba Prónai

Basic information on Gypsy (Roma) migration in Hungary

The IOM research project

The data presented here is chiefly drawn from a research project[1] carried out in Hungary between March and May 2000 and financed by the Geneva-based International Organization for Migration (IOM). The research covered two main areas, which were quite distinct. Firstly, we tried to gain insight into the migration strategies and attitudes of Gypsies living permanently or temporarily in Hungary. Secondly, we collected and analysed Hungarian media coverage of Gypsy migration between September 1997 and January 2000. The overall project manager was András Kováts of the International Migration Research Centre, attached to the Political Institute of the Hungarian Academy of Sciences and the media analysis was carried out by Katalin Bognár and Dorka Sík of the Shelter - Foundation to Assist Migrants. Post-migration processes were not surveyed within the framework of the IOM research project, although a certain amount of information was gathered on this aspect of migration in various projects. However, discussion of these is beyond the scope of the present paper.[2]

The initial part of the research consisted of ten case studies based on previous individual and group interviews and, in some cases, on participant observation. These studies were undertaken by the following researchers with the specific Gypsy groups listed below:

---

[1] Apart from my own research experience, I have made use of the following Hungarian publications: Bognár 2000, Hajnal 2000, Kállai 2000a, Kováts 2000, Vajda and Prónai 2000. I have also drawn on the following Hungarian manuscripts, written within the framework of the IOM research project: Wizner 2000a and 2000b and Bognár and Sik 2000.

[2] For example, see Krasznai 2000 or Puporka 2000 on the case of the Zámoly community. Similarly, the Gypsies who emigrated to Canada have been filmed by György Kerényi and László Endre Hajnal has researched this group using participant observation.

- Endre László Hajnal, a student of the Department of Cultural Anthropology, Eötvös Loránd University, has been doing participant observation for several years in a prosperous Vlach Gypsy group who were planning to emigrate to Canada.
- Ernő Kállai, a researcher for the Minority Research Institute of the Hungarian Academy of Sciences, carried out interviews with a group of young intellectuals from Budapest and also with amateur and professional Gypsy musicians making regular trips abroad.
- Balázs Wizner, a researcher of the Sociological Institute of the Hungarian Academy of Sciences, conducted two group interviews. One was with Gypsies living in the west of Hungary, who had taken jobs abroad, and the other with Gypsies who made their living providing attractions at funfairs and fairs.
- However, the greatest number of interviews, with five different groups, was undertaken by Imre Vajda, a Vlach Roma researcher for the Minority Research Institute of the Hungarian Academy of Sciences, and myself.[3] We interviewed a poor Vlach Gypsy community living in the countryside, who later attracted international attention as the Zámoly community seeking legal protection at the European Court of Human Rights in Strasbourg. In addition, we conducted interviews with four distinct groups of Gypsies migrating from Romania to Hungary, which are described in more detail below.

Amaro Drom

This paper also drew on numerous articles from the Romani periodical *Amaro Drom* on the Gypsy migration to Canada.[4] This source is particularly important, partly due to the fact that György Kerényi, head of the editorial board, went to Canada to make a film[5] about Gypsy immigrants.[6] In fact, he was first persuaded to do so by József Krasznai, one of the relatives of the Gypsies living in Zámoly and who

---

[3] I was also fieldwork co-ordinator for the project as a whole.
[4] E.g. Puporka 2000, Kerényi 2000a.
[5] The film has not yet been screened.
[6] Those interested in the issue of Roma migration to Canada from Hungary should also consult the reports by Kerényi published in the periodical *Élet és Irodalom*.

later ended up as their spokesperson in Strasbourg.[7] Kerényi also helped us to interview the Zámoly group, then in Budapest, at the beginning of their journey in search of justice. *Amaro Drom* continued to focus on this issue by publishing translations of two papers from the Cambridge Review of International Affairs, which dealt with Roma migration.[8] These were Braham and Braham 2000 and Lee 2000.

Difficulties with migration data

No exact data is available on Gypsy emigration from Hungary, since 'most of this data is secret or at least not accessible to the public' (Kováts 2000:79). Under international law, the relevant regulations prohibit data concerning immigrants to be revealed to the authorities of their home countries. However, this restriction still leaves considerable latitude for rumours to circulate and political manipulation to occur. As Kováts put it, 'the data published by the various Gypsy interest groups and political groups provides insight into their own current positions in the political battlefield but not into the migration process as such' (2000: 78). The review of relevant newspaper articles also suggests that there are widely different estimates of numbers of migrants, depending on the political stance of their source.

In recent years several research projects have been carried out that studied the migratory patterns of the Hungarian population as a whole (Laki 1999). However, in these surveys the actual question put to respondents was: 'Would you emigrate if you could?' The findings revealed that Gypsies were more prepared to emigrate than others, even though 'in the group of those who answered "yes, we would" the percentage of Gypsy respondents is slightly higher than their proportion in the total population, so that they are over-represented. While only 4 per cent of the sample were Gypsies, their proportion of those

---

[7] His standpoint on this issue was published in *Amaro Drom*, see Krasznai 2000a and 2000b. For more on the question of the Hungarian Gypsies in Strasbourg, see Kerényi 2000c and Dobszay 2000.

[8] These were Braham and Braham 2000 and Lee 2000. The original articles in English were: Braham, M. and Braham, M. (2000) 'Romani Migrations and EU Enlargement', *Cambridge Review of International Affairs*, 13, 2, spring-summer, 97–116 and Lee, R. (2000) 'Post-Communism Romani Migration to Canada', ibid., 51–70.

answering 'yes' was 9 per cent' (Kováts 2000: 79). In Hungary, however, the Gypsies have the least chance of all of realising their migration plans. Over and over again, by every possible statistical indicator, all research has shown that the situation of Gypsies remains far more unfavourable than that of the majority population. For example, their expected life span is well below average, their unemployment rate is three times more than average, while their opportunities for higher or, indeed, secondary education are virtually non-existent (see Krémer 1999: 90).[9] Nevertheless, great care must be exercised in interpreting the figures about the proportion of Gypsies contemplating emigration. What they do show very clearly is that of the whole Hungarian population, Gypsies tend to be more prepared to emigrate than non-Gypsies. These empirical surveys investigating the migratory intentions of Hungarian citizens of Hungary have reported the following findings:

- the migration potential has not changed significantly throughout the 1990s;
- approximately 3-4 per cent of the population would go abroad to work, but only 2 per cent would go and settle in another country;
- within the group of those willing to leave the country the following groups are over-represented: men, students, the unemployed, the young and those with larger families, more valuable flats or higher education;
- those willing to work abroad would prefer to go to Austria or Germany, while those wanting to emigrate would prefer to go to the United States (see Kováts 2000: 79).

As mentioned above, data about the number of Hungarian citizens arriving in other countries as refugees is not available from the countries where they seek asylum. Therefore, it remains unclear how much the Hungarian authorities responsible for migration and refugees and the Ministry of Foreign Affairs know about refugees arriving in Western Europe from Hungary (see Kováts 2000: 96). This is either because there have been very few instances of such refugees in recent

---

[9] Also found by Andorka (1996: 12), Kertesi (1995: 19) and Havas and Kemény (1995).

years or because the data is simply not accessible. The case of the forty-six Gypsies from Zámoly[10] seeking asylum and justice in Strasbourg is an exception in reaching the public domain.

Canada seems to be the only country where Hungarian citizens have sought and have been granted asylum in recent years, or at least the only country we know of, due to the fact that the relevant information was sent to the Roma Press Centre in Hungary by the Immigration and Refugee Board of Canada. This data is given below in Table 1:

Table 1: *Asylum claims and outcomes for Hungarian citizens in Canada: 1998, 1999*

Year	1998	1999
Claims submitted	982	1,579
Decisions made	395	958
Refugee status granted	153	74
Claims rejected	64	378
Status expired	95	155
Withdrawal/Other	83	351

Source: Canadian Immigration and Refugee Board

From this table it can be seen that in 1998 and 1999 a total of 2,561 Hungarian citizens applied for refugee status and in 227 cases this was granted it (cf. Kerényi 2000b: 12).

Even though 'the Canadian data is broken down by citizenship and not by ethnicity' and consequently 'we can only guess the ethnic identity of those listed', Kováts thinks that, on the basis of information given on the home page of the Canadian Immigration and Refugee Board and publishished decisions setting a precedent, 'we can safely say that those

---

[10] The exact number was specified by József Krasznai (2000: 4): 'when you are responsible for 45 people in the middle of nothing'. A slightly different figure was given by Kerényi (2000b: 12) who wrote: '47 people left for France in a coach'. However, these accounts are nor incompatible, since we know from the report of Háberman and Kende (2000: 8) that there was an extra person in the coach – Katalin Katz, a professor of the Department of Social Work at the University of Jerusalem.

applying for refugee status are of Gypsy ethnicity, or at least identify themselves as Gypsies' (2000: 80).

IOM case studies

The ten communities studied within the framework of the IOM case studies were categorised into three main groups by Kováts (2000: 83).

Firstly he described those 'personally involved in migration as refugees', who all identified Canada as their destination. This included the Vlach Gypsy community in Budapest observed by Hajnal[11] as well as the other rural Vlach community, which is considering emigration because of incessant conflict with the non-Gypsy population. The latter community, from Zámoly, was the group that eventually applied for refugee status in France rather than in Canada[12]. The third such group consisted of young intellectuals from Budapest, most of whom have relatives or acquaintances who have already emigrated.

Secondly, Kováts identified a non-refugee group, termed as 'those with an above average migration potential'. He divided this group into three types: migrant workers and their families living in the northern and south-eastern Hungary, musicians regularly working abroad for shorter or longer periods and finally Gypsies earning their living providing attractions at fairs – referred to as *búcsús* in the vernacular. Research revealed that even though members of this *búcsús* group are very mobile, 'their migration is strictly regional without involving any travel abroad' (Wizner 2000b: 1). While migrant workers predominantly identify Germany as their goal (Wizner 2000a: 1), musicians tend to list – apart from Germany – other Western countries such as Austria or England and even overseas destinations like the USA, Canada and Australia (Kállai 2000a: 98–99).

Kováts' third category consisted of 'those using Hungary as a transit country' and four such groups were identified by the IOM research

---

[11] Currently also in Canada

[12] The personal interviews conducted by Imre Vajda and myself revealed that the idea of going to France came up spontaneously. The original intention of this group was to travel to Canada.

project. Since all of these had come to Hungary from Romania, it might be more appropriate to call them 'Romanian Gypsy migrants to Hungary'.

Policy makers' views of Gypsy migration

If we ask whether decision makers in Hungary regard Gypsy emigration as a profound social problem, the answer has to be a definitely 'no'. The 1999 *Government Report on the Situation of the National and Ethnic Minorities living in Hungary* (see Kormánybeszámoló 2000) and the document entitled *Government Measures Taken in order to Improve the Social Integration of Gypsies in Hungary* (Kormányzati Intézkedések 2000) contain no reference whatsoever to Gypsy emigration. Neither do any governmental reports, legislative documents or specific programmes during the 1990s, as a comprehensive review has revealed (Kállai 2000b).

Likewise, the Hungarian Prime Minister Viktor Orbán told the daily newspaper *Magyar Hírlap* (29 October 1999) that 'the number of Gypsies arriving in Canada from Hungary is not high enough to require diplomatic measures. No ethnic group in Hungary has any reason to leave Hungary as political refugees' (see Bognár 2000: 91). The deputy secretary of the Ministry of Justice voiced the same opinion at the November 1998 hearing of the Canadian Immigration and Refugee Board (see Kende 1999: 8) and shortly after in a press interview to *Magyar Hírlap* in January 1999 (see Bognár 2000: 86).

The fact that decision makers in Hungary do not see Gypsy emigration as a serious social problem is quite evident from government statements concerning the group of Gypsies seeking justice in Strasbourg (see Kerényi 2000c: 5). In the words of Toso Doncsev, head of the Office of National and Ethnic Minorities, the emigration of the Zámoly community was not an issue involving all Gypsies but was a problem limited to the six families concerned. In similar vein, the Minister of Welfare and Families said that the Gypsy families had gone to Strasbourg with the intention of shaming Hungary. When his statement was strongly criticised by several Gypsy politicians, the Prime Minister not only publicly defended his colleague but furthermore added the advice that Gypsies should work and study harder.

Motivations for Migration

The prosperous Vlach family and young Gypsy intellectuals, both from Budapest, as well as the Gypsy musicians and the Gypsies regularly working abroad, all said that their motivation for migrating was economic. The same can be safely said about all Gypsy groups travelling to Hungary from Romania. In contrast, the Zámoly community professed different motives – political considerations. They asserted this while at home in Budapest, when they were thinking of leaving for Canada, and József Krasznai still maintains the same position in Strasbourg.

However, we need to ask whether these motives are necessarily mutually exclusive? To resolve this question it is helpful to adopt a holistic perspective, characteristic of cultural anthropology[13]. Viewed in this way economy and politics are simply two different aspects or dimensions of a culture. However individual dimensions never exist in isolation but are interrelated. From the perspective of cultural anthropology, therefore, separating and contrasting political and the economic explanations results in a false and misleading dichotomy. Instead, when trying to explain the migratory pattern of a group of people, we should always take both dimensions into account simultaneously, as well as other factors such as their kinship and legal system, etc., since every culture exhibits a whole variety of such dimensions.

Even if the migration of Hungarian Gypsies appears to be entirely motivated by economic considerations, the political atmosphere in Hungary should not be disregarded as a relevant factor. A review of publications during the 1990s covering the issue of violations of the human rights of Hungarian Gypsies and the Gypsy civil rights movements that have emerged in response (see Prónai 2000) make us

---

[13] See, for example, Crapo 1993: 5, Haviland 1978: 11, Howard 1993: 136, Peoples and Bailey 1991: 6.

realise that Hungarian Gypsies have suffered discrimination in many ways. On the other hand, financial aspects should also be taken into account when considering the case of the Zámoly community, even if these are overshadowed by József Krasznai's heroic battle, symbolic of the current conflict between Gypsies and non-Gypsies. As Károly Mannheim put it, 'in the world it's not only partial group interests fighting one another but it's worlds fighting worlds, and ... the whole cultural process is the result of this basically existential battle' (1995: 317).

One of the things the IOM research project has shown us is that both the Gypsies living in Hungary and those using Hungary as a transit country have adopted a wide variety of migration strategies. Indeed, these strategies are just as diverse as the Gypsy communities themselves. Even if we consider just the Vlach Gypsies, the prosperous Budapest community migrates in a completely different way from that of a poorer community from the countryside. Also there are various groups within the community of musicians: those playing mainly classical music, those playing in bars and restaurants, and a further, younger group playing authentic Vlach Gypsy music. Interviews revealed that the musicians' willingness to emigrate was less committed but that besides economic motives they identified discrimination as a reason for leaving Hungary (Kállai 2000a: 92). Similarly, the answers of the young intellectuals suggested a kind of 'siege mentality' (Heusch 1966: 89) – a 'constant sense of being under threat and of segregation experienced when in contact with the majority, which significantly lessens their opportunities in terms of economic success' (Kováts 2000: 87).

There are also significant differences between the individual groups migrating from Romania. One group, the 'Gábors', is involved in flourishing commercial enterprises, while in contrast the entrepreneurs of the so-called Hungarian Gypsy group are less organised and lack sufficient capital. The members of another group depend for their livelihood on their physical strength as unskilled casual labourers, while the money-making opportunities of yet a further group – beggars – are even more precarious.

Although information gathered from interviews by Imre Vajda and myself is beyond the scope of the present paper, it is worth drawing attention to the diversity of strategies used during migration. This is hardly surprising if we consider how very varied the groups are. In fact, the question of diversity is immediately raised as soon as an attempt is made to communicate with members of any group, since a decision has to be made about which language to use. It turns out that one of the groups speaks Hungarian as well as *Romanes* (Romani language) and Romanian (the 'Gábors'), another speaks only Romanian (the manual labourers), while yet another speaks both Hungarian and Romanian but not *Romanes* (the Hungarian Gypsies), or speaks only *Romanes* and Romanian (the beggars). This factor, in itself, determines the opportunities of specific groups and the extent of their disadvantage, etc.

In seeking a general interpretative framework Leonardo Piasere's theory of 'commercial eclecticism' is helpful. Piasere asserts that each Gypsy group[14] 'fills a niche within the wider context of non-Gypsy society – offering goods and services (sometimes their own labour power) in exchange for basic goods or their exchange value' (1991a: 211). In order to avoid having to rely entirely on the majority, Gypsies have developed what can be termed eclectic forms of commerce, meaning that they can offer multiple services and/or goods to non-Gypsies. 'One family can pursue various activities simultaneously or at different times, or concentrate on one type of product for several years on end.' This also implies that their choice of economic activity at a given moment is strongly influenced by the market situation.

Utilising this framework we can answer the question concerning the target country by saying that the migratory destination is largely determined by a combination of the economic strategy adopted and the market situation at the given moment. Since Gypsy culture is a multi-ethnic culture (Formoso 1986: 17), we can never limit our account to a single strategy or solution, not even within one country. Moreover, Gypsy culture is transnational (Kende 1994: 152, Acton 1994: 86) and consequently the geographic scope of a group's activity may well

---

[14] By which, of course, he means the groups of the Gypsies in northern Italy.

extend across national borders. However, this does not imply that we should equate Gypsy identity with nomadism (Manna 1996: 55) or with migration, since neither of these categories can adequately reflect its multifaceted nature (Reyniers 1989: 73). According to Piasere, 'being settled, migrant or in-between are all transitory, not constant situations' (1986: 46). Migration, then, is the product of a given social and economic system (cf. Reyniers 1986: 73), therefore only the former can be explained by the latter and not vice versa.

All scholars analysing Gypsy cultures from a cultural anthropological perspective agree that in dealing with Gypsy cultures, it is necessary to discuss the mechanisms by which Gypsies adopt and adapt non-Gypsy features in a flexible way, while avoiding uniformity and continuing to maintain their distinctive identity.[15] Gypsies constantly try to identify themselves as different from non-Gypsies and at the same time distinguish themselves from all the other Gypsy groups. In Piasere's words, 'the flexibility of the individual groups is due to their economic activities and their diasporic existence' among non-Gypsies, which gives them opportunities to learn about non-Gypsy culture, 'and also their ability to change. In short, the Gypsies are perfect at building intercultural contacts' (1991a: 216).

On the basis of all this research we can be fairly sure that they, the Gypsies, know more about us, non-Gypsies, than we know about them. Therefore, it would be very wrong to assume that they have no preliminary knowledge about their target countries before emigrating. What is undoubtedly true is that they gather information about their prospective destinations, mainly from relatives and acquaintances. What needs to be emphasised here is that they trust Gypsy sources of information much more than non-Gypsy ones. And while they try to keep these information channels hidden from non-Gypsies, information from non-Gypsies is always welcome (cf. Piasere 1995: 84). Otherwise they would be unable to gain the intercultural insights (cf. Piasere 1991a: 219) needed to create successful migration strategies.

---

[15] See, for example, Formoso 1994: 129; Okely 1983: 77; Piasere 1989: 137, 1991b: 1; Reyniers 1989: 85; Reyniers and Williams 1990: 103-104; Salo 1981; Salo and Salo 1977: 219; San Román 1975; Silverman 1982: 395; Sutherland 1977: 389; Williams 1982: 315, 341; 1990: 173; 1994: 177-8.

References

Acton, T. A. (1994) 'Unity in diversity', in Zs. Bódi (ed.) *Studies In Roma (Gypsy) Ethnography* 2, Budapest: Magyar Néprajzi Társaság, 79–88.

Andorka, R. (1996) 'A társadalmi egyenlőtlenségek növekedése a rendszerváltás óta', *Szociológiai Szemle* 1: 3–26.

Bognár, K. (2000) 'A roma migráció kronológiája a magyar sajtó alapján', *Mozgó Világ* 26 (10): 78–91.

Bognár, K. and Sik, D. (2000) *Roma migráció megjelenése az írott és elektronikus sajtóban 1997 szeptember és 2000 január között*, Kézirat (manuscript).

Braham, M. and Braham, M.(2000) 'Roma migráció és az EU bővítése', *Amaro Drom* 10, 11: 6–9.

Crapo, R. H. (1993) *Cultural anthropology*. 3rd edn., Guildford: Dushkin.

Dobszay, J. (2000) 'Hazai cigányügy: Magyar vándor', *Heti Világgazdaság* 22, 31: 7–10.

Formoso, B. (1986) *Tsiganes et sédentaires: La reproduction culturelle d'une société*, Paris: L'Harmattan.

Formoso, B. (1994) 'Diversité des itinéraires et uniformité des stéréotypes', *Études Tsiganes*, n.s. 2, 2: 127–38.

Háberman, Z. and Kende, Á. (2000) 'Úgy láttam, hogy a semmibe menekülnek', *Amaro Drom* 10, 10: 8–9.

Hajnal, L. E. (2000) 'Budapesti oláh cigányok migrációs stratégiái: Kivándorlás Kanadába az 1990-es évek második felében', *Mozgó Világ* 26, 10: 104–8.

Havas, G. and Kemény, I. (1995) 'A magyarországi romákról', *Szociológiai Szemle* 3: 3–20.

Haviland, W. A. (1978) *Cultural anthropology*, 2nd edn., New York: Holt, Rinehart and Winston.

Heusch, L. de (1966) *A la découverte des Tsiganes: Une expédition de reconnaissance* (1961), Bruxelles: Institut de Sociologie.

Howard, M. C. (1993) *Contemporary cultural anthropology*, 4th edn. New York: Harper Collins.

Kállai, E. (2000a) 'Cigányzenészek és külföldi lehetőségeik', *Mozgó Világ* 26, 10: 96–101.

Kállai, E. (2000b) 'Kormányzati intézkedések, jogszabályok, politikai programok', in *A magyarországi cigányság az elmúlt tíz év kutatásainak tükrében*, Kézirat, 132–43.

Kende, Á. (1999) 'Jó hely-e Magyarország', *Amaro Drom* 9, 3: 6–8.

Kende, P. (1994) 'Kisebbségi helyzetek: van-e megoldás?', in P. Kende *Miért nincs rend Kelet-Közép-Európába*, Budapest: Osiris/Századvég, 149–59.

Kerényi, Gy. (2000a) 'Továbbra is Kanada', *Amaro Drom* 10, 8: 4.

Kerényi, Gy. (2000b) '...s majdan sírod is', *Élet és Irodalom* 44, 30: 12.

Kerényi, Gy. (2000c) 'Egy menekülés utóélete', *Amaro Drom* 10, 9: 5.

Kertesi, G. (1995) 'Cigány foglalkoztatás és munkanélküliség a rendszerváltás előtt és után', *Esély* 4: 19–63.

Kormánybeszámoló a Magyar Köztársaság területén élő nemzeti és etnikiai kisebbségek helyzetéről (2000) in *Kisebbségek Magyarországon 1999*, Demeter Zayzon Mária (ed.) Budapest: Nemzeti és Etnikai Kisebbségi Hivatal, 35–224.

Kormányzati intézkedések a cigányság társadalmi integrációjának elősegítése érdekében (2000) in *Kisebbségek Magyarországon 1999*, Szerk, Demeter Zayzon Mária, Budapest: Nemzeti és Etnikai Kisebbségi Hivatal, 225–44.

Kováts, A. (2000) 'Magyarországon élő romák migrációja', *Mozgó Világ* 26, 10: 77–96.

Krasznai, J. (2000a) 'Valamit megmozdítok vele', *Amaro Drom* 10, 10: 3–7.

Krasznai, J. (2000b) 'Magyarországon élő roma testvérek!', *Amaro Drom* 10, 10: 5.

Krémer, B. (1999) 'Javaslatok és dilemmák a cigányság helyzetének javítását célzó terv(ek)hez', in *Tanulmányok 'A cigányság társadalmi helyzetének javítását célzó hosszú távú stratégia alapkérdéseiről'*, Budapest: Nemzeti és Etnikai Kisebbségi Hivatal/Európa Tanács. 88–115.

Laki, T. (co-ord.) (1999) *A munkaerő migrációja és az Európai Unió*, Budapest: Miniszterelnöki Hivatal, Integrációs Stratégiai Munkacsoport.

Lee, R. (2000) 'Posztkommunista roma migráció Kanadában', *Amaro Drom* 10, 9: 8-12.

Manna, F. (1996) 'Rom abruzzesi: nomadi o sedentari?', in L. Piasere (ed.) *Italia Romaní* Vol. 1, Roma: CISU, 43–58.

Mannheim, K. (1995) *A gondolkodás struktúrái. Kultúraszociológiai tanulmányok*, Budapest: Atlantisz.

Okely, J. (1983) *The Traveller Gypsies*, Cambridge: Cambridge University Press.

Peoples, J. and Bailey, G. (1991) *Humanity*, 2nd edn, St. Paul: West Publishing Company.

Piasere, L. (1986) 'Les slovensko roma: entre sedentarité et nomadisme', *Nomadic Peoples* 21-22: 37-50.

Piasere, L. (1989) 'Parte antropologica', in *Il fenomeno della migrazione in riferimento alle difficolta di adattamento sociale delle componenti nomadi*, Roma: Instituto Internazionale di Studi Giuridici, 91–163.

Piasere, L. (1991a) 'Relazione transculturali e cooperazione allo sviluppo in Italia', in P. Inghilleri and R. Terranova-Cecchini (eds) *Avanzamenti in psicologia transculturale*, Milano: Franco Angeli, 205–22.

Piasere, L. (1991b) 'Prefazione', in L. Piasere, *Popoli delle discariche. Saggi di antropologia Zingara*, Roma: CISU, 1-3.

Piasere, L. (1995) 'I segni "segreti" degli Zingari', *La Ricerca Folklorica* 31: 83–105.

Prónai, Cs. (2000) 'Tanulmányok a jogsértés és a jogvédelem témakörében a magyarországi romák vonatkozásában, 1990-2000', in *A magyarországi cigányság az elmúlt tíz év kutatásainak tükrében*, Kézirat, 82–93.

Puporka, L. (2000) 'Mindenhol jobb, mint Magyarországon', *Amaro Drom* 10, 8: 3.

Reyniers, A. (1989) 'Le nomadisme des Tsiganes: une attitude atavique ou la réponse a un rejet séculaire?', in P. Williams (ed.) *Tsiganes: identité, évolution*, Paris: Études Tsiganes/Syros Alternatives, 73–85.

Reyniers, A. and Williams, P. (1990) 'Permanence tsigane et politique de sédentarisation dans la France de l'apres-guerre', *Études Rurales* 120: 89–106.

Salo, M. T. (1981) 'Kalderas economic organization', in M. T. Salo (ed.) *The American Kalderash: Gypsies in the New World*, Hackettstown: Gypsy Lore Society, 71–97.

Salo, M. T. and Salo, S. (1977) *The Kalderas in Eastern Canada*, Ottawa: National Museums of Canada.

San Román, T. (1975) 'Kinship, marriage, law and leadership in two urban Gypsy settlements in Spain', in F. Rehfisch (ed.) *Gypsies, Tinkers and other Travellers*, London: Academic Press, 169–99.

Silverman, C. T. (1982) 'Everyday drama: impression management of urban Gypsies', *Urban Anthropology* 11, 3-4: 377–98.

Sutherland, A. (1977) 'The body as a social symbol among the Rom', in J. Blacking (ed.) *The Anthropology of the Body*, London: Academic Press, 375–90.

Vajda, I. and Prónai, Cs. (2000) 'Romániai romák Magyarországon: Koldusok, "Gáborok", munkások', *Mozgó Világ* 26, 10: 101–4.

Williams, P. (1982) 'The invisibility of the Kalderash of Paris: some aspects of the economic activity and settlement pattern of the Kalderash Rom of the Paris suburbs', *Urban Anthropology* 11, 3-4: 315–346.

Williams, P. (1990) 'Nomadisme et situation minoritaire: un essai de catégorisation. A propos d'un ouvrage de Aparna Rao', *Études Rurales* 120: 171–174.

Williams, P. (1994) 'Structures ou stratégies? Le mariage chez les Rom Kalderás', *Études Tsiganes*, n.s. 2, 2: 169–82.

Wizner, B. (2000a) *Magyaroszági cigány vendégmunkások Nyugat-Európában*, Kézirat.

Wizner B. (2000b) *Búcsús cigányok migrációja*, Kézirat.

The Gypsies in Bulgaria and their Migrations

Elena Marushiakova, Vesselin Popov, Mirella Decheva

Migration and Gypsy traditions

To understand properly the nature of contemporary Gypsy migrations, we must first look at how these are connected to Gypsy nomadic traditions. One of the primary ethnocultural features of any given community is the predominant way of life and in the case of the Gypsies there is a close relationship between this and the manner in which they make a living – their professional specialisation. In this respect the situation of Gypsies is highly problematic, since it cannot be established with reliability whether their original, 'traditional' way of life was settled or nomadic. It is uncertain whether the ancestors of present-day Gypsies in the Indian sub-continent were sedentary or not, or if the nomadic way of life was adopted during the long journey to Europe. This fundamental doubt was raised at the very outset of Gypsy studies and still remains an open question today. On reflection, it seems quite likely that there is no simple answer, as indeed with so many other queries concerning the origin of the Gypsies. Therefore, it is quite possible that the distinction between 'settled' and 'nomadic' already existed at the time these people left India and that some groups within the wider Gypsy community were bound by tradition to one way of living, while others followed another different pattern.

This distinction between the 'settled' and 'nomadic' way of life has been drawn since the Gypsies first arrived in the Balkans and Europe and still continues to be made today. Even where a process of enforced sedentarisation was backed by the law in the 1950s and 60s (mainly in the countries of Eastern and Central Europe), the former nomads preserve a marked taste for a life on the move. In contrast, sedentary Gypsies retain their preference for permanent settlement, even when they have been forced by circumstances beyond their control to leave home and move elsewhere, as in the recent migrations from former Yugoslavia to Italy. Of course, the boundaries marking the distinction between 'settled' and 'nomadic' are very fluid and indeterminate and can often change, for example nomads may settle and adopt the main features of the way of life of sedentary Gypsies. Nevertheless, these distinctions are still relevant. At the same time, the link between a way of life and customary occupation (i.e. professional specialisation) is not rigid, although the practice of certain crafts and occupations definitely requires a nomadic or semi-nomadic way of life. Different variants may emerge and in such situations it is hard to decide which occupations should be associated with nomadic as opposed to sedentary Gypsies. Indeed, it is not uncommon that particular crafts are practised reciprocally by both groups.

During the period of state socialist rule in Bulgaria people were legally required to register their place of residence. This administrative system of controlling residency made it difficult to migrate within the country. Nevertheless, in spite of these restrictions, Gypsies always managed to find their way around existing regulations and continued their travels, albeit in different forms, which for some became a mid-seasonal migration.

Migration after 1989

More recently, there emerged a new type of travelling abroad and the numbers involved are rapidly growing. This change began in the autumn of 1989. After the collapse of the former regime one of the first measures taken by the new government was to allow Bulgarian citizens to obtain passports and to abandon visa requirements for foreign travel. However, they were prevented from entering other European countries by conditions such as humiliating visa requirements and various financial stipulations. Those states restricting free entry of Bulgarian citizens included some former Eastern bloc countries that still did not require visas from them.

Here it must be said that the visa regulations and long lines of visa applicants waiting in front of Western embassies in Sofia did not present a serious obstacle to anyone who really wanted to leave Bulgaria. Many were able to do so, and still can, including large numbers of Gypsies. It is hard to give precise information about how many people left the country because there is no way of differentiating between those who emigrated and those temporarily working abroad. In

1992–3 the total number of emigrants per year was roughly 60–65,000 but what percentage of these were Gypsies was not specified. In later years these numbers definitely decreased but more specific information would be needed for reliable estimates.

The border crossings of Bulgarian Gypsies should not be regarded solely as emigration, since these journeys are very varied in their nature and scale and consist of a range of basic types, which are often interrelated or overlapping.

Long-term emigration

Firstly, there are Gypsies who migrate from Bulgaria to Western Europe, as well as the USA and Canada, with the aim of remaining there for good, although these are comparatively few in number. Formerly such emigrants sought political asylum but currently they arrange marriages with citizens of European countries, which are often marriages of convenience. Many European countries recently restricted the possibility of being granted political asylum and nowadays would-be emigrants attempt this strategy only where the anticipated response to applications is not a swift administrative decision and extradition but rather an extended legal process, as in Great Britain, the USA and Canada. Precise data is not available and it should be noted that there are frequent cases of ethnic Bulgarians declaring themselves as 'Gypsy victims of racial discrimination', who claim to have 'forgotten their mother tongue because use of the Romani language was banned during the communist period'. Among those originally involved in what might be termed 'emigration business' were a number of non-governmental organisations (NGOs) from various countries.

Variants of these permanent migrants are those seeking a temporary, though long-term, stay in a foreign country. The Kardarasha were trail-blazers in pioneering this migratory route, even before the changes of 1989. This type of migration can be characterised as 'invisible' since it does not appear in official records. Individuals go to another country, investigate the situation and, if it seems promising, then establish a base and arrange for their relatives to join them. Preferred destinations of such emigrants are the Benelux countries, as well as Scandinavia and

Germany. During 1999 and 2000 the severe economic situation in Bulgaria brought stagnation to the business activities of some of the Kardarasha community, who opted for more permanent settlement in Western Europe, especially in Belgium, where several thousand Kardarasha families were already established.

Asylum seeking

In contrast, at the start of the 1990s the migration of settled Yerlii Gypsies, especially 'Turkish Gypsies' from north-east Bulgaria, were much larger in scale and extremely 'visible'. Their initial destination was Germany, partly since it was relatively easy to enter via the former socialist countries, which do not require visas, but mainly because of its liberal laws and generous social assistance by Bulgarian standards. These Gypsies travelled in larger groups, usually organised on the basis of kinship or those inhabiting the same territory in Bulgaria, and did not make links with Gypsies from other countries. They camped near the German frontier in Poland and the Czech Republic and attempted to make illegal border crossings to Germany. On arriving in Germany (and also other Western countries), they mainly employed the strategy of demanding political asylum, usually claiming to be Turks who had suffered from measures to strip them of their ethnic identity as part of the Bulgarian 'national revival' process. However, refusal of their asylum claims did not bring them tragic consequences. Due to social assistance payments for their large families, work in the black economy, illegal petty-trading and similar activities they were able to return to Bulgaria with enough foreign currency and goods to ensure them a decent standard of living.

Data relating to this type of migration reveals that 3,927 claims for political asylum by Bulgarians were lodged in Germany in 1991, of which only 14 were granted. The others were either rejected or settled in some other way. Usually the 'political refugees' simply left the country shortly before the review period for their claims ended. Unfortunately we do not know the proportion of Gypsies among these applicants, but all the indications suggest that it was substantial. In 1992 those termed 'political immigrants' from Bulgaria to Germany numbered 31,540 and in 1993 more than 23,000. Subsequently, following changes in German law at the end of 1993 that limited assistance for such 'refugees', the flood rapidly subsided in 1994 and present-day Bulgarian Gypsy migrants seek other destinations.

Short-term emigration for work

Another relatively common type of migration concerns seasonal or irregular trans-border migration of Bulgarian Gypsies. To a certain extent these journeys are related to the revival of the Gypsies' former nomadic or semi-nomadic way of life, as already mentioned, although they often assume new forms. Sometimes smaller numbers of settled Gypsies are also involved. This pattern is followed by hired workers, usually in the construction industry, as well as by musicians. The latter often have formal contracts to work in countries of the former Soviet Union and/or the Middle East, and at times even in Western Europe. There is widespread interest in this type of migrant work among non-Gypsies and consequently Gypsies only occasionally manage to be included as part of a larger group of workers. Musicians, however, form an exception since they compete successfully with other workers, occupying a niche market for a specific style of music.

The most favoured manner of working abroad is as illegal 'black workers', without official documents or approval from the country where they work. The undisputed leaders in this type of migration are the Rudari communities, whose preferred destinations are Greece and Cyprus where they work in agriculture, mostly harvesting. At the same time Rudari women are employed as domestic workers and also care for the sick. In these countries the Rudari turn to related Gypsy groups for assistance. They usually cross the Bulgarian–Greek border illegally, sometimes through Macedonia, but the Greek authorities have adopted a comparatively liberal attitude towards their presence and almost encourage them as a source of cheap labour. Rudari also travel to Italy where they work as unskilled labourers, have odd jobs in farming and only occasionally engage in speculative trading. In Italy their situation is somewhat easier than in Greece as they speak a related language. More recently Spain has become the most popular destination where a relatively substantial Rudari community has become established, working illegally in agriculture. There are no precise details about the extent of this migration but it is hard to find a Rudari family without a member employed in temporary work abroad.

Horahane Roma are also active participants in these foreign journeys, preferring Turkey, Cyprus, and less frequently Italy, where they often pass themselves off as Turks. Migrations in search of work are usually made by small groups of men, where relatives or neighbours travel together. Increasingly, whole families take part in these trips including children, at least those capable of working.

Travel abroad for trade

A further common type of border crossing made by Bulgarian Gypsies is the regular return trip abroad for trading purposes. This pattern began in 1989 when the frontier with former Yugoslavia was opened, allowing the widespread transport of Bulgarian goods and foodstuffs to Yugoslavia to be sold for hard currency. At the same time, the unification of Germany provided the opportunity for travel abroad to speculate in hard currency. These trade routes were later extended to include the markets of Central and Eastern Europe (Romania, Hungary, Poland). The Turkish city of Istanbul provided a plentiful source of cheap goods of mostly Turkish and Middle Eastern origin, which were then sold in Bulgaria. These trips, popularly called 'shopping tours', have become a regular feature of Bulgarian life. Between 1990 and 1995 dozens of tourist companies flourished by meeting the demand for such trips. Among the permanent 'tourists' travelling in buses overflowing with goods throughout the former Eastern bloc are many Gypsies, mostly those settled in urban ghettos. While 'Turkish Gypsies' from Eastern Bulgaria, who usually speak Turkish, mainly choose Turkey as the destination for their trips, the Gypsies from Western Bulgaria tend to travel to the countries of former Yugoslavia and Central and Eastern Europe. This type of activity expanded to wholly new dimensions with the embargo on trade with former Yugoslavia and the closure of the Greek frontier with Macedonia, when whole border regions would make a living from this kind of trade. In 1996–7 there was a certain decrease in this sort of commercial activity, but it still exerts a significant influence over the lives of many Gypsies. This is especially true of the 'Turkish Gypsies' from north–eastern Bulgaria who travel regularly to Poland, spending months in the markets of different cities.

In this particular context it is remarkable that the Kardarasha, who had been heavily involved in speculative trading as early as the communist period, swiftly pulled out of this business as soon as such activities became widespread. Instead, they redirected their cross-border journeys elsewhere in order to pursue their traditional female occupation of pick-pocketing in affluent Western Europe, occasionally in the airports of the Persian Gulf and even as far afield as Singapore.

While Gypsies commonly complain that foreign countries' visa requirements affect all Bulgarians, the Bulgarian media frequently condemns Gypsy migrations alone as motivated by criminality. However this accusation is both conjectural and one-sided. Gypsies do not play a significant part in the most lucrative forms of illegal smuggling such as trafficking in prostitutes, drugs and stolen cars, which are monopolised by non-Gypsy Bulgarian citizens. The extent to which they are involved in these activities is completely marginal – as cheap prostitutes or as petty speculators taking merchandise from Bulgaria to Poland.

At the present time other Gypsy groups have begun to look for ways of resuming their former trans-border nomadic travels but so far only a few small-scale attempts have been made, such as a handful of families of 'Thracean Kalajdjii' going to Macedonia where they tin household utensils.

Another great migratory wave?

All these myriad patterns clearly indicate that the transition from a nomadic to a settled way of life is by no means unidirectional. Depending on the specific social and economic conditions that prevail, new forms of traditional nomadism may emerge and have the effect of 'resuscitating' this way of life.

This possibility raises interesting questions about perspectives of cross-border Gypsy migrations and whether we can speak about a new great wave of migration following the 'great Kelderara invasion' of the nineteenth century and subsequently the 'Yugoslav wave' of the 1960s. We can certainly speak about a third wave of international Gypsy migration in Europe, particularly in respect of Gypsies from Romania and former Yugoslavia. However, the extent to which Bulgarian Gypsies might participate in this process remains a question that still cannot be answered with any certainty. No doubt there is great potential for mobility but the direction this might take will depend both on the development of the Gypsy community in Bulgaria and the assistance it receives from abroad. However, of even greater significance is the overall situation in Bulgaria, which is far from promising.

References

Klímová, I. and Pickup, A. (eds) (2000) 'Romani Migrations: Strangers in Anybody's Land?', *Cambridge Review of International Affairs*, XIII, 2, spring/summer, 13–118.

Reyniers, A. (1995) 'Gypsy Populations and their Movements within Central and Eastern Europe and towards some OECD Countries', *International Migration and Labour Market Policies, Occasional Papers*, no. 1, Paris: OECD.

Migration by Roma from former Yugoslavia

Dragoljub Acković

Nationality data in twentieth century Yugoslav censuses

Introduction

During the period from 1884 to 1910 there was a significant increase in data about nationality in Serbian censuses through the inclusion of questions about native language and religion. This change complied with decisions and recommendations of international statistical institutions. At the same time efforts were also made to take full account of the Roma population. Accordingly, instructions for the 1900 Census specifically required that '… the native language of each and every person should be noted, for example Serbian, German, Hungarian, Romanian (Vlachian), Greek, Turkish, French, Italian, Gypsy, etc. **For Gypsies whose native language is Romanian (Vlachian) or Serbian, a note should be made that they are Gypsies.** The same note should be made for Jews if they declare a language other than Jewish as their native language' (emphasis added).

After the First World War the Constitution guaranteed all Yugoslav citizens complete freedom to declare their nationality and Roma appeared in the classificatory schemes of all five Yugoslav censuses during the inter-war period. However, if we examine the variation in Roma numbers from census to census, which is far more extreme than for other nationalities, we cannot avoid querying the shrinking number of Roma. According to these figures Roma appear to be a 'vanishing nation' and the official Yugoslav census statistics seem to reflect an irreversible 'Roma decline'. In the inter-war Yugoslav censuses of 1921 and 1931, more emphasis was placed on questions about native language and religion in order to obtain additional information about the ethnic structure of the Yugoslav population. More specifically, there was a question about nationality in the 1931 census, but the results were never published. Apart from this single occasion, the obvious intention was to present all South-Slavic groups as a unified

'Yugoslav' nationality, while other nationalities were to be recorded by ethnic group (for example: German, Hungarian, Turkish, etc.).

In these inter-war censuses, **there was no place for Roma in any of the classifications used to present data about the ethnic structure of the Yugoslav population.** However, Frenchmen and Englishmen were separately categorised, even though Yugoslavia was hardly their ethnic home territory in 1921. **The official statistics of that time 'hid' Roma in the nameless ethnic category of 'others'.** Such a procedure represented a complete break with the longstanding practice of identifying Roma in Serbian census statistics. This tradition can be traced back to the mid-nineteenth century, to the 1866 Serbian Geography, where it was estimated that Roma (Gypsies) formed 2.1 per cent of the population of Serbia.

In comparison with other censuses, only those of 1953 and 1961 included short explanations, with examples, about how to complete answers to questions about nationality. An important difference between these explanations was that Roma were excluded from the list of nationalities in the 1961 census, although they were mentioned in both the list and explanations in 1953.

Demographic data about Roma in Yugoslavia

Natural population trends

Until the last decade of the twentieth century and the violent break-up of the former Federal Republic, the population of the whole state was increasing. This population growth was particularly marked among Roma for one of their basic demographic characteristics is a high birth-rate. In 1981, the birth-rate for Yugoslavia as a whole was 16.5 per thousand. At that time Roma shared second place with Turks, with a birth-rate of 25.5, while Albanians had the highest rate of all at 31.7.

Other demographic changes affected the Roma population in specific ways. In recent years the absolute number of births, deaths and overall population growth has been increasing. On the other hand, the death-rate decreased to a level of 6.2 per cent by 1986, while the birth-rate remained at the high level of 25 per cent, resulting in a population increase of about 20 per cent. It was discovered that younger generations of Roma women are having fewer children than their predecessors. At the same time, however, young women of fertile age are now having children, regardless of whether they are formally married or not.

While the direct effect of a reduced birth-rate is in purely demographic terms, it also has significant social and economical implications. Families with low birth-rates are small in size and their structure and relations are simplified. Such families consist of two generations, frequently incomplete because divorce is common. These factors, as well as other characteristics, make them modern families but the situation is quite different in the case of other families. The average Romani family consists of many members, often contains several generations, includes numerous children with limited employment prospects in a modern economy, and is based on specific marital and family relations which have certain advantages but also disadvantages for its members.

Roma are an ethnic group with a youthful age structure and consequently in 1981 their overall mortality rate of 6.1 was below the Yugoslav average of 9.0. Nevertheless, the infant mortality rate for the same year – one of the most telling indicators of the standard of living and level of general education – presents a completely contrasting picture. In 1981 the average mortality rate for newborn babies in Yugoslavia was 30.8 per thousand, while the corresponding figure for Roma was 51.5. Although this is half the 1971 rate of 95.3, it is still indicative of the very poor living conditions of this community.

Mortality statistics, broken down by age, over the fifteen-year period from 1971 to 1986 emphasise the high mortality rate of Roma babies even more dramatically, as well as raised Roma mortality in the early years of life. The diminished life expectancy of many Roma is illustrated by the shocking mortality balance between those who died in the first year of life (26.1 per cent) and those who died after the age of retirement (30.4 per cent). However, this balance is illusory for if we split the wide age interval – 'aged 65 and over' – into narrower age groups, the infant mortality rate upsets this apparent balance, revealing that Roma babies mostly die within a few days of birth. The mortality rate for Roma is above average in all age groups except for those who die after the age of 64, where Roma mortality is less than half the average. However, the infant mortality rate for Roma is almost four times higher than average – 26.1 per cent compared to 6.8 per cent.

Above all, the effects of falling birth and death-rates are seen on age structure by gender, following the increase in the average length of life and population growth. As with every other similar community, the Roma population became younger as the proportion of younger people increased to a total of 40 per cent.

Demographic distribution of Roma:
cities, towns, villages and characteristic Roma enclaves (quarters, ghettos)

Roma quarters, a form of Balkan urban ghetto, and gypsy tents are not only characteristic forms of dwelling for sedentary and nomadic Roma, but also represent authentic ethnic symbols for them. However, the Romani lifestyle, romantically referred to as 'gypsy tents', is not typical today for the territories of former Yugoslavia. Ethnological studies and other sources reveal that quarters or settlements still remain the predominant type of Roma dwelling in towns and villages.

Originally, these ethnic islands formed suburbs on the outskirts of towns, although nowadays some have been gradually transformed into districts of city centres as a result of rapid urban expansion during recent years. However, urban Roma settlements remain largely ethnically segregated and are pervaded by an atmosphere of lethargy – unmistakable proof of continuing poor social and material conditions. These settlements' 'historic role' of protecting ethnic homogeneity and preserving Roma cultural identity was achieved at great cost – by the almost total marginalisation of Roma in every area of socio-economic and cultural life.

In national censuses Roma mostly declare themselves as Serbs, since this is the most populous nationality in the Serbian Republic. However, Roma sometimes identify themselves as members of other nationalities where these groups form a significant part of the population in local areas where they live. These variations in ethnic declaration by Roma are usually presented as a sign of their growing assimilation, in spite of the lack of any clear empirical evidence to support such an interpretation and regardless of historical counter-examples contradicting this view.

Roma migration from the territory of former Yugoslavia

Data from the 1981 census yielded evidence of past internal migration of the Yugoslav population and revealed that the representation of Roma among Yugoslav migrants (0.5%) was less than their proportion of the total population (0.7%). In the light of migration rates by ethnicity (i.e. the number of migrants per 1,000 ethnic group members), Roma were categorised as a community with low mobility. Classification of the data by republics and provinces with larger Roma populations, demonstrated that Roma from Bosnia and Herzegovina (0.2%), Vojvodina (0.7%) and Serbia, excluding its provinces, (0.8%) migrated less than Roma from Macedonia (1.2%) and Kosovo (2.6%).

The statistics revealed Roma to be a group extremely reluctant to move from where they are living. This attachment to their place of permanent residence is hardly surprising, because for Roma quarters and similar urban settlements still represent the safest and most protective environment in which to live and they return there after occasional journeys in search of opportunities to boost their income. Apart from these Roma, a number of nomads without permanent residence registration could not be recorded as migrants since they were entered as residents of the place where they happened to be at the time of the census. A further difficulty, which complicates recording Roma migrations, is that Roma frequently ignore legal requirements for registering and deregistering at their place of residence. It can be assumed that increased Roma mortality might have been a factor influencing the lowered number of Roma migrants during the entire period up to the 1981 census. However, all the reasons mentioned above are of minor importance since it can be argued that frequent change of residence is not typical for Roma. Since the Second World War the strongest migratory pressures stemmed from the combined processes of industrialisation and urbanisation. The major postwar occupational shift from agricultural into non-agricultural employment, usually involving change of residence or urbanisation, by-passed Roma living in small groups in rural areas. Consequently, the low numbers of Roma in employment was the precondition that allowed many of them to join the streams of economic migrants that often resulted in permanent emigration.

From a total of 44,601 Roma migrants, 21,704 (49%) Roma moved between municipalities within the same republic or province, 11,676 (26%) changed their place of residence within the same municipality, while 10,353 (23%) migrated permanently from one republic or province to another. The remaining 868 comprised foreign immigrants and 'unknown' cases.

As we have seen, almost a quarter of Roma migrations are between republics or provinces. However, if we look more closely at the migratory balance, three administrative-territorial units are particularly significant – the republics of Serbia, excluding its provinces, (+2153), and Macedonia (+1138) and the province of Kosovo, with a negative migratory balance (-4272). Roma migrating from Kosovo to Serbia proper in the period up till the 1981 census and from Macedonia constitute 38 per cent of all Roma migrating between republics or provinces.

Economic migration for temporary work

If people who did not declare their nationality are excluded (where 'Yugoslav' was among the official categories), Roma had the highest growth index for persons temporarily abroad (274.8) in the 1971-1981 inter-census period. According to these figures, those temporarily working abroad together with their families formed 5 per cent (8,167) of the entire recorded Roma population of Yugoslavia (168,197).

Migration of Roma from Kosovo – 1998-2000

According to unofficial statistics gathered by Roma societies and individuals, there were about 120,000 Roma in Kosovo and Metohija around 1981. This estimate of Roma numbers is almost four times that recorded in the census and is extremely significant since it reveals a huge difference in numbers between those who declared themselves as Roma and those who concealed this fact for various reasons. Whether this ethnomimicry by Roma from Kosovo and Metohija was deliberate because of pressure or unintentional, the effect was to inflate the recorded population of Albanian, Serbian or Turkish nationalities. Some, however, declared themselves as Yugoslavs during this period. More recently, with the disintegration of the Federal Republic, the category of Yugoslav has disappeared, so that Roma who formerly chose this option now declare themselves as one of the three nationalities mentioned above.

Reasons for wide variations in statistical data about Roma from Kosovo

There are numerous reasons why the numbers of Roma in Yugoslavia vary widely according to both statistical and unofficial data. To those reasons, valid throughout Yugoslavia, should be added pressure on members of the Roma nationality living in Serbia, Montenegro, Kosovo and Metohija. A remarkable fact as regards constitutional rights is that no Roma declared themselves as such in the first version of 1981 census. A revised version of the census was substituted following protests from Roma activists in Kosovo and Metohija.

Economic factors

Until the beginning of 1998 there were several tens of thousands of Roma in Kosovo and Metohija who were capable of work but mostly remained unemployed. Those who did have some sort of job did not generally work for state or private companies, but were mainly occupied in petty trading or the service sector. Roma living in villages were mostly landless and worked in the fields of richer Albanians or

Serbs. Many of them went to Vojvodina and elsewhere to work as seasonal wage labourers on the land of richer people or on larger farms.

During this period a far smaller number of Roma subsisted on help sent by relatives abroad, who either worked there or lived as refugees. Only a very few Roma in Kosovo and Metohija managed to escape economic penury and poverty by starting private businesses – mostly small-scale but occasionally more substantial.

During the last two years of the twentieth century, however, the idea of migrating abroad was wide-spread among the Roma of this region. The main destination was Western countries where they usually claimed and were granted asylum. Asylum seeking was a very popular choice among Roma from Kosovo and Metohija, especially for those who managed to save some money and build houses or start businesses. The usual strategy was for some of the family to go abroad, obtain asylum and then send money they had saved with great difficulty from their unemployment benefit to support other family members who had stayed at home. Initially this provided basic subsistence for those remaining behind, who eventually were able to build better houses or start small businesses.

Pressure from surrounding ethnic groups

Roma in Kosovo and Metohija have been pressurised in various ways by Albanians and Serbs since the end of the Second World War until the present day. The most common form of pressure was exerted when Roma came to make their census declarations. A subtler kind of pressure occurred during the enrolment of their children for elementary and other schools. Local Roma were further pressurised when seeking employment in state companies because the chances of getting a job were better it if they presented themselves as Albanians or Serbs rather than as Roma. Some Roma were quite content with this situation and took advantage of it on other occasions.

Continuing expulsion of Roma from Kosovo – autumn 1998 to spring 1999 – resulting in greatly increased numbers of displaced Roma

In spring 1998, a large number of Roma left Kosovo and Metohija for various reasons, but above all because of armed conflict between the Yugoslav army and police and the Kosovo Liberation Army (KLA). Most of these Roma fled to Serbia, Montenegro or abroad. However, the majority migrated to Serbia. Their main destinations were Belgrade and other larger Serbian towns, especially where they had relatives and friends, though Roma often went to places where they knew nobody. There were many such cases where families found themselves in a desperate situation, since their only means of subsistence was any money they had managed to bring with them. Roma associations from their home areas provided most help to these wretched Roma families, but the support was inadequate to meet their needs. According to the information at our disposal, at that time there were roughly 3,000 Roma from Kosovo and Metohija in Belgrade alone. The public was not made sufficiently aware of their problems, even though serious family crises occurred such as occasional deaths of newborn babies. Meanwhile it was known that pregnant women in such families had to pay for expensive deliveries in local hospitals because they had no documents or health cards. Likewise, the purchase of medicine caused great problems. Roma associations managed to acquire some medicine from *Caritas* and other humanitarian organisations for distribution to those in most need. These displaced families were often forced to live in unhygienic conditions and consequently most were infected with fleas and lice, requiring Roma associations to obtain large quantities of insecticide.

The desperate situation of Roma expelled from Kosovo and Metohija

Before the NATO campaign in Yugoslavia about 150,000 Roma lived in Kosovo and Metohija but during 1998 at least 10,000 Roma fled to Serbia, Macedonia, Montenegro, Albania or other European countries for various reasons. The data is quite precise for this period, when about 3,000 people moved to Belgrade and roughly 2,000 to Montenegro. At the same time there is evidence that a few dozen families moved to Italy and several hundred Roma migrated to the Czech Republic and other countries.

Most Roma expelled from Kosovo at that time were without documents, so they were unable to claim their entitlements under Yugoslav laws. The same is true of Roma who migrated to Serbia, especially to Belgrade and its surroundings. The most fundamental entitlement denied to them was health insurance. Roma organizations tried and partially succeeded in helping in the most acute situations – childbirth, death, and equally serious circumstances. There were up to a hundred cases of severe hardship and some were reported in the national and foreign press.

According to our information, at least 2,000 Roma fled from Kosovo and Metohija during the 1999 NATO campaign in Yugoslavia. The problems faced by these new refugees were similar to those suffered by Roma previously expelled from Kosovo. The majority arrived with only the minimum of baggage and many had been unable to bring their essential documents, let alone personal belongings.

For the first few days of the influx, the state tried to organize the reception of these wretched refugees but later, partly due to war problems and partly because of increasing numbers, state authorities ceased supplying aid to them. Whether from fear or other reasons, some did not register at all as refugees with the Red Cross or any other organisation and consequently were unable to receive any help. Roma organisations soon recognised this problem and started to register Romas refugees from Kosovo and Metohija and provided them with humanitarian aid packages, although this was insufficient to meet even their most basic needs.

After the NATO campaign ended, instead of a stabilisation of the situation to enable 30,000 Roma to return to their homes in Kosovo, there began a larger and more bloody exodus of Roma refugees. At that time even more Roma left Kosovo and Metohija, mostly out of fear of the KLA and ethnic Albanians. They were driven out by individual and mass murders, as well as by ethnic cleansing carried out by KLA groups and individuals.

Leaving aside whether their reasons for leaving were justified, it is now known that more than 40,000 Roma left Kosovo and Metohija after the end of NATO hostilities against Yugoslavia. We also know from personal communications that many villages and towns in Kosovo and Metohija are now without a single Roma inhabitant and hundreds of houses have been burnt to the ground, amounting to entire settlements in some areas.

If the statistics of Roma expelled from Kosovo and Metohija during all three periods discussed are added together, this produces a total of over 80,000 refugees who fled to various parts of Serbia and elsewhere. Recalling that prior to 1998 150,000 Roma lived in Kosovo and Metohija, this means that more than half the original Roma population left the province.

However, for a full appreciation of the situation and problems of the Roma who abandoned Kosovo and Metohija, particularly during the last two years of the twentieth century, it is necessary to discover the whereabouts of all the Roma expelled from Kosovo and to appreciate under what conditions they are they now living and whether they want to return home or leave for another country? Answers must be found as soon as possible because many of these refugees have been away from home for months or years. Some have nowhere to return to because their houses have been destroyed and some cannot return for fear of reprisals. The need for a swift resolution is all the more imperative for the following reasons. All those expelled from Kosovo can only obtain temporary rather than permanent residence, they cannot be employed in places where they are living and their children are unable to attend school. Whatever money they may have possessed has been spent and the resources of humanitarian and other organizations have been exhausted and only limited funding has been made available for this purpose. One way or another the Government and state authorities are trying to return refugees to their original place of residence, meanwhile Albanian nationalist extremists are seeking an ethnically cleansed Kosovo and to this day are expelling the remaining Roma, demolishing their houses and threatening to kill anyone who returns to Kosovo. The interim coalition government of Albanians and Serbs, formed at the instigation of the international community, excludes Roma. A good example of this practice is the Juridical Council in Kosovo, consisting of Albanian, Serbian and Turkish judges. Not a single Roma judge is included, in spite of the fact that qualified Roma judges are present in Kosovo.

The state authorities of Serbia and Yugoslavia pay little attention to Roma expelled from Kosovo because they are preoccupied with the problems of Serbs and Montenegrins who have arrived in Serbia. At the present time, what particularly worries the Roma population in Serbia is the fact that the authorities are consulting and negotiating with Roma representatives from cultural-artistic societies, in this way by-passing the authentic political representatives of the Roma nation, just as they had formerly. When it is appreciated that the majority of these Roma cultural-artistic societies are dominated by members of the former ruling gang, then it is easy to see where this might lead.

Proposals for solving some of the most urgent problems of Roma expelled from Kosovo and Metohija

To solve the problems of these refugees, it is necessary above all to work with local activists to make complete records of the number of Roma from Kosovo, to assess their economic situation and to make a list of their priorities. The poorest need to be provided with temporary or permanent accommodation. At the same time funds are required for rent or some other kind of assistance, such as food, to be given to families who took in these refugees. Families and individuals without financial resources need accommodation in camps for refugees and displaced people. Considering that large numbers of Roma, more than 10,000, were expelled from Kosovo and Metohija to Belgrade, it is necessary to identify a site and start building a camp capable of housing such large numbers. The camp should be suitable for winter accommodation since, according to their statements at roundtables organised by the Roma Congress Party, Roma refugees 'do not want to return to Kosovo until normal living conditions have been established' and this will not happen soon.

It is evident that some Roma cannot return to Kosovo because they fear they might be killed by the KLA and ethnic Albanians in retaliation for their previous collaboration with the Serbian government. This must be borne in mind, because such families might be returned to a place where their lives and those of their families would be in danger. These Roma want the chance to travel, even temporarily, to a country that is willing to accept Albanian, Serbian or other refugees.

For some time now there has been the need in Belgrade and other towns for the formation of councils for Roma from Kosovo and Metohija. Such institutions should be established in Kosovo as well. The Organisation for Security and Co-operation in Europe (OSCE), UNHCR and similar organisations should help to establish and support the work of such councils. This justifiable demand was made and accepted in 2000 at the *International Conference on the Position of Roma expelled from Kosovo*, held in Sofia. The opinion of the OSCE representatives was clear but until now no such council has been convened. Recently, The recently founded Roma humanitarian organization *Romano Ilo* should play a leading part in finding and supplying humanitarian aid for Roma, since at present Roma cultural-artistic societies are handling this kind of 'work', even though it is definitely outside the proper scope of their activities.

Roma Migration: Experience from the IOM Prague Project with Returning Roma Asylum Seekers

Míťa Castle-Kaněrová

This is a brief overview of the experience gained from a one-year IOM pilot project, sponsored by the European Commission and three EU member states – Belgium, The Netherlands and Finland. The International Organization for Migration project started in January 2000 and its aim was to assist with the voluntary repatriation of predominantly Roma asylum seekers who wished to return home to the Czech Republic. In practice, Roma were 99.9 per cent of those involved. The reasons why they wanted to come back or, indeed, the reasons why they had left their homeland in the first place, were not key questions at the start of the project. Assistance was offered on humanitarian grounds, not for political or any other reasons.

Of course, there were certain basic criteria for eligibility. To be considered for the scheme people had to be legal migrants, who had stayed in one of the three participating EU countries for at least three months before applying for help from the project. This restriction was imposed because the objective was to assist only those who were deliberately returning to their homeland with the serious intention of remaining there. There was a real danger that a project offering an air ticket and a small amount of cash to survive the first two weeks after arriving home, might provide support for what could be termed 'migrant tourism'.

The countries to which asylum seekers were repatriated under this scheme comprised not only the Czech Republic, but also Slovakia and Romania. Therefore the entire project was international in scope and included the former Eastern European countries that had provided the bulk of recent Roma migration to the EU. Hungary also took part in the project but in order to provide comparative research material on Roma migration in general.

Roma migration and EU accession

It is not difficult to guess why the project was supported by the EU. In the late 1990s levels of migration to the EU increased dramatically at times, and Roma involvement was particularly noticeable. The EU faced an unprecedented situation of 'unpredictable' arrivals of migrants quite unlike any other previous groups. Roma migrants were European and capable of reaching EU countries relatively easily, where they demanded political asylum on arrival. However, in the opinion of EU immigration authorities, there were no justifiable reasons for their claims to be accepted, with the exception of a few verified cases. Even more puzzling was the fact that numbers of Roma arrivals were not related to any specific events, political or otherwise. This differed from the usual pattern of cases where political asylum was granted under the 1951 Geneva Convention, as in outbreaks of systematic persecution, war, natural disaster, etc. In these circumstances Roma migrants began to be characterised not only as unpredictable but also as undesirable. Their demands for refugee status soon came to be considered an abuse of the asylum system.

Roma migration clearly contravened a general trend, which is currently emerging in the EU. The growing tendency is to promote and support freedom of movement for those who have something to offer, that is skilled or specialised labour. Such freedom of movement among EU member states has increasingly received encouragement and protection at the level of EU social policy. Roma migration posed implicit questions by default, in highlighting the very unequal situations of individuals from EU member states and non-EU countries, as well as raising the sensitive issue of what might happen after EU enlargement.

However, the accusation that Roma were misusing the asylum procedures did not stimulate new ways of thinking about free movement within Europe, but instead led merely to a tightening of EU immigration policies and repatriation programmes.

The situation became more complex when Roma individuals and families seeking asylum began to give evidence to EU and international organisations of the discrimination they had suffered in their home countries. This often included total unemployment of entire communities, increased marginalisation in the aftermath of changes since 1989, as well as racial ostracism and attacks. As a result the newly developing democracies of Europe, as applicants for EU membership, had to answer uncomfortable questions about economic, political and social aspects of their 'transitions'. In addition, they were required to demonstrate that their human rights records met European standards.

Undergoing such scrutiny was often a difficult process but as EU accession negotiations took a more realistic turn, the urgency to deal with Roma migration became more pressing for both the EU and candidate countries. Following many bilateral discussions a kind of a compromise was eventually reached, whereby it was concluded at official level that Roma migration is a form of economic migration. From the point of view of candidate countries, this was not such a negative outcome, since investment to achieve economic and social integration of Roma – by implication a long-term process – might lead to a satisfactory solution at some future point in time. The Czech Republic also proposed that Roma migration was a Europe-wide issue and therefore not the sole responsibility of the migrants' countries of origin. The human rights issue became increasingly submerged at EU level, since candidate countries could no longer be accused of being undemocratic while the issue of economic change was seen as a matter of long-term domestic development. In this way the issue of Roma migration was relegated to a less significant status, and even the EC annual report for 2000 on the progress of accession countries affirmed that there was no racism in the Czech Republic.

Achievements of the IOM project

This complex situation was the context for the IOM project. This project, co-ordinated by the IOM in Brussels, was given the original remit of assisting 780 people returning from all three participating EU countries to the three countries from which they had come (the Czech Republic, Slovakia and Romania). Aid comprised providing practical support both at departure and on arrival, monitoring the returnees and offering counselling in aspects of reintegration that the returnees might find most difficult, such as housing, social benefits, schooling, medical insurance, employment opportunities, etc. In fact, the project eventually succeeded in providing help to 1,235 returnees, exceeding its predicted target, although the distribution of those assisted was very uneven. The bulk of the returnees went to Slovakia (over 1,000), 156 to the Czech Republic, and the remainder – the smallest number – to Romania (59). The relatively low numbers returning to the Czech Republic can be explained by the fact that, around this time, the largest groups of Czech Roma seeking asylum had travelled to the UK and previously to Canada. Since the UK was unwilling to participate in a voluntary repatriation programme, Roma in Britain were ineligible for the project.

The project can be said to have been successful insofar as it was the only project of its kind that offered help to Roma returnees, apart from notable exceptions of some non-governmental organisations (NGOs). This is undoubtedly the case, even though that help might have been limited in relation to the substantial difficulties that awaited Roma migrants after their return. The project mapped out at national level the realistic needs of returnees, it gained practical experience by dealing with real people and carried out a survey of migratory trends among Roma in the Czech Republic. This information was shared with others, either organisations and institutions working in the same field or those who may not have known about each other. It also served to highlight extremely effectively the shortcomings of domestic national policies concerning the integration of the Roma ethnic minority.

In addition, the project revealed weak points in EU policies as well as in those of the migrants' home countries. On the basis of the experience of other recently repatriated groups, EU member states envisaged, and in fact assumed, that voluntary repatriation, as it came to be known, would lead to permanent resettlement of Roma in their homelands. To the contrary, Roma migration is not only failing to decrease but, in the Czech Republic at least, returnees form at least 30–40 per cent of all those contemplating and planning repeated migration abroad. The apparently attractive package offer of a voluntary flight home, a pledge of no stigmatisation and copious information disseminated in advance to relevant authorities and municipalities did not seem to lead to reintegration into the community, regardless of the optimistic expectations in official circles.

The shifting focus of the project

Faced with this perplexing situation we had to start asking different questions and shift the agenda of the project somewhat. In the process the two poles of Roma migration, departure and return, became inextricably linked. The evident fact that many returnees do not wish to resettle permanently in their homeland cannot be explained adequately without looking at why they left in the first place. Up till now there has been insufficient analysis and comprehension of the causes and motivation underlying recent Roma migration. In their place are only fragments of analysis and partial comprehension. Roma movement westwards is not economic migration, but neither is it political migration in the strict sense of this term. Least of all is it ethnic 'tourism', as some commentators claim. Nevertheless, on the basis of our experience, we can safely conclude that Roma migration, and repeated migration, will continue regardless and independently of the IOM project. It will also continue regardless of various piecemeal official attempts to resolve the situation at national as well as international level.

One plausible explanation is that the Roma who emigrate from the Czech Republic feel deeply alienated from mainstream society in almost every way. Their stated reasons for migrating are predictable enough – long-term unemployment, bad housing, apprehension about the future of their children, fears for their own safety, etc. – but the lingering question underlying these accounts is straightforward enough. Why have they experienced such systematic marginalisation – even neglect?

The survey commissioned by the IOM and carried out by Gabal Analysis and Consulting[1] revealed that perceptions of migration among

---

[1] Gabal (2000) *Analysis of the Migration Climate and Migration Tendencies to Western European Countries in Romany Communities in Selected Cities in the Czech Republic*, Research report for IOM Prague, Praha: Gabal Analysis & Consulting, May.

administrators and officials are almost diametrically opposed to those of the Roma population itself. This represents total misunderstanding of each other by two communities that for many years have lived together, side by side, have shared the experience of communism and post-communist changes, and yet still see the world through quite different eyes. It simply cannot be because Roma are unwilling to adjust to a new reality.

That Roma are reluctant to adapt is refuted by the experience of migrants who travel into the civilised world of EU countries and comment on the very different conditions they find there. They praise the high levels of personal tolerance and social acceptance, the welcoming reception of their children into mainstream education, the congenial behaviour of officials with whom they come into contact, etc. While there are many who are confused by these differences, many more raise their own expectations – both of themselves and of their children. Emigration is essentially a learning experience. Emigrants feel a new desire to better themselves, to improve their standard of living, to change the reality surrounding them, to raise their ambitions and, above all, they feel the desire to be taken seriously by the world around them.

Unfortunately, this new spirit of hope does not always survive the return home. Instead, there is often a feeling of deep disappointment, especially among those who came back from Holland. There, the message spread through the community of Roma asylum seekers that conditions for Roma at home had improved during the period of their absence. However, they came back only to be faced with an unchanged situation. This is not to say that returnees should be given different treatment from other people – whether Roma or non-Roma. There is no justification for preferential treatment of any kind. Yet, the unanswered question remains. Why does the Roma population as a whole fare so badly in all social situations?

Hopefully the IOM project has contributed in a small way towards addressing these issues, raising key questions, and indicating that a full analysis of the reasons for migration is the only way to develop a coherent strategy for integrating Roma, the vast majority of whom still remain in their homelands which they have never left. The migrants who do leave are those who have acknowledged their dissatisfaction and alienation. They are drawn from the so-called Roma 'middle classes' and consequently should have the capacity and motivation to regenerate their community, bringing to this task their new experience from abroad.

Dissemination of results

The IOM project addressed people at local as well as at national level. Through the Steering Committee, we communicated the results of the repatriation and the problems associated with integration to relevant ministries, to the representatives of the donor countries, that is the embassies of Belgium, The Netherlands and Finland, as well as to the Delegation of the European Commission in Prague. We also expressed our view that repatriation was sometimes used as an alternative to deportation and that the EU should continue to pay attention to monitoring the situation after families had been repatriated to their home countries. Among the activities initiated by the project were various roundtables and seminars, where we brought together a mixture of people ranging from labour exchanges and local authorities' social services and housing departments to Roma advisors and representatives of local NGOs. From this series of meetings we accumulated a wealth of information about unresolved issues in specific localities, and often why they had not been dealt with.

Failures in communication

In many problem situations the crucial aspect appears to be lack of communication, or rather lack of adequate or appropriate communication. On both sides people tend to jump to hasty conclusions with predictable results. Since the local authority is a seat of power, its employees frequently argue about the detail of legal codes or regulations in a way that may not be comprehensible to their listeners. Alternatively they may not disclose relevant information about rights and entitlements. Misinformation, partial information and inadequate information all play their part in provoking mutual hostility, lack of trust and unwillingness to co-operate. Our project clearly identified significant gaps in communication between local authorities and Roma representatives. The exception was the role of Roma advisor, which in some cases was brilliantly well executed but in others became an excuse for lack of action by the local authority itself.

Another important gap in communication was found to exist between local authorities and central government. No matter how adamantly central government insists that its policies to achieve integration are in place, their successful implementation requires co-ordinated action from local authorities and central government in localities where Roma communities live and to which returnees are repatriated. Yet since people actually live in specific towns and villages, the expectation is that these towns and villages should bear the responsibility of solving their own local problems. In this way policies devised at the top often fail to correspond to execution on the ground and consequently intention and realisation seem to be two different entities. Political history provides many instructive examples suggesting that that those who formulate lofty ideas and concepts should also pay attention to how these are to be translated into everyday practice.

In some respects the IOM project may have exceeded its original brief by addressing issues at European level, where the current trend in EU immigration policies is to shift responsibility for the plight of migrants to their home countries. However, the project also focused on domestic issues, but in this case whatever relevant policies already exist are fragmentary and disjointed, requiring further co-ordination. To sum up, the project has revealed that Roma migration it is not an irrelevance and will not go away. It is evident that free movement is a form of migration but we need to be clear why some groups are freer to migrate than others.

Asylum in Perspective: Roma Migration to the UK

Will Guy

At a time of European Union enlargement eastwards, when the integration of Roma minorities of Central and Eastern European applicant countries has been a political criterion for their entry, the arrival in existing member states of significant numbers of Roma asylum seekers has been a discordant and destabilising phenomenon. This paper considers the growth of Roma migration[1] westwards since 1989 from the formerly Communist-ruled states of Central and Eastern Europe (CEE) with particular reference to some of the most high-profile Roma refugees, from the Czech Republic and Slovakia. It challenges the still prevalent myth that their migration can be explained as a 'traditional' cultural pattern unrelated to wider events. Further, it argues that Roma have been assigned a significant role in the highly politicised discourse surrounding all asylum seekers and the search for more effective measures to deter them. The paper develops this argument with reference, first, to three revealing studies on the motivations of Roma, and, second, to the reception of these migrants in one of their main destination countries, the United Kingdom.

In 2000, debates about Roma refugees had intensified, prompting systematic research to understand their reasons for departure. One of the studies undertaken at this time investigated Roma asylum seekers while still living in Western Europe, carried out by the Czech NGO *Člověk v tísni* (People in Need 2000). Findings were based on semi-structured interviews with Czech and Slovak Roma refugees in south-east Kent, many of whom had migrated to England in 1997 and 1998, supported by statistics derived from the Kent social services database.

The People in Need project coincided with somewhat similar research, sponsored by the European Commission (EC) and three EU member states – Belgium, Finland and the Netherlands, which was

---

[1] The term 'migration' is used here to refer to Roma who have left their home countries for whatever reason This includes a whole range of motivations, such as the search of a better quality of life and/or protection from discrimination and attack. In the case of Roma these motives are often interwoven.

commissioned by the International Organisation for Migration (IOM) in the Czech Republic, Slovakia, Hungary and Romania. The stated aim was 'to investigate the migration potential among the Roma population in these countries, the socio-economic profile of the potential and the real migrants, as well as the motives and the triggering mechanisms for their migration'. It was hoped the findings would provide background knowledge to inform an IOM resettlement programme, following the repatriation of Roma from the sponsoring EU states (IOM 2000b).

This research was undertaken in the emigrants' homelands and included interviews with returned migrants and together represented a comprehensive, in-depth picture of Roma migration at the turn of the century. Since reports from these IOM projects are drawn on elsewhere in this collection (c.f. Castle-Kaněrová, Prónai, Uherek and Weinerová), selective use will be made of only two of them to supplement findings from the People in Need project. These are the studies carried out in the Czech Republic under the direction of Ivan Gabal (Gabal 2000) and in Slovakia by a team including the researchers Imrich and Michal Vašečka (Vašečka, M. et al. 2000).[2]

Problems of tracking and counting Roma migrants

Assessing the extent of Roma migration poses particular problems, which partly arise from the methods by which the statistics are generated. In most migration statistics, Roma are not identified by their ethnicity but by their state citizenship. Such procedures avoid the bureaucratic assignment of imputed ethnicity, as was common practice in making counts of Roma during the Communist period. However, this does mean that numbers of Roma asylum seekers can be hard to identify. While it is a safe assumption that all asylum seekers from Czech and Slovak Republics are almost certainly Roma, this is less true for Romania and Hungary. Roma were by no means the only CEE migrants heading westwards after 1989 for many other citizens of former Communist states also left home, taking advantage of the new freedom of travel in search of better employment prospects and higher pay. Indeed, a number of ethnic Romanians and Magyars have

---

[2] This discussion draws mainly on chapter five by Imrich Vašečka (Vašečka, I. 2000).

attempted to increase their chances of being allowed to stay in the West by presenting themselves as Roma and claiming asylum on the grounds of suffering discrimination.[3]

Another problem is that even if it can be assumed that all those appearing in official statistics are Roma, these figures do not reflect the true scale of migration, that is all who initially migrated. Illegal immigrants making no asylum claims are entirely absent from the records. Moreover, published statistics do not include those who have been prevented from continuing during the course of their journey or persuaded to return after arrival but only those who have eventually lodged an asylum claim.

A particular difficulty with UK statistics is that, unlike elsewhere, the figures do not show individuals but asylum claims, so numbers are not directly comparable with other countries. For this reason, UNHCR tables either state 'without dependants' or use a multiplier of approximately 1.3 persons per claim for all UK figures.[4] In the case of Roma refugees the real numbers are likely to be higher, because migration is generally in family groups. This last factor is relevant to the distinct manner of Roma migration, which is only rarely as individuals as is the common pattern with others. Roma usually prefer to migrate in family groups – either as nuclear families or not infrequently including members of extended families (Matras 2000: 36–7).[5]

Given these complications it is little wonder that estimates of asylum seekers are rarely consistent with each other. Figures published by UNHCR, by the UK Home Office, in academic studies and in the media often appear incompatible. All statistics, however reputable their

---

[3] For Ireland, see McNiffe and Lane (2000). Such examples of reverse passing are rare instances of Roma identity being more advantageous than that of a majority ethnic group!

[4] To be more precise, the UNHCR multiplier in 2002 was 1.289 persons per claim (UNHCR 2002b).

[5] Matras claims this was 'never a migration by individuals', though some Roma men did go to Canada in advance of their families following a more convention pattern of emigration (see Lee 2000: 61).

origin, must be treated warily since it is probable that none are accurate.

Roma migration westwards from Central and Eastern Europe

Although Roma migration to the United Kingdom is the main focus of this paper, this should not be viewed in isolation since Roma arriving in the United Kingdom from particular CEE countries also chose other target countries as destinations. Therefore, comparison with the experience of different Western states is helpful. In the past there had always been sporadic Roma migration in Europe, mainly in small groups and often from east to west, including to Britain. During the Communist period this meant entering Western countries either illegally or else legitimately on a tourist visa, but then perhaps overstaying the permitted period or seeking asylum under the 1951 Geneva Convention. The main exception to the general pattern was West Germany where migration for work was possible, particularly from the former Yugoslavia (as from Greece and Turkey) but bilateral agreements for such 'guestworkers' (*gastarbeiter*) were cancelled in 1973.

From 1990 onwards Roma migration westwards intensified dramatically with the principal source countries being located mainly in Eastern Europe and the Balkans (Matras 2000: 34–5). At this time most Roma migrants to the West came from Romania, Bulgaria and former Yugoslavia (not only the most war-affected regions but also from Macedonia).[6] However, from 1995 onwards, they were joined by raised numbers of Roma migrants from Central Europe (Matras 2000: 34–5). These new migrants came from Poland, the Czech Republic and Slovakia, and to a lesser extent from Hungary, but in smaller numbers than those from further east and south. At the end of the 1990s the savage war in Kosovo drove out a fresh wave of refugees (Kenrick 2001: 413–7, Acković 2003). Substantial flows of refugees from disintegrating former Yugoslavia continued throughout the 1990s but the proportion of Roma among them is impossible to determine.

---

[6] See Dragoljub Acković in this collection for migration from Macedonia, before the inter-ethnic flare-up in 2000, and from Kosovo.

Initially the target area for Roma migrants was nearby West-Central Europe, particularly countries having common borders with former Communist countries such as Germany, Austria and Italy, but also France. Others did not travel so far but remained in East-Central Europe, including some Romanian Roma who were markedly visible in former Communist countries.[7] Later preferred target areas extended to Scandinavia and Western Europe and beyond. Destinations included the United Kingdom and Ireland, the Netherlands and Belgium, Norway, Sweden and Finland, as well as Canada.

Germany was particularly important as an early migratory destination for Roma since, in addition to being one of the nearest Western states, it had a buoyant economy as well as the most liberal policy on refugees. In some cases kinsfolk were already established there, either as refugees or as former *gastarbeiter*, especially from Yugoslavia, Poland and Romania (Matras 2000: 42–3). 'In 1992 ... approximately one quarter of the 438,191 asylum seekers in Germany were from Romania, and of these an estimated 100,000 were Romanies' (Tebbutt 2001: 276). However, the liberal policy on refugees was revoked in early 1990s, as it was seen as attracting asylum seekers from all over the world. In 1992–3, as for other 'front-line' states like Austria and Italy, there was a tightening of border controls and entry procedures. As a further defence against continuing immigration Germany concluded bilateral arrangements, as in November 1992 with Romania, whereby source countries agreed to the return of recent migrants to Germany in exchange for money to reintegrate them and improve conditions in their homelands (Matras 2000: 43, Tebbutt 2001: 276).[8]

---

[7] For the situation in Poland, see Mróz (2001: 263–4) and Barany (2002: 242–3).

[8] 'German authorities reported that over half of the 35,345 Romanians who entered Germany in 1990 were Gypsies, while in 1992, 33,600 Romanian Gypsies reached that country, ... [prompting] an upsurge of neo-Nazi and right-wing violence that resulted in a growing number of Roma deaths'. The November 1992 repatriation agreement with Romania was 'aimed at illegal Romanian refugees without proper documentation' and legislation the following month, which 'made it more difficult for political refugees to enter the country', was prompted partly by violent attacks on Romanian Roma (Crowe 1994: 147).

Considerable emigration of Roma might have been anticipated from the Czech Republic following the peaceful dismemberment of former Czechoslovakia, when many Czech Roma were denied citizenship of the newly formed state by the strict conditions of its 1993 citizenship law (Gross 1994, Guy 2001: 297–9). However, this uncompromising act of exclusion conveyed to even those Roma with citizenship an unambiguous message that they were unwelcome in the near ethnically homogenous state in which the 'basic solution … [was] seen as mutual segregation rather than integration' (Gabal 2000: 7).

Some Roma did leave after 1993 but it was only in 1997 that sizeable departures occurred, when independent Czech TV documentaries depicted first Canada (6 August) and, shortly after, the UK (30 September) as tolerant sanctuaries for Roma.[9] After the screening of the first documentary around 1,500[10] Czech Roma claimed asylum in Canada from 7 August to 8 October1997, when the Canadian government re-imposed visas for Czech citizens.[11]

The numbers of Roma refugees arriving in the United Kingdom following the second documentary were roughly equivalent to those who had gone to Canada but prompted quite different official action. Whereas the Canadian government resorted to visa requirements, a measure that practically cut off Roma migration from the Czech Republic, the British response was less drastic, tightening asylum application procedures by reducing the time for claimants to substantiate their case from 28 to 5 days (Braham and Braham 2000: 97). In spite of less rigorous controls, numbers of Roma refugees initially decreased but rose once more during the following year when Roma from Slovakia claimed asylum. In all, 1,350 asylum claims were

---

[9] The documentaries, called *Na vlastní oči* (See for Yourself), were screened by the *Nova* TV station.

[10] Numbers making the journey were undoubtedly higher as some were persuaded to return before making a claim, while others were removed en route in Germany (Lee 2000: 55). Among these migrants were also Roma who were Slovak citizens (Braham and Braham 2000: 98). By June the following year, 600 of the recorded 1,500 Roma migrants to Canada had returned home (Radio Prague, 1998).

[11] After talks to lift visa requirements had remained deadlocked, the Czech government eventually retaliated by imposing visa restrictions on Canadian citizens from 1 April 2002 (Associated Press, 1 February 2002).

recorded from the Czech and Slovak Republics during 1998 (Home Office 1999a).[12] The British government promptly responded by imposing visa requirements on Slovak citizens on 8 October 1998, unlike its more lenient treatment of the Czech Republic a year earlier. In spite of increased restrictions there was further immigration to the UK of Roma from the Czech Republic during 1999. Claims by Czech Roma started in April with 110, increased to a high point of 255 in August and then fluctuated around 200 per month until the end of 1999, totalling 1,565 for the year.[13]

In response to UK visa restrictions, the main destination of Slovak Roma switched to Scandinavia and the Benelux Countries. Of the total of 4,960 and 4,390 Slovaks seeking asylum in Europe in 1999 and 2000, UNHCR statistics recorded no Slovak claims in the UK (UNHCR 2001a, UNHCR 2000a, UNHCR 2001b). In contrast, Finland registered over 1,000 Slovak Roma asylum claims in June and July 1999, at the time of assuming the rotating EU presidency, and consequently introduced visa restrictions for Slovaks (7 July). Norway (27 July) and later Denmark (30 November) soon followed suit (Cahn and Vermeersch 2000: 78). The subsequent lifting of Finnish visa requirements (7 November) led to 407 new claims over the next 3 months, after which controls were re-imposed,[14] although in that country Slovaks were replaced by Poles (1229 claims) and, to a much lesser extent, Czechs (129 claims).[15]

---

[12] In 1998, there were 498 claims in the Netherlands, while in the same year there were 125 claims by Slovak Roma in Germany and 176 in Canada (all figures exclude dependants) (UNHCR statistics quoted Braham and Braham 2000: 98).

[13] Monthly Home Office figures for the Czech Republic were April 110 claims, May 110, June 150, July 195, August 255, September 195, October 180, November 165 and December 205 (Home Office 1999b: 1). CTK gave the rather different figures of 140 claims for June and a drop to 85 in July, which according to the accompanying news story alleviated the threat of visas being imposed (CTK, 29 July 1999).

[14] Norway, too, re-imposed visa restrictions on 7 December, the same day as Finland and a month after lifting them, in response to the arrival of 219 Slovak Roma asylum seekers (Slovak Spectator, 13-19 December 1999).

[15] Figures for Poland and the Czech Republic are for the 12-month period, July 1999–June 2000 (Gheorghe and Hedman 2000: 5).

Meanwhile Belgium had registered 2,015 asylum claims from Slovak Roma, from January 1997 to August 1999 inclusive, of which 1,498 were immediately refused while only three Slovak citizens were granted asylum (Cahn and Vermeersch 2000: 77). In October 1999 Belgium acted on an earlier reciprocal agreement with Slovakia by peremptorily returning a group Roma whose claims had still to be fully processed (ibid.: 77–82). In spite of this enforced repatriation, Belgium was still the main destination of Slovak Roma in 2000 (1,392 claims), closely followed by the Netherlands (998 claims), while for the first time 721 Slovak Roma sought refuge in the Czech Republic.[16] At the same time, smaller numbers still continued to travel to Scandinavia.[17]

Roma migration in theoretical and historical context

The arrival of Czech and Slovak Roma asylum seekers in Canada and the UK attracted wide international media coverage and focused attention on the apparently growing tide of Roma abandoning their homelands in Central and Eastern Europe for the West. The very fact that that were Roma, prompted some to explain this perplexing phenomenon as a reversion to what were presumed to be ancestral patterns of behaviour, deeply ingrained in the Roma psyche.

The thesis had been advanced far earlier that '[t]he Gypsy is primarily and above all else a nomad. His dispersion throughout the world is due less to historical or political necessities than to his own nature' (Clébert 1967: 246). This '"primordialist" theory of ethnicity' (Hobsbawm 1992: 24) has long been thought particularly applicable to Roma. Therefore, it is not altogether unexpected to find it resurfacing in policy documents and occasionally in academic discourse, identifying recent Roma migration as a 'cultural' pattern unique to this group.

A 1997 report by the United Nations High Commissioner for Refugees (UNHCR) started its section on Roma asylum and migration with the sentence: 'A common characteristic of almost all Roma communities across Europe is their nomadic lifestyle' (UNHCR 1997: box 6, 2). In

---

[16] For more detailed information, see Zdenek Uherek and Renata Weinerová in this collection.

[17] Norway (460), Finland (346) and Sweden (92) (UNHCR 2001b).

similar vein, the European Commission opened its 1999 listing of EU support for Roma communities in Central and Eastern Europe by explaining Roma difficulties in the region in 'defending their basic human rights' as '[d]ue to their nomadic way of life' (European Commission 1999: 2).[18] Perhaps these accounts took their lead from the chair of the Specialist Group on Roma/Gypsies at the Council of Europe (CoE), who declared Roma migration during the 1990s to be 'merely a return to the normal mobility of Gypsies' (Verspaget 1995: 13).[19]

Given the far higher numbers of settled Roma in comparison with nomads in Central and Eastern Europe, the claim that nomadism is a core, defining element of Romani identity is unfounded. Equally, the assertion that the absence of 'traditional' nomadism on a wide scale in the region was the result of Communist anti-nomadism laws in the 1950s ignores the fact that the vast majority of Roma in the region were settled long before the advent of Communist rule. The confusion about recent Roma population movement arises partly from romanticising the Gypsy figure as the exotic 'other', a variant of Said's 'orientalism' (1995). However, it stems more from a failure to distinguish between nomadism as means of subsistence – an established pattern characteristic of the relatively smaller, more scattered Roma communities of Western Europe[20] – and migration from the larger, often more concentrated and predominantly settled Roma populations of Central and Eastern Europe.[21]

---

[18] The subsequent listing in 2002, substituted the explanation 'As a minority group' for 'Due to their nomadic way of life' (European Commission 2002: 4).

[19] For more details of Verspaget's view of Roma migration, see Kovats (2001: 100).

[20] Characterised as 'economic nomadism' (Acton 1974: 254, 257) and as 'service nomadism' (Mirga and Gheorghe 1997: 5). For further discussion of the east-west 'divide', see Guy (2001a: 5–8).

[21] These are broad generalisations, of course, for different groups of Roma have always pursued very diverse ways of life. Particularly in south-eastern Europe, for example, some groups remain nomadic to this day although adapting as always to contemporary conditions (see Marushiakova, Popov and Decheva in this collection). Likewise, even before 1989, previously nomadic Polska Roma began to reinvent and redirect their former trading migrations (see Mróz 2001). In Great Britain, however, some Roma have sought to settle in houses from the fifteenth century onwards.

Equally misplaced is Clébert's suggestion that historical or political factors are unhelpful in explaining the travels of Roma. To the contrary, major Roma migrations have always been associated with seismic shifts in wider society. The initial diaspora across Europe coincided with Ottoman invasions, flight from persecution in Western Europe with regulation of the landless poor, the mid-nineteenth century exodus from Romania with the abolition of slavery and the ending of feudalism in that area and, more recently, westward emigration of some who escaped the Holocaust with the ending of the Second World War. Like earlier substantial Roma migratory flows, their post-1989 population movement was directly linked to external events – in this case the collapse of Communism and its political, social and economic repercussions.

Such confusions are not only misleading but dangerous, since they mask the diverse motivation of Roma journeys and can lead to misinterpretation of the actions of many Roma. Instead of seeking explanations that are specific for Roma, we should seek the same sorts of reasons for Roma migration as we would for any other people, that is similar push and pull factors such as deprivation and discrimination, employment and security. This is by no means to say that these elements operate equally for all groups. Such an approach offers the best prospects for understanding Roma migration since the ending of Communist rule.

Motivation of Roma migrants

In an influential article discussing the significance of CEE Roma migration westwards after 1989, Yaron Matras (2000) dismissed the idea that this could be explained as 'nomadism'. The reality is quite the opposite, for in his view 'the extraordinary feature of Romani migration is that so many Roma are prepared to take the risks of migrating **despite their lack of nomadic traditions** (Matras 2000: 32, emphasis in original). Nevertheless, Matras noted that while sharing some motivations with non-Roma migrants, 'such as to improve their economic status', reports 'repeated[ly] mention … "insecurity due to community tensions and occasional violent incidents", a motivation which is peculiar to the Roma' (Matras 2000:36). Linked to this, he

174

identified 'a significant distinctive feature of Romani migration patterns', which he characterised as:

> **Lack of confidence in the social structure and institutions** of their countries of residence, and a consequent loose attachment to those countries, [which] has led Roma to **explore the opportunities offered by migration, even at the risk of repeated expulsion and clandestine, self-sufficing existence** on the fringe of western societies.
>
> (Matras 2000: 35–6, emphasis in original)

The article went on to single out particular causes of Romani migration: social conflict, ethnic tension, severely restricted employment, single acts of violence and change of status (e.g. citizenship) (ibid: 37–9). Matras' conclusions were based on secondary analysis of reports (e.g. UNHCR, CoE and NGO) but further revealing evidence of the motivation of Czech and Slovak Roma refugees was provided by sociological research carried out among asylum seekers in the three empirical studies. Their findings were compatible with the analysis of Matras and also provided more contextual detail.

The People in Need study estimated that in April 2000 a total of around 3,000 Czech and Slovak Roma were living in the UK, roughly equal in numbers at that time. Of these, half were living in London and somewhat less than a half in south-east Kent. Data from a UK charitable organisation suggested that Slovak arrivals had peaked between July and September 1998 but had then been reduced to a trickle after the imposition of visa requirement in October 1998. However, the origins of Slovak Roma were almost entirely concentrated in the eastern region of the country, whereas Czech Roma came from all over the Czech lands.[22]

Though many migrated in family groups, sometimes three-generational, many left parents behind and likewise adults sometimes left grown-up children.[23] A breakdown by age reveals a broad pattern of young adults

---

[22] In the Czech Republic: Chomutov, Jirkov, Kladno, Litvínov, Louny, Ostrava, Přerov, Rokycany, Žatec.
In Slovakia: sources were concentrated in Košice and Michalovce (People in Need 2000, January: 6–7).

[23] See Lee (2000: 61) for Canada.

migrating with children. Of the whole sample 58 per cent were children under the age of eighteen, while of adults over two-thirds (69 per cent) were younger than 36. Many children attended local schools but this varied greatly, depending on location.

Interviews were carried out only in south-east Kent and no attempt was made to collect detailed information on educational and financial circumstances but migrants included some who had been in work ('in their own words financially well-off') as well as long-term unemployed. This suggests that many of these migrants were similar to those who had travelled to Canada where Roma asylum seekers were said to be 'mostly the better-educated middle-class élite who had small businesses or assets they could sell to raise money for the trip' (Lee 2000: 54).[24]

The table below shows predominant reasons given for migrating, although the study emphasised that the decision to leave home usually involved a combination of motives.

Main motives given by Czech and Slovak Roma for seeking asylum in UK

- **repeated racist attacks (verbal & physical)** on themselves or someone close (more often by ordinary 'decent' citizens rather than by skinheads)
- **inaction of police in defending them**
  and the light sentences delivered to perpetrators of racially-motivated crimes
- **discrimination at work,** particularly lower pay than whites for similarly qualified work and impossibility of finding employment because of their racial origin
- **discrimination against children at school,** particularly placing them in Special Schools[25] and impossibility of taking part in all activities like white children (school outings etc.)
- **pessimistic vision of the future**
  - constant worsening of general situation of Roma in Czech Republic

  (Source: People in Need 2000, January: 6)

---

[24] However, see Renata Weinerová in this collection. Weinerová points out that the term 'middle class' is misleading when applied to CEE Roma since it refers to 'the former "socialist" middle class, ... literate but unqualified people', who 'in relation to overall stratification in society ... still formed part of the lower class'.

[25] Special remedial schools for children with learning disabilities.

The study stressed the primacy of migrants' concern for the future security of their families and, as noted by Matras, 'the fear and great mistrust of [their own] state authorities' (ibid., April: 5), challenging the common view that the migration of these Roma asylum seekers was undertaken wholly on economic grounds.

> The British and Czech media often speak of economic migrants. However, on the basis of the interviews obtained, it is possible to state that the number of purely economic migrants is minimal. Undoubtedly the poor economic situation of Roma in the Czech Republic was often a contributory factor in their departure but it was evidently never the primary cause. On the contrary many asylum seekers were better provided for financially in the Czech Republic than in Great Britain.
>
> (People in Need, January: 6)

The overriding importance of the family to Roma also featured strongly in the findings of the other two empirical studies. In the words of Roma interviewed in Gabal's research, family values played a crucial role in the decision whether to emigrate. These Roma felt the need to ensure financial security to 'protect the family' and also maintain cohesion for 'the family should live together' (Gabal 2000: 25). This latter factor often led to remigration in cases when death or other misfortunes afflicted members of the extended family. While sharing the view that motivation for migration was invariably mixed, Gabal placed considerably more emphasis on economic considerations than the People in Need study. According to his respondents, their motives for emigrating, in decreasing order of importance, were high unemployment, lack of housing, insecurity (fear of racially motivated attacks) and the rising cost of living (ibid.).

In the opinion of Czech officials interviewed by Gabal's team, there were sufficient jobs available for Roma but they had no interest in taking them since the wages were too low to compensate for the consequent loss of benefit payments (Gabal 2000: 26). Similar opinions had been expressed in the 1997 government report (Czech Government 1997: I 17–18).[26] According to these officials 'the main stimuli for [Roma] emigration are unequivocally economic motives'. At the same time they also saw Roma behaviour as 'economically rational', since

---

[26] Also cited by Gabal (2000: 26–7).

they were often able to conceal the fact of their emigration and continue to draw substantial social welfare payments consisting of unemployment and housing benefits, as well as child support.[27] This was in addition to whatever support they might receive abroad as refugees (Gabal 2000: 25). However, their views about economic rationality did not prevent officials reverting to stereotypical explanations of Roma behaviour in terms of their assumed cultural patterns, maintaining that Roma were 'very impulsive and traditionally tend towards migration' (ibid.: 26).

In Gabal's view, the surge in Roma migration from the Czech Republic from 1997 onwards was indeed economically motivated, but in a rather different sense, being partly prompted by a deep economic recession in the last third of the 1990s, which impacted most severely on the poorest and on the areas of heavy industry where most Roma lived. The economic crisis was heightened by an 'accompanying moral crisis ... [with] both main political parties debilitated by financial scandals as well as unprecedented and deliberate ... [asset-stripping] by businesses and banks' (ibid.: 6). Gabal wryly commented:

> In these circumstances minor fraud in the areas of welfare payments and unemployment payments, which usually became part of the process of the emigration of Romany families abroad, can be understood as tolerable misdemeanours or even a manifestation of inventive socio-market behaviour.
> (Gabal 2000: 6)

However, while admitting that benefit fraud undoubtedly occurred, he contested the negative image of Roma as simply passively gathering all manner of support payments. He found that to Roma refugees 'it does not matter that in the target countries they will not receive money (just checks or in-kind support) [as] they say it is always possible to find work there' (ibid.: 34). Gabal agreed that Roma migration is rational but in a much broader sense, as 'active, determined social-market behaviour ... with which Romany families react to their social and ethnic marginalisation in the Czech Republic' (ibid.: 34).

---

[27] These benefits were quantified for a family with four children at approximately 15,000–20,000 Czech crowns per month (400–500 Euro).

This interpretation was compatible with that of Imrich Vašečka in his analysis for the Slovak IOM report. While he, like Gabal, gave greater prominence to economic motivation than the People in Need report, he saw this as a triggering mechanism rather than an underlying cause of emigration. He also pointed out that to make a substantial sum of money while abroad was not easy, or achievable by every migrant. According to one informant his success, 'require[d] a strict consumption discipline and an ability to obtain durable goods by collecting them on the streets and subsequently repair[ing] them' (Vašečka, I. 2000: 169).

Vašečka concluded that the migration of Slovak Roma to the West was largely due to the loss by the Roma 'middle-class' of their former, hard-won, socio-economic status, the blocking of channels of upward mobility for their children and the decline of the previously 'achieved degree of integration into particular local communities' (Vašečka, I. 2000: 185). All these were 'a consequence of the enormously high rate of unemployment among the Roma' (ibid.).[28] In addition, however, he also saw migration as a consequence of attitudes among some Roma, 'characteristic of the culture of poverty',[29] as well as of 'distrust of non-Roma institutions and organisations' by some Roma (ibid.).

It is important to realise that the earlier progress in social mobility made by Roma during the Communist period derived from their ability and willingness to work, often extremely arduously, as migrant workers in the Czech lands. In Vašečka's words: 'Our elder respondents are still very proud that they have acquired their current status by the sweat of their brows and by leading a life full of privations' (ibid.: 176). While

---

[28] A 1997 nationwide survey by the Slovak Ministry of Labour, Social Affairs and Family had shown that 80 per cent of the Roma population were dependent on state welfare (Vašečka and Džambazovič 2000: 50). 'In 1999, unemployment among Roma ranged from 60 per cent in integrated settlements, to nearly 100 per cent in the most segregated settlements' (World Bank 2002: 27). Also in 1999, the Czech government estimated Roma unemployment at 70 per cent, compared with 10 per cent of the total population (Ringold 2000: 16).
[29] Some of these, such as chronic dependency on state welfare, are attributed to the corrupting 'influence of the Communist regime', which in some cases undermined Romani initiative by the provision of 'special benefits and various social security measures' (Vašečka, I. 2000: 177).

the overwhelming majority of Roma men had worked as manual labourers,[30] many of whose families were categorised by Vašečka as 'middle class', a thin stratum of entrepreneurs as well as a small, educated Romani intelligensia had emerged during the period of Communist rule (Lemon 1996: 29, Guy 2001b: 296, Gheorghe 1997: 157–8). Some of these, too, migrated in the bleak, post-Communist climate since they felt that in spite of their previous level of integration, they now suffered blanket discrimination as Roma *per se*. Vašečka reported that 'some of our respondents, mostly members of the Roma intelligentsia and representatives of Roma entrepreneurs, perceive their exclusion on the nationwide level' as depriving them of 'the feeling of human dignity and freedom of choice' (Vašečka, I. 2000: 167).[31] In their own view and irrespective of social status, 'for many Roma ... migrating remains the only viable chance to improve their situation' and that of their children and 'the one solution which they could influence and decide upon themselves (ibid.: 166, 174). The IOM research report stated its main conclusion quite bluntly:

> Our findings indicate that the main reason for Roma migrating into EU member states is their endeavour to maintain the level of emancipation they have achieved. Every single Roma who we have spoken with claimed that for Roma it was easier to live in this country before 1990. As one of them put it: 'It is necessary to return the Roma where he was ten years ago'.[32]
>
> (Vašečka, I. 2000: 172)

---

[30] 90 per cent in the Czech Republic, according to research by the Dženo Foundation for the 1997 report (Czech Government 1997: I 17), but 68 per cent according to the 1991 Slovak population census (Vašečka and Džambazovič 2000: 49).

[31] A Romani refugee in London, impeccably dressed and speaking perfect Czech, explained how he had felt humiliated in his ministry post as an adviser on integrating the Roma minority by witnessing fellow (non-Roma) officials sending, as a joke, totally unqualified Roma for job interviews as computer programmers. However, the decision to flee as refugees was only made after his disabled wife had been beaten up on a Prague street (Will Guy, field notes, 2000).

[32] Vašečka also mentions 'examples of how Roma were abused during the Communist period', illustrating his point with the extreme case of the stigmatised east Slovak settlement of Rudňany, where Roma were resettled by the local authority in derelict and dangerous housing in the vicinity of mine workings and a highly toxic waste tip (Vašečka, I. 2000: 177–8).

Attempts to counter this catastrophic loss of status and despair about the future go far beyond what is termed 'economic motivation' but impoverishment is nevertheless at the heart of Roma experience. Vašečka chronicled the processes of impoverishment and fears of the consequences of falling into debt (ibid.: 174) and while there is no space to expand on this here, Uherek and Weinerová explore this topic further in this collection, including the exploitative practice of usury. Vašečka also discussed growing ethnic segregation, including the example of the removal by the local authority of all rent defaulters in a single east Slovak district to the town of Čierna nad Tisou, which non-Roma are consequently leaving. The authorities are warned that their actions run the risk of creating 'a showpiece ghetto of Roma poverty, exclusion and despair' (ibid.: 174).

The People in Need study found that most interviewees had been thinking about leaving their homeland for an extended period before their departure, which was sometimes triggered by specific incidents. One case was the departure of several Roma families from South Bohemia, who reacted in this way following the murder of a Rom nearby (People in Need 2000, April: 4). In this case the migrants had not been directly attacked themselves but the incident had heightened their already acute sense of vulnerability. This example illustrated Matras' point that 'it is often difficult to document a direct link between ethnic violence or other human rights violations and specific cases of migration of individual families' (Matras 2000: 37).

Gabal also found that migration could be triggered by 'at first glance negligible motives (e.g. news about inter-ethnic conflict in other parts of the Czech Republic)' (Gabal 2000: 26). However, he viewed such responses as indicative of the broader climate of deep-rooted fear for 'it is necessary to take into consideration not only the occurrences or the number of reported physical racial attacks, but also the overall ethnic climate in Czech society'. Gabal pointed to 'the existing deep alienation of both communities, ... xenophobia ... [and] tense and alienating ethnic conditions in which a minority justifiably can feel threatened and discriminated against' (ibid.: 33). A Roma participant to a roundtable discussion in Slovakia on Roma migration took the same view, arguing that 'in many respects, migration is a security issue: the Roma want to live in safety' (PER 2000: 11).

The overwhelming importance of inter-ethnic relations was emphasised by the explanation why some areas generated lower numbers of Roma migrants. Although varying regional levels of unemployment in the locations researched did not influence the uniformly high Roma emigration rates (Gabal: 28), closer integration of Roma with their local majority communities seemed an important factor in inhibiting their departure. Gabal noted that 'Roma are apparently least inclined to emigrate from southern and eastern Bohemia ... [which are] regions with long-standing and stable (if smaller) Romany communities' (ibid.: 36).[33] Vašečka came to the same view in Slovakia, finding that Slovak Roma in Banská Bystrica, central Slovakia, and Hungarian Roma in south-east Slovakia had much closer links with local populations than the larger numbers in east Slovakia and consequently felt far less pressure to leave (Vašečka, I. 2000: 161–2). On the basis of the evidence 'a logical conclusion then would be that Roma's decisions on migration are rather influenced by the degree of their integration into particular local communities' (ibid.: 162).

Knowledge and expectations of Roma migrants

All three empirical studies noted high levels of information exchange among Roma, although the question whether further migration is prompted by news from those who have already made the journey was not elaborated in the People in Need report. However, there were evidently frequent communications between migrants in Kent and family members who had remained at home (by letter, phone and even by occasional visits!) (People in Need 2000, April: 4). The other reports were more explicit about information networks and their significance.

Gabal concluded that 'experiences gained and knowledge about conditions and circumstances in individual countries are quickly communicated and shared in Romany communities' (Gabal 2000: 40)

---

[33] However, these two regions were not investigated in Gabor's research because they were not 'areas ... with the largest concentration of Roma populations'. This view was based on interviews with experts (Gabor 2000: 3, 36).

and was in no doubt that increased migration was 'associated with effective sharing of relevant information and accumulated experiences' (ibid.: 34). Likewise, for Vašečka, 'information and assistance provided on an informal basis among members of the Roma community' was 'the immediate catalyst' triggering 'mass migration' (Vašečka, I. 2000: 185).

Vašečka found that 'Roma living in rural settlements and urban colonies seemed to rely on collective activities when seeking solutions to their difficult situation' (ibid.: 159). After giving examples of common strategies for making a livelihood adopted by individual settlements in the Spiš region of east Slovakia, he argued that Roma emigration 'can also be considered a locally implemented strategy, which is adopted by the entire community through mass emulation' (ibid.). In his view, this characteristic way of social organisation for mutual support explained the peculiarly localised emigration from specific locations in Slovakia, noted in the People in Need report, as opposed to the more diffuse migration from the Czech Republic. Vašečka remarked: 'To an outside observer, this may appear as organising. But in fact it is merely information provided in an informal way, which spreads through the community's communication channels as a steppe fire' (ibid.: 169). To reinforce the point, he cited the example of 'the village of Pavlovce [where] one can find streets referred to by the locals as English Street, Finnish Street, etc.' (ibid.: 168).

This interpretation went some way to answer accusations of 'organised emigration' by Slovak politicians, who alleged that some migration has been deliberately engineered for political purposes by Roma pressure groups or others. Such explanations were offered of the arrival of Slovak Roma in Helsinki at the Finnish accession to the EU presidency in July 1999.[34] Here, it should be noted that there was a general switch in Roma migratory patterns towards northern European countries during early 1999, well before Finland assumed the presidency.

---

[34] The Slovak daily *Pravda* headlined its front-page story 'Organised Exodus' (*Pravda*, 6 July 1999), while President Schuster believed the migration was a plot, insisting that 'time will confirm how these Roma were organised, in what manner, and why they were chosen' (Naegele 1999).

However, this is not to deny that some emigration may have been politically motivated[35] or, far more plausibly, was encouraged and planned by usurers and speculative traffickers in people, as Uherek and Weinerová explain in this collection.

The general lack of success of Roma refugees in gaining asylum prompts the question whether they had a realistic view of their prospects when deciding to emigrate. Only Canada relented when confronted by Roma asylum seekers and in 1998 eventually accepted 85–95 per cent of initial Czech Roma applications, recognising that 'Czech Romani refugees ... have a valid claim for [Geneva] Convention-status based on ethnic persecution in the Czech Republic' (Lee 2000: 61).[36] All other Western states, even supposedly more liberal Scandinavia, showed comparable determination in expelling Roma asylum seekers as soon as their procedures allowed or even in advance of this, as in the case of Belgium.[37] In spite of criticism by the Finnish prime minister of harsh treatment of Roma in their homelands, the outcome was no different for recently arrived Slovak Roma refugees. Some were returned to Belgium as a 'safe third country',[38] which responded by deporting 74 Slovak Roma to their country of origin in defiance of the European Court of Human Rights (Cahn and Vermeersch 2000: 72, Raeymaekers 1999).[39]

---

[35] The 'direct appeals of [Czech] Roma leaders for all Roma to emigrate' in 1999 (Gabal 2000: 9) could be regarded in this light.

[36] However, this tolerant approach was not extended to Hungarian Roma who arrived later, although even in their case up to 12 per cent of asylum claims were successful - a higher rate than for Roma refugees in the European Union (Lee 2000: 63).

[37] It should be noted that the southern European countries of Spain, Portugal, Italy and Greece had a somewhat more relaxed approach to illegal immigrants and during the 1990s enacted amnesty programmes, resulting in a total of 1.2 million people being granted legal residency (IOM 2000a; Reuters, 29 April 2002).

[38] The 1990 Dublin Convention specified that refugees should claim asylum in the first 'safe' country they had entered, where there was presumed to be no risk of persecution. Supplementary rules in 1992 allowed the return of refugees to a 'safe third country', while all EU states were designated 'safe' in the 1997 Treaty of Amsterdam (Buirski 1999: 3). On this basis some Slovak Roma were returned to the Czech Republic.

[39] In 2002 the European Court of Human Rights ruled in a test case against the Belgian government that the expulsion had 'violated ... European human rights rules' (Associated Press, 5 February 2002).

The stance of the UK was no different from that of its EU partners. According to Home Office statistics, up to the end of 2001 the UK had initially granted asylum to only 1 or 2 Czech Roma families in 1999 and a further 10 in 2000 and none in the preceding years or in 2001 (Home Office 2002b). These figures represented less than 1 per cent of the 1,200 applicants from the Czech Republic in 2000 and only a tiny proportion of the 1,790 in 1999 (Home Office 2002a), in marked distinction to the general success rate for all UK asylum claims. In 1999, 36 per cent of all initial decisions resulted in applicants being granted asylum, although in the following years this rate plunged to only 10 per cent in 2000 and 9 percent in 2001, perhaps related to heightened sensitivity about the issue of asylum seekers (Home Office 2000: 1, 2001: 1, 2002c: 1).

Unsurprisingly, all three studies noted a marked change over time in Roma expectations, linked to failure to obtain asylum, more restrictive asylum policies and stringent procedures for processing claims in the West, which 'considerably sobered the views and attitudes of emigrating Roma' (Gabal 2000: 34). In response, Roma migration strategies were modified to take account of bleaker prospects. Gabal reported that unlike previous practice, 'emigrating families now do not sell their flats and possessions and do not close off avenues for return' (ibid.: 33). Similarly, the People in Need researchers found that 'the majority [of their respondents] were aware that eventually they would have to return home'. Although 'roughly half [said they] would return voluntarily if the situation in the Czech Republic changed so that they would not have to go in fear of their lives', at the time of interview little optimism was expressed about such developments and '[i]n general it can be said that no-one is returning voluntarily as a matter of principle'. However, 30 per cent of interviewees were adamant they would not return home for good when their asylum claim was rejected but would emigrate again to the UK or elsewhere. The remainder were undecided about what they might do (People in Need 2000, April: 5). Both other studies came to the same conclusion that many failed asylum seekers would attempt to re-migrate and that new migration was likely to occur in the future.

Positive aspects of Romani experience in the West

Any indication of positive aspects of the Romani experience of emigration was strangely absent from the People in Need account, although negative features such as painful separation from family members, health problems, accommodation difficulties and the tedium from enforced idleness were included (People in Need 2000, April: 6). It is not clear whether the refugees in Kent lived a life of unmitigated dreariness or whether the interviewers failed to probe sufficiently but other research has spoken eloquently of what Roma appreciated about living in a Western country. The Roma experience is sometimes described as 'tourism', mostly in accusatory although occasionally in comprehending tones, but an awareness of those aspects of life in the West most valued by Roma, and how they are perceived, is an important key to understanding Roma emigration.

Gabal's report included, as a short appendix, the summarised experience in the UK of one extended family of Romani migrants from the Czech Republic (Gabal 2000: 41). Although mostly not in the emigrants' own words, the account threw light on many of the themes in the People in Need report. This was exactly the kind of personal testimony generally missing from the UK media coverage of Roma refugees and which might have made their motives and human situation more comprehensible.

Mr. B. left Ústí nad Labem in North Bohemia in May 1999 to travel to London with his wife, three children and six grandchildren. He said he had left a week after his daughter had been assaulted in his home by the skinhead son of a neighbour, who had constantly harassed them. A brother from Plzeň joined them, making a group of thirty Roma journeying together.

One of their main impressions in their new home was of the kindness of everyone, not just friends who helped them find their feet but also the officials they dealt with. In Mr. B.'s words: 'Officials in England are worth a million. You can't even compare them with here. Here they scream at us if they just see us. There they are all very nice'. He particularly valued living in a Black neighbourhood in London, declaring: 'Blacks are our brothers. We really miss them. We have very good friends there'.[40] One neighbour had given them a bed and cabinet when they first moved in. Mr. B. was quite frank about how they survived, explaining that they were financially secure in London as 'everyone worked ... "on the black"' and although the officials apparently knew about this, they turned a blind eye. Meanwhile the grandchildren went to school and learned English.

Yet young children were the cause of their return, crying constantly and wanting to go home, so most of the group left for the Czech Republic in early 2000, even though they had a residence permit until March 2001. They passed on all their furnishings to newly arrived Roma migrants from North Bohemia as 'everyone helps out there'. On their return they found that they had lost their municipal flat and initially had to live with relatives but were now building a new home with their savings. Other Roma at home found their decision strange and Mr. B.'s family all came to regret leaving England. However, they were planning a holiday trip to Mr.B.'s brother, who had remained in England. Mrs. B. said she wanted to see the sea again before she died and ruefully reflected on her experience: 'An old [proverb] says, "everywhere good, at home the best". In the Czech Republic that is no longer true.'

Writing of the emigration of Czech Roma, Gabal tried to summarise both the push factors making life unbearable in their homeland and the pull of a more emancipated life in the West. This involved not just the possibility of making a viable livelihood, although this was seen as extremely important by Roma, but of being treated as human beings.

> The foundation of ethnic relations between Roma and the majority population in ... Czech society is fear, suspicion and distrust. An important driving motive for emigration therefore is not only better security, more open and ... uncontaminated access to officials in the target countries, but in particular the greater ethnic diversity and openness of Western societies, the lower level of xenophobia and positive ethnic climate where the level of *a*

---

[40] Romani interviewees from Slovakia in the IOM research also stressed the kindness they had encountered but linked this to supposed redressing of racial discrimination: 'Coloured people often sit in managerial posts in England, we felt good there' and 'They are kind to a person in England, [because] the country is run by the coloured, not by the white' (Vašečka, I. 2000: 176, 178).

priori prejudice towards people with a different skin colour is basically lower. The above average xenophobic, ethnically and culturally homogeneous Czech society of today decidedly does not have these qualities.

(Gabal 2000: 30–1)

UK immigration discourses and the role of Roma

Chauvinistic discourses are nothing new in British society but xenophobia in public debate increased in response to successive waves of immigration, particularly from the West Indies and Indian sub-continent after the Second World War.[41] The paradox is that while the labour of these newcomers has been needed, their difference is resented and consequently attitudes to immigrants living in the UK have always been deeply ambivalent. In the mid-twentieth century, populist media and politicians voiced their active hostility to the emergence and consolidation of non-indigenous, minority communities, which were portrayed as threatening the cultural homogeneity and ultimately the stability of British society. The subsequent immigration acts of 1962, 1968 and 1971 aimed at restricting entry to the United Kingdom and thereafter all UK governments have sought to keep the politically sensitive immigration of non-whites to a minimum, often with the aid of questionable administrative procedures (Fenton 1996: 147–8).

While migrants from the 'New Commonwealth' (member states from non-white parts of the former British Empire) were still able to migrate to the UK, with difficulty, on the basis of kinship links and marriage, these grounds were not available to others from the Third World. Nor could they be utilised by migrants from the former Communist-ruled states of Central and Eastern Europe who travelled to the Britain and elsewhere in Western Europe after exit restrictions were removed in their home countries after 1989. Those from East-Central Europe were generally able to come to the UK as tourists without visas, even if they were intending to work as seasonal agricultural workers or in other sectors of the economy.[42] However, the general requirement of visas for states at the periphery of Eastern Europe and in the previous Soviet Union severely limited this possibility. While many entered Britain

---

[41] For a fuller elaboration of this argument, see Guy (2003: 68–70).
[42] Many others obtained short-term permission to work as domestics or au pairs.

188

illegally and do not appear on any statistics, others claimed asylum and are consequently visible.

The highest proportions for citizens of CEE states of all asylum claims lodged throughout Europe during the 1990s came from the former Yugoslavia (24%), Romania (8%) and Bulgaria (2%) (UNHCR 2000b). That the bloody civil wars of Yugoslavia should have generated up to a million refugees during this period is fully comprehensible but explaining the flight of asylum seekers from the other two states is more problematic. Nor is it clear to what extent Roma were involved. Over half of all claims made by Romanians in the decade had been lodged in 1992 and 1993 and at that time Germany was the main destination for CEE migrants including refugees. Romanian refugees decreased in numbers over the following years and they travelled to different countries but by 1999 two-thirds of their asylum claims were made in the British Isles, divided roughly equally between the United Kingdom and Ireland (UNHCR 2000c, 2000d).

During the later years of the 1990s a corresponding redirection by refugees had taken place and in 2000 the UK overtook Germany for the first time as the European country registering the highest number of asylum claims (UNHCR 2001e). Until the closing years of the twentieth century Britain had not attracted significant numbers of refugees but, by 1999, 21 per cent of all asylum claims in Europe were lodged in the UK. Of these, however, only 25 per cent were made by citizens of European states, mostly from the former Yugoslavia (82% of European claimants in the UK) (UNHCR 2000c).

Nevertheless, the increase in refugees posed particular political problems, since the start of a noticeable growth in asylum claims coincided with the first electoral victory of the Labour Party for eighteen years. Consequently, the incoming first government of Tony Blair was faced with an immediate challenge to prove its credentials on contentious 'law and order' issues as a safe replacement for the outgoing Conservatives. Barely six months after taking office, the new administration was confronted with an event that attracted widespread media attention and highlighted the increasingly vexed issue of refugees.

In the autumn of 1997, Roma asylum seekers from the Czech Republic were greeted on the day after their arrival at the main entry port to the United Kingdom with a front-page banner headline, complete with half-page photograph, 'Gypsies invade Dover, hoping for a handout' (*The Independent*, 20 October 1997). The accompanying story, referring sceptically to 'would-be immigrants ... claiming racial persecution at home', was indicative of the hostile assumptions made about Roma refugees from the outset. Even more disquieting was the fact that these views were not the prejudices of a populist tabloid but appeared in one of the most creditable, liberal daily broadsheets. Meanwhile, the tabloids were not slow to follow suit, as when the Evening Standard headline (13 November 1997) used a derisive pun to make the same allegation, announcing 'Giro Czechs hit London' (UK benefit payments were paid by Post Office (Giro) cheques).[43]

The arrival of these refugees was seen by the UK media as highly newsworthy and described as an 'invasion' or 'tidal wave', even though the estimated 1,500 or so Roma formed less than 4 per cent of all asylum seekers to the UK in that year.[44] Almost no attempts were made to discover the refugees' side of the story and the tone of the reporting was almost invariably hostile with the term 'bogus asylum seekers' becoming almost standard usage.[45] This extensive and antagonistic coverage thrust the issue to the forefront of the political agenda of the day.

The instant and widespread supposition, shared by media and politicians alike, was that these newcomers could be nothing but economic migrants, whose journeys were entirely motivated by the lure

---

[43] For a comprehensive discussion of UK media reaction, see Clark and Campbell (2000).

[44] Relatively low numbers of Roma had travelled to the United Kingdom soon after the ending of Communist rule but had attracted little attention (Kenrick 1997: 108–10).

[45] The only exceptions were more liberal UK newspapers such as *The Guardian* which, while reporting the almost unanimous condemnation by politicians of 'bogus asylum seekers', also published articles about myths about refugees (17 February), the need of the West for immigrant labour (22 March) and the positive contribution of immigrants to British life (19 April). These articles were followed by a special investigation into asylum and immigration, *Welcome to Britain* (June 2001).

of high levels of social support in the UK. On a visit to Prague, soon after their arrival, the then home office minister, Jack Straw, declared that Britain was no 'soft touch for Czech Gypsies' (*Daily Telegraph*, 28 November 1997). On the same occasion, he also voiced the scepticism of the UK Government about Roma claims of suffering persecution in the Czech Republic. Nevertheless, a junior home office minister insisted that 'each of the [asylum] cases was being considered individually' (*The Independent*, 20 October 1997). The official view, like that of other Western governments, was that although sporadic racist attacks might occasionally occur, as indeed in the West, the post-Communist regimes were democratic. By this reasoning CEE states could be regarded as safe countries, where citizens could turn to state institutions to protect their human rights and therefore had no need to emigrate as refugees.[46]

Yet, at that time, this belief was challenged by mounting evidence, not only of racist attacks by skinhead groups but also of racism within the Czech police force. Confirmation was contained in reports by domestic and international NGOs, and even by the Czech government. These suggested that the state was not only failing in its duty to offer adequate protection to its Roma citizens but, in view of its manifest inaction, could be said to be unwilling to do so. Consequently, whether actually assaulted or not, Roma were living in a general climate of fear.

In 1997, over 150 racist attacks were reported in the Czech Republic. The following year the number decreased to 138 (including two deaths) but a spokesperson for the Czech human rights organisation HOST stated that the NGO had registered 40 per cent more racist crimes than were officially recorded (Lidové noviny 1999). Only a month before Mr. Straw's speech, an authoritative Czech government report had concluded that figures for racist crimes underestimated the extent of the problem. It explained that Roma interpret the inadequate prosecution of such attacks as official 'approval and passive support [for them], and so

---

[46] This same view was upheld by the UK law lords in July 2000 when dismissing the appeal of Milan Horvath, a Roma asylum seeker from east Slovakia. Their judgement stated that 'the authorities in Slovakia are willing and able to provide protection to the required standard, and Gypsies [sic] as a class are not exempt from that protection' (*The Guardian*, 7 July 2000; *The Times* 2000).

they often do not even report these attacks' (Czech Government 1997: I 22). This was hardly surprising since the same report also revealed that 'there are ... sympathisers, even members, of the skinhead movement among the police' (Czech Government 1997: I 23).[47] Two years earlier 'an internal study by the [Czech] Interior Ministry ... [had] determined that racism was a serious problem within the police force' (Human Rights Watch 1996: 7–8).[48] The Czech judiciary was also criticised for leniency in cases of racist crimes (Czech Government 1999a: 8–9, Mladá fronta dnes 1999). There were even cases where judges refused to recognise them as such, as when a district court decided an attack could not be racist since 'the injured Roma are of the same Indo-European race as the perpetrators' (Czech Government 1999b: 4).[49] Two years later, during a period of frank reassessment of government policy towards Roma, the Czech minister of the interior made the startling admission that Roma refugees 'were right when justifying applications for asylum abroad by saying they are persecuted by skinheads' (Grohová 1999).[50]

In a critical assessment of the handling of deteriorating inter-ethnic relations between the majority population and Roma in the early years after the formation of an independent Czech state in 1993, Gabal, a leading Czech sociologist, charged the government and parliament of 'total passivity and incompetence' (Gabal 2000: 7). In his IOM report, he argued that 'the Czech government, legislature and judiciary did not react with adequate means of repression [of racism] and elevated

---

[47] Also see Jakl (1998).

[48] This charge was met with a flat denial by a police spokesperson who did not even feel the need to resort to the familiar 'just a few rotten apples' defence: 'There is no racism in the police. It's just a matter of their [police officers'] personal experiences. And a lot of them have had bad experiences with Roma. And someone dealing with them on a day by day basis could even say that every Roma is a thief. It's an individual matter' (Human Rights Watch 1996: 7–8).

[49] A Slovakian court in Banská Bystrica made a similar ruling in May 1999 (Fenyvesi 1999).

[50] In Slovakia, although there were fewer racist attacks by the public, there were reports of a more systematised violence (ERRC 1998). For example, the 1995 incident when over 100 armed and masked police, allegedly searching for stolen property, raided the largest Roma settlement of Jarovnice, attacking the inhabitants with batons, knives, chemical sprays and electric cattle prods (ERRC 1997: 36–44).

security protection of the afflicted and those at risk' (ibid.: 29). Instead of taking action, 'the Czech government continually refused to adopt any ethnic interpretation of the problem [but] ... viewed ... the growing ethnic tensions and racist violence as a fringe aberration of small groups of extremists' (ibid.: 6). While acknowledging progress since the 1997 government report and the electoral defeat of the centre-right in 1998, Gabal noted the 'paradox ... that ... [Roma] migratory behaviour has the tendency to increase exactly in the time when the ethnic climate in the Czech Republic, minimally on the level of central politics, markedly changed for the better' (ibid.: 26). In other words the damage had already been done and real changes to the situation of Roma were too slow in coming, for 'despite gradual improvements in the situation ... there have not yet been any significant repercussions on Roma status and conditions in any way' (ibid.: 9).

In early 2000, little more than two years after the arrival of Roma from the Czech Republic, it was Roma asylum seekers from Romania who were to capture the headlines,[51] although this country generated less than 5 per cent of UK claimants at this time.[52] However, the women were highly visible in their voluminous skirts as they begged with their children and their menfolk attracted criticism for alleged aggression when seeking payment for washing car windscreens. Stories were printed about Romanian villages subsisting on the illicit earnings of asylum seekers, and of gangs trafficking in people.[53] Little attempt was made to undertake serious investigation of the background to these stories and so, whatever their truth, once more Roma were presented simply as archetypal scroungers, exploiting the generosity of the UK benefits system.

---

[51] For a more detailed discussion, see Guy (2003: 70–1).
[52] For the United Kingdom figure for January 2000 was 280, for February 305 and for March 255 (UNHCR 2000f).
[53] For example, 'Town that lives off London's beggars', *Evening Standard* (UK), 29 March 2000; 'Romanians send home £20K a day', *Sunday World* (Ireland), 14 May 2000.

Extensive media coverage of the issue of asylum seekers[54] had the effect of raising this to an incredible third place in the ranking of topics of most concern to the UK public in March 2000 (Travis 2000). Meanwhile, politicians were not slow to capitalise on public opinion. The Conservative manifesto for the May 2000 local elections employed the most emotive clichés, warning that 'Labour has made this country a soft touch for the organised asylum racketeers who are flooding the country with bogus asylum seekers' (Barkham 2000b). For its part, the government demonstrated its resolve by a new immigration and asylum act, which came into force in April shortly before the elections. This introduced controversial measures such as the replacement of welfare benefits with a food voucher system of £35 a week for an adult where no change was given and forcible dispersion of asylum seekers into accommodation around the UK (Barkham 2000a). The following year the question of refugees also featured strongly in the build-up to the June 2001 general election, when the Conservative leader proposed compulsory detention of all asylum seekers. In March of that year, the Council of Europe strongly criticised the UK media for 'xenophobic and intolerant coverage' of refugee issues and the British government for 'increasingly restrictive asylum and immigration laws' (Black 2001).

Although insignificant in terms of overall numbers of refugees arriving in Britain, Roma nevertheless served a convenient symbolic purpose. Already bearing an established negative stereotype, Roma had few supporters in the UK and least of all their home states, where they were mostly despised by majority populations as marginal outsiders. Their defenceless situation allowed them to be vilified in a way unimaginable for any other group,[55] helping once more to place asylum seekers high on the political agenda of the day. However, they had a further important role to play in UK efforts to deter refugees.

---

[54] The populist, right-wing tabloid, the *Daily Mail*, published over two hundred articles on asylum seekers and refugees between 7 September 1999 and 11 July 2000 (Moller 2000).
[55] Claude Moraes of the Joint Council for the Welfare of Immigrants commented on the public response: 'this has produced more hostile calls than we have ever had before. There is an instinctive reaction just because they are Gypsies' (Clark and Campbell 2000: 58–9).

Roma as guinea pigs for new asylum measures

The People in Need report on Czech and Slovak Roma refugees in south-east England viewed proposed new UK measures for asylum seekers as seeking to improve the situation of claimants during the asylum process (People in Need 2000, April: 6-7). However, there is a manifest contradiction between different aspects of refugee policy. For while government ministers and state officials formally adhere to the spirit of the Geneva Convention, where each individual case is to be decided on its merits and treated fairly and with compassion, they are at the same time sharply aware of the pragmatic requirement to reduce refugee numbers to counter criticisms of political weakness and administrative incompetence. Therefore, while social services and NGOs, such as Migrant Helpline with Home Office support, genuinely seek to provide information and support to claimants, this takes place within a context of steadily tightening constraints on asylum seekers.

Jeanette Buirski is a leading NGO representative, currently involved in CEE Roma integration projects supported by the UK Department for International Development (DFID). In her considered view, 'current legislation in the UK is purposefully and unashamedly designed to deter refugees or asylum seekers from ever reaching the UK, and once having arrived to make it most difficult for them to stay' (Buirski 1999: 1).

Buirski drew attention to another significant consequence of the vulnerability of Roma, suggesting that they were convenient guinea pigs on which to test questionable projected measures (Buirski 1999: 15–16). She argued that 'Roma are already experiencing many of the changes proposed for other asylum seekers', listing among other such procedures '"one-stop" asylum interviews without legal representation, "presumption of detention" after refusal [of claims], ... "payment in kind" of one-off emergency payments ... [and] vetting in the near future by British immigration officers inside ... the Czech Republic' (ibid.).

One way in which Roma were singled out for special attention in 2001 was their incorporation in a short list of eight named groups, whose members were to be regarded from the outset as *prima facie* impostors when claiming asylum. They were be subjected 'to a more rigorous examination than other persons in the same circumstances', following a ministerial order in April 2001 which allowed 'discrimination on the grounds of ethnic or national origin' (Young 2001). This inequitable treatment would have breached race relations law had not the immigration service been exempted, the previous year, from the provisions of the Race Relations (Amendment) Act 2000. The justification offered by ministers was that the ruling had been made in order 'to make it easier to discriminate in favour of, say, Kosovan refugees' (ibid.). Well before the introduction of this measure, The UNHCR had earlier concluded about the reception of asylum seekers in the UK, that 'the merits of individual cases were rarely considered' (O'Nions 1999: 18).

The last measure mentioned by Buirski caused great controversy shortly after it had been introduced on 18 July 2001, when a team of twelve British immigration officers was sent to Prague. Czech TV tested the impartiality of the vetting of prospective travellers at Prague airport by attempting to send two reporters to England and filming the outcome with a hidden camera. Both reporters were provided with identical sums of money and the same story of going on holiday but while the pale-skinned Czech woman was allowed to proceed, her dark-skinned Roma male colleague was taken aside and informed he would not be permitted to enter the UK. After resulting protests by Roma activists, NGOs and Czech politicians, the scheme was suspended on 9 August, only to be resumed shortly afterwards on 22 August.[56]

British embassy officials insisted throughout that this procedure was neither a breach of Czech sovereignty nor discriminatory[57] and was

---

[56] Czech Roma activists appealed to the EC ambassador in Prague to intervene but were told that the EU could do nothing as the checks were 'the result of an agreement between two sovereign states' (Associated Press, 7 August 2001).

[57] In a case brought by a group of Czech Roma, supported by the NGO Liberty, a UK high court judge ruled in October 2002 that the checks 'were legal under international law and "no more or less objectionable" than a visa control system'. He added that that 'the existence of an "anti-Roma diatribe" and other criticism in the Czech press did not amount to evidence of racial discrimination'. The NGO launched an immediate appeal (Travis 2002b, CTK 25 October 2001).

preferably to the imposition of visas (CTK, 30 July 2001), while in the role of Roma defender appeared the unlikely figure of former premier and centre-right opposition leader, Václav Klaus, condemning the targeting of Roma in screening as 'ethnic discrimination' (ibid.).[58] The Czech premier, Miloš Zeman, who had 'signed a bilateral agreement with Britain in February [2001] introducing the scheme, publicly denounced it as racist and discriminatory but only after [the] investigative programme'[59] (Travis and Connolly 2001) and soon acquiesced to its re-introduction (CTK, 22 August 2001). Meanwhile the government's human rights commissioner, Jan Jarab,[60] also appeared to reverse his earlier position that the 'immigration checks carried out by British authorities … are likely to be discriminatory and should end as soon as possible' (Associated Press, 3 August 2001), as three weeks later he reluctantly 'welcomed … the re-imposition of the controls' as 'the best solution' (Czech radio, 23 August 2001). Mikulaš Horváth of the Romani Civic Initiative had earlier suggested that something beyond the avoidance of visa controls prompted government compliance with the scheme, saying that 'the Czech Social Democratic government wanted to enter the EU at all costs … [and] if the government had not made the agreement … Britain would have threatened to impede Czech EU entry' (CTK, 19 July 2001). Whether or not such a threat was likely, the Czech government was worried, following earlier criticism by the European Commission. In its view, progress in the 'solution of the integration of Roma into society will influence the integration of the Czech Republic into Europe' (Czech Government 2000: 24, Guy 2001b: 303).

---

[58] Klaus was the dominant politician when the 1993 Czech citizenship law was planned and approved. He scornfully dismissed widespread international and domestic criticism of anti-Roma bias as 'insignificant' (Gross 1994, Guy 2001b: 298). In 2003 he was elected president of the Czech Republic.

[59] The Czech culture minister, Pavel Dostal, admitted ' that the film had persuaded him that "skin colour plays an important role" in such checks', but the Czech minister of foreign affairs, Jan Kavan, brushed criticism aside, declaring 'Mr. Broucher [the British ambassador] has assured me that it was not a case of discrimination' (Agence France Presse, 27 July 2001).

[60] Jan Jařab was a co-founder of the influential HOST/Tolerance Foundation NGO, which played a leading role in exposing human rights abuses of Roma in the Czech Republic.

The screening continued intermittently[61] on the bizarre legal basis of 'an addendum to a consular agreement between Britain and the then [Communist-ruled] Czechoslovakia of 1975' (CTK, 24 July 2002). While the immigration officers could not directly prevent those described by the British ambassador as 'undesirable' from flying, carriers were warned that if they ignored official recommendations, they would be liable for the costs of any delay and of deportation when entry was refused – which in practice amounted to the same thing (CTK, 18 July 2001). A Czech News Agency report explained that 'airliners [sic] who denied them [Roma] access [to flights for which they had bought tickets] have done so since they fear problems with British authorities (CTK, 24 July 2001).

In an attempt to defend the scheme, Deputy Foreign Minister Martin Palouš, a former human rights activist, had argued on Czech TV that 'the checks were no limitation of people's rights and that Romanies can apply for asylum at the [British] embassy in Prague'. This claim had been flatly contradicted the following week by a British embassy spokesperson, who insisted that 'in the Czech Republic it is only possible to ask for a permit to enter Britain'. 'Any request for asylum submitted in Prague will be rejected, he stressed, adding that all previous requests for asylum in Britain had been turned down [initially]' (CTK, 24 July 2001). Although the Czech Republic 'is the only country in the world where British immigration officials quiz passengers before they get on a plane for the UK' (Mitchell and O'Flynn 2001), this '"pre-entry clearance" scheme ... could have [been] extended across the Balkans if it had proved a success' (Travis and Connolly 2001).

In a more recent innovation, in September 2002, Roma were the first asylum seekers to be filmed when being deported as they were put aboard a charter flight to Prague. On the same day, a new round of

---

[61] Vetting was re-introduced whenever there was a marked increase in numbers of passengers attempting to claim asylum in the UK and allowed to lapse when numbers fell. The 23 June – 11 July period of screening was already the twelfth round of such checks since the scheme started (CTK, 24 July 2002). At this time the Czech Republic ranked twelfth among countries whose nationals were seeking asylum in the UK (Mitchell and O'Flynn 2001).

screening began after a two-week pause (CTK, 9 September 2002). The filming exercise served a double function. Following only a week after the admission by the home secretary, David Blunkett, that an earlier target for removal of failed refugees was 'over-ambitious',[62] it 'was designed to demonstrate to the public both in Britain and the Czech Republic that rejected asylum seekers were being removed from the UK' (Travis 2002a, iDNES 2002).[63] It was predicted that the filmed deportations would be shown on Czech TV, perhaps in the hope that if a rose-tinted TV documentary had attracted Czech Roma to the UK in the first place, another screening conveying a far less positive message might deter them.

At the same time the Czech government was also pursuing a more constructive strategy as Premier Vladimir Spidla appealed to Roma to stay: 'I call on our citizens belonging to the Roma community – do not leave. ... Let's try to tackle your problems here, in the Czech Republic' (Associated Press, 1 August 2002). Deputy Premier Petr Mareš followed, pledging a government-funded 'action plan' comprising projects to support education and employment of Roma, as well as taking action against the usurers who preyed on the impoverished Roma (CTK, 4 August 2002). However, the hard line was still maintained, as failed asylum seekers were to 'lose [the] right to receive social allowances retrospectively after their return to the Czech Republic (ibid.). Likewise, deputy premier and Czech Justice Minister Pavel Rychetský argued that 'the mass exodus of Czech Romanies to Great Britain should be solved by the prepared tightening of British asylum laws ... [to] allow for the return of those whose applications are rejected to happen within hours instead of months or years as is the case today' (CTK, 9 September 2002). This declaration was made shortly before the deportation, following a meeting with Lord Irvine, his British legal counterpart. A month later the home secretary confirmed the 'white list' status of EU applicants as 'safe countries'

---

[62] The target was '30,000 removals a year of failed asylum seekers. The number is running at 12,000' (Travis 2002a).

[63] 'It is believed that the previous home secretary, Jack Straw, rejected on human rights grounds the idea of filming deportations when immigration officials first raised the idea'. Experimental TV screenings of deportations were first attempted in the US on local stations along the Mexican border but 'the scheme backfired' (Travis 2002a).

and cited the arrival that summer of asylum seekers from two states, the Czech Republic and Poland, in justification of new criteria for withholding benefit payments from refugees in the UK (BBC 2002).

Future prospects

By 2002, several CEE applicants for EU membership, most notably Hungary, the Czech Republic, Slovakia, Romania and Bulgaria, had adopted comprehensive strategies to integrate their Roma minorities, supported by EU funding to promote political change and economic restructuring under the Phare programme (European Commission 2002). As part of this change, some progress has also been made in introducing legislation against discrimination. Nevertheless, the prognosis of the two most economically advanced states with large Roma populations, the Czech Republic and Hungary, is that socio-economic equalisation for Roma will not be achieved for about twenty years. In the meantime, CEE governments continue to be both embarrassed and politically threatened by the fluctuating westward haemorrhage of their Roma citizens. Consequently, to avoid appearing to violate the political criteria on minority rights of the accession partnerships, governments of the region – of whatever political colour – have been complicit in sharing the Western view of Romani migration as overwhelmingly if not entirely motivated by economic considerations.

For their part Western governments, including the UK, have shown no little hypocrisy in unwaveringly proclaiming this interpretation when confronted by Roma refugees, whatever the situation in their homelands. This stance has been maintained in the face of repeated charges by the EC of continuing discrimination in CEE countries and some scepticism about the implementation on integration programmes. For example, in October 1999 the EC concluded that

> deep-rooted prejudice in many of the candidate countries continues to result in discrimination against the Roma in social and economic life. There has been an increasing incidence of racially-motivated violence against the Roma which has not received the unequivocal response from the authorities which it demands.
>
> (European Commission 1999: 4)

Moreover, in spite of the introduction in June 2000 of the EC anti-discrimination directive 'to combat discrimination on the grounds of racial or ethnic origin', on the basis of article 13 of the Amsterdam Treaty, the response of the UK soon afterwards was to increase its levels of ethnic discrimination. Perhaps the hope was that the ministerial order naming specific ethnic groups and the vetting of would-be travellers at Prague airport, together with other measures, would have done their job by July 2003 when the directive was due to come into force for EU member states (European Commission 2002: 5–6).

The studies in 2000, discussed in this article, revealed that while economic considerations were of great importance to migrants, these formed part of a far more complex picture of motivation which frequently involved a desperate bid to cling on to their previously achieved status, both for themselves and their children. For many Roma, migration was far more than a means of making money but was seen as the only course open to them to avoid being thrust back into the ghetto of stigmatised debtors. At the same time it was an attempt to gain respect and freedom from fear in what Roma experienced as more tolerant, multicultural societies and, paradoxically, where many found it easier to integrate than in their own homelands in spite of cultural and language barriers. To them, therefore, the act of migrating represented an affirmation of their identity as full human beings.

What the studies also reported was that migration was likely to continue. Gabal was scathing about ill-informed Czech officials, who believed in Spring 2000 that the situation had already stabilised, whereas everywhere the researchers visited they found 'Roma in [a] very pro-migratory mood' (Gabal 2000: 39). Likewise, Vašečka noted that the previous pattern of emigration from very specific places in Slovakia was changing, for 'the strategy of migration has begun to be applied by new Roma communities living in other localities ... [widening] the group of potential migrants'. He offered a 'tentative estimate of ... anywhere from 20,000 to 50,000 people from eastern Slovakia' (Vašečka I. 2000: 167).[64]

Since these predictions were made in early 2000, Roma migration from Slovakia has continued although UNHCR statistics show decreasing numbers of claims from 4,977 in 1999, to 4.543 in 2000, and 2,800 in 2001 (UNHCR 2002a). However, the figure for the first six months of 2002 was already 1,829, suggesting an increase (UNHCR 2002c).[65] No claims by Slovak Roma were recorded in this half year for the UK but Czech (600) and Romanian Roma (540) returned once more in significant numbers (UNHCR 2002d, 2002e).[66] In response, further rounds of vetting were introduced at Prague airport (CTK, 12 July 2002). Like Slovak Roma, those from the Czech Republic also travelled to Scandinavia as did Roma from Romania and Bulgaria (CTK, 26 June 2002; Agence France Presse, 4 June 2002).

Until now the UK remains the largest recipient of those lodging asylum claims in Europe, taking a full 25 per cent in spite of stringent measures to reduce refugee numbers (UNHCR 2002b), and a similar proportion of those arriving are granted asylum (ECRE 2002a). Meanwhile, the estimated UK refugee population of 169,370 at the end of 2000 represented only 0.29 per cent of the UK population as opposed to around 1 percent in the Netherlands and Germany and approaching 2 percent in Sweden (ECRE 2002b).

---

[64] Vašečka characterised potential migrants from east Slovakia as 'members of the so-called Roma middle class, young to middle-aged, who do not live in shacks in [rural] Roma settlements' but possess 'relatively high social prestige'. Important factors, but less so, were 'a low degree of integration of Roma and non-Roma ... [in] the local community' and, interestingly, 'an increased degree of anomie among the dominant population of the local community' (Vašečka, I. 2000: 167).

[65] For the first six months of 2002 the Slovak migrants' destinations were Sweden (482), Norway (222), Germany (384) and Belgium (374), while a smaller number (126) sought asylum in the Czech Republic. These figures include dependants, unlike those for the UK (UNHCR 2002d, 2002e).

[66] During these months 602 Romanian Roma lodged asylum claims in Ireland (UNHCR 2002d, 2002e).

EU enlargement, scheduled to start in 2004, is expected to make the situation even more problematic and the first applicants to be admitted are likely to include the Czech and Slovak Republics, Poland and Hungary. While the general process of globalisation encourages mobility of labour, the EU in particular posits free movement for citizens of member states (Castle-Kaněrová 2001). However, a September 2001 survey in Poland by leading Western consultants PricewaterhouseCoopers 'found that 40 per cent of the adult working population, or 6 million people, would like to live and work in another European country (*The Guardian*, 29 September 2001). Although some form of limitation may be introduced to prevent a sudden population influx from new entrants, according to a UN study on migration in 2000 'Europeans will need to rely increasingly on immigrants to pay their pensions because of declining birth rates' (Ellison 2000). In the UK the alternative of raising the retirement age is now being actively considered (Haurant 2002). Such potential developments rather put Roma migration and asylum seeking in perspective.

References

Acković, D. (2003) 'Migration by Roma from former Yugoslavia', in this collection.

Acton, T. (1974) *Gypsy Politics and Social Change*, London: Routledge and Kegan Paul.

Barany, Z. (2002) *The East European Gypsies: Regime Change, Marginality, and Ethnopolitics*, Cambridge: Cambridge University Press.

Barkham, P. (2000a) 'How does asylum work?', *The Guardian*, 9 February.

Barkham, P. (2000b) 'Are our politicans racist?', *The Guardian*, 19 April.

BBC (2002) 'Today', *BBC Radio Four*, 7 October.

Black, I. (2001) 'UK "most racist" in Europe on refugees', *The Guardian*, 3 April.

Braham, M. and Braham, M. (2000) 'Romani migrations and EU enlargement', *Cambridge Review of International Affairs* XIII, 2, spring-summer.

Buirski, J. (1999) 'The Rom [sic] and UK immigration and asylum law', *The Legal Protection of Rom in Contemporary Europe*, European Information Centre, Charles University, Prague, 28–29 June.

Cahn, C. and Vermeersch, P. (2000) 'The group expulsion of Slovak Roma by the Belgian government: A case study of the treatment of Romani refugees in Western countries', *Cambridge Review of International Affairs*, vol. XIII/2, spring/summer.

Castle-Kaněrová, M. (2001) 'Romani refugees: The EU dimension', in W. Guy (ed.).

Clark, C. and Campbell, E. (2000) 'Gypsy invasion: A critical analysis of newspaper reaction to Czech and Slovak Romani asylum seekers in Britain, 1997', *Romani Studies*, series 5, vol. 10, no. 1.

Clébert, J.-P. (1967) *The Gypsies*, Harmondsworth: Penguin.

Crowe, D. M. (1994) *A History of the Gypsies of Eastern Europe and Russia*,
New York: St. Martins Griffin.

Czech Government (1997) *Report on the Situation of the Romani Community in the Czech Republic and Government Measures Assisting its Integration in Society*, (known as the Bratinka Report), Prague: Office of Minister without Portfolio, accepted 29 October.

Czech Government (1999a) *Information about Compliance with Principles set forth in the Framework Convention for the Protection of National Minorities according to Article 25, Paragraph 1 of this Convention*, Government of the Czech Republic, April.

Czech Government (1999b) *Draft Conception of Government Policy towards Members of the Romani Community designed to facilitate their social integration*, Decision 279, Government of Czech Republic, draft approved 7 April 1999.

Czech Government (2000) *Conception of Government Policy towards Members of the Romani Community designed to facilitate their social integration*, Decision 599, Government of Czech Republic, approved 14 June 2000.

ECRE (2002a) 'Recognition rates as a percentage of total decisions', *The Real Facts about Asylum and Migration in the EU*,

European Council on Refugees and Exiles, figures from Population Data Unit, UNHCR.

ECRE (2002b) 'Refugees per 1,000 inhabitants in the EU', *The Real Facts about Asylum and Migration in the EU*, figures from Population Data Unit, UNHCR.

Ellison, M. (2000) 'Immigrants needed to save west from crisis', *The Guardian*, 22 March.

ERRC (1997) *Time of the Skinheads: Denial and Exclusion of Roma in Slovakia*, European Roma Rights Center, Country Reports Series, 3, Budapest: ERRC, January.

ERRC (1998) 'Police raid in Rudňany, central Slovakia', *Roma Rights*, Budapest: ERRC, summer.

European Commission (1999) *Enlargement Briefing*: *EU Support for Roma Communities in Central and Eastern Europe*, Brussels: European Commission, December.

European Commission (2002) *Enlargement Briefing*: *EU Support for Roma Communities in Central and Eastern Europe*, Brussels: European Commission, May.

Fenton, S. (1996) 'Counting ethnicity', in R. Levitas and W. Guy (eds) *Interpreting Official Statistics*, London: Routledge.

Fenyvesi, C. (1999) 'The Romani flight to Helsinki - neither the first nor the last', *RFE/RL Watchlist*, 1, 26, 15 July.

Gabal (2000) *Analysis of the Migration Climate and Migration Tendencies to Western European Countries in Selected Cities in the Czech Republic*, Research report for IOM Prague, Gabal Analysis and Consulting, Prague: IOM, May.

Gheorghe, N. (1997) 'The social construction of Romani identity', in T. Acton (ed.) *Gypsy Politics and Traveller Identity*, Hatfield: University of Hertfordshire Press, 153–63.

Gheorghe, N. and Hedman, H. (2000) 'Visa versus vision: The survey of Roma asylum seeking in Finland 1999-2000', working paper, *Meeting on Roma Migration*, Tarnów, 22-24 July.

Grohová, J. (1999) 'Stále více lidi sympatizuje s extremisty', *Mladá fronta dnes*, 15 July.

Gross, T. (1994) 'A blot on the conscience: Czech attitudes on citizenship for gypsies come under fire', *Financial Times*, Supplement on Czech Republic, 19 December.

Guy, W. (2001a) 'Romani identity and post-Communist policy', in W. Guy (ed.).

Guy, W. (2001b) 'The Czech lands and Slovakia: Another false dawn?', in W. Guy (ed.).

Guy, W. (ed.) (2001) *Between Past and Future: the Roma of Central and Eastern Europe*, Hatfield: University of Hertfordshire Press.

Guy, W. (2003) '"No soft touch": Romani migration to the UK at the turn of the
21st century', *Nationalities Papers*, Vol. 31, no. 1, March.

Haurant, S. (2002) 'State pensions age may rise', *The Guardian*, 20 September.

Hobsbawm, E. J. (1992) 'Who's fault-line is it anyway?', *New Statesman and Society*, 24 April.

Home Office (1999a) *Home Office Statistical Bulletin: Asylum Statistics United Kingdom 1998*, 27 May (cited Braham and Braham 2000: 98).

Home Office (1999b) *Asylum Statistics: January - December1999 United Kingdom*.

Home Office (2000) *Asylum Statistics United Kingdom 1999*, 12 October.

Home Office (2001) *Asylum Statistics United Kingdom 2000*, 25 September.

Home Office (2002a) 'Table 2.1. Applications received for asylum in the United Kingdom, excluding dependents, by nationality, 1993 to 2001', *Asylum Statistics United Kingdom 2001*, 31 July.

Home Office (2002b) 'Table 3.1. Cases recognised as refugees and granted asylum , excluding dependents, by nationality, 1993 to 2001', Initial decisions made on applications received, *Asylum Statistics United Kingdom 2001*, 31 July.

Home Office (2002c) *Asylum Statistics United Kingdom 2001*, 31 July.

iDNES (2002) 'Britové deportují stále více Čechů', *iDNES*, 20 September.

Human Rights Watch (1996) *Roma in the Czech Republic: Foreigners in their Own Land*, Human Rights Watch/Helsinki Report, 8, 11(D), NewYork: Human Rights Watch.

IOM (2000a) *World Migration Report*, International Organisation for Migration, IOM: Geneva.

IOM (2000b) 'Brief summary of findings', *Return and Counselling Assistance of Asylum Seekers from Czech Republic, Romania and Slovakia Currently Living in Belgium, Finland and the Netherlands*, IOM research on Roma migration from four former East European countries, (Hungary was included later), Prague/Bucharest/Bratislava/Budapest: IOM.

Jakl, R. (1998) 'Police struggle with own racial prejudice', Prague Post on-line, March 4.

Kenrick, D. (1997) 'Foreign Gypsies and British immigration law after 1945', in T. Acton (ed.) *Gypsy Politics and Traveller Identity*, Hatfield: University of Hertfordshire Press.

Kenrick, D. (2001) 'Former Yugoslavia: A patchwork of destinies', in W. Guy (ed.).

Kovats, M. (2001) 'The emergence of European Roma policy', in W. Guy (ed.).

Lee, R. (2000) 'Post-Communist migration to Canada', *Cambridge Review of International Affairs*, vol. XIII/2 spring/summer.

Lemon, A. (1996) 'No land, no contracts for Romani workers', *Transition*, 2, 13, 28 June.

Lidové noviny (1999) 'Rasových trestných činů ubylo, počet skinheadů naopak vrostl', 15 July.

Matras, Y. (2000) 'Romani migrations in the post-Communist era: their historical and political significance', *Cambridge Review of International Affairs*, vol. XIII/2 spring/summer.

McNiffe, M. and Lane, D. (2000) 'Ruthless gangs prey on refugees', *Sunday World*, Ireland, 14 May.

Mirga, A. and Gheorghe, N. (1997) *The Roma in the Twenty-First Century: a Policy Paper*, Princeton: Project on Ethnic Relations (PER).

Mitchell, A. and O'Flynn, P. (2001) 'Airport screening halts flow of bogus refugees', *The Express*, August 28.

Mladá fronta dnes (1999) 'Za rasové motivované činy bývají často nízké tresty', 15 July.

Moller, T. B. (2000) 'Are we a tolerant nation?' *Reader's Digest UK - Magazine*, September.

Mróz, L. (2001) 'Poland: The clash of tradition and modernity', in W. Guy (ed.).

Naegele, J. (1999) 'Slovak authorities suspect "plot" behind Romany exodus to Finland', *Radio Free Europe*, 14 July.

O'Nions, H. (1999) 'Bonafide or bogus?: Roma asylum seekers from the Czech Republic', *Web Journal of Current Legal Issues*, Blackstone Press.

People in Need (2000) *Zpráva z Doveru* (Report from Dover), Phare-funded project, *Člověk v tísni* (People in Need), January and April.

Radio Prague (1998) 'Romanies come home', *Radio Prague*, 15 June.

PER (2000) *Roma and the Government in Slovakia: The Debate over Migration*, Project on Ethnic Relations roundtable in Bratislava, 13-14 March, Princeton: PER.

Raeymaekers, T. (1999) 'A Western European failure to respect human rights', *The New Presence*, November.

Ringold, D. (2000) *Roma and the Transition in Central and Eastern Europe: Trends and Challenges*, Washington, D.C: The World Bank, September.

Said, E. (1995) *Orientalism: Western Conceptions of the Orient*, London: Penguin.

Tebbut, S. (2001) 'Germany and Austria: The "Mauer im Kopf" or virtual wall', in W. Guy (ed.).

The Times (2000) 'Horvath v Secretary of State for the Home Department', *The Times*, Law Report, 7 July.

Travis, A. (2000) 'Fast-track curb on beggars', *The Guardian*, 20 March.

Travis, A. (2002a) 'Home Office films Roma deportation: Asylum policy critics say tactic "verges on the obscene"', *The Guardian*, 21 September.

Travis, A. (2002b) 'Blunkett wins challenge on Roma rights', *The Guardian*, 11 October.

Travis, A. and Connolly, K. (2001) 'Britain forced to end "discriminatory" watch on would-be Czech migrants', *The Guardian*, 8 August.

UNHCR (1997) *The State of the World's Refugees: A Humanitarian Agenda*, United Nations High Commissioner for Refugees, Geneva: UNHCR.

UNHCR (2000a) 'Table 6a - Slovakia, Monthly asylum applications lodged in Europe, 1999', *Asylum Applications in Europe, 1999*.

UNHCR (2000b) 'Table VI.7. Origin of asylum applicants by year of application, 1990-1999', *Refugees and others of concern to UNHCR, 1999 Statistical Overview*.

UNHCR (2000c) 'Table VI.1. Origin of asylum applicants, 1999', *Refugees and others of concern to UNHCR, 1999 Statistical Overview*.

UNHCR (2000d) 'Table VI.8 Asylum applications submitted in Ireland, 1996-1999', *Refugees and others of concern to UNHCR, 1999 Statistical Overview*.

UNHCR (2001e) 'Table V.2 Asylum applications submitted in selected countries, 1990-1999', *Refugees and others of concern to UNHCR, 1999 Statistical Overview*.

UNHCR (2000f) 'Table 4. Top-10 nationalities by country of asylum in Europe, January-March 2000', *Asylum Applications in Europe, First Quarter 2000*.

UNHCR (2001a) 'Table 4. Origin of asylum applicants in Europe, 1999 and 2000', *Asylum Applications Submitted in Europe, 2000*.

UNHCR (2001b) 'Table 6. Origin of asylum applicants in Europe by country of asylum, 2000', *Asylum Applications Submitted in Europe, 2000*.

UNHCR (2002a) 'Table 4. 'Top-40 nationalities of asylum applicants in 28 industrialised countries, 1999-2001', *Trends in Asylum Applications in Europe, North America, Australia, and New Zealand, 2001: updated tables*, 1 March.

UNHCR (2002b) 'Table 1. 'Monthly asylum applications submitted in 29, mostly industrialised, countries, 2002', notes, *Trends in Asylum Applications in Europe, North America, Australia, New Zealand and Japan, January–June 2002*, 2 September.

UNHCR (2002c) 'Table 3. 'Quarterly asylum applications submitted in 24 European countries, 2002', *Trends in Asylum Applications in Europe, North America, Australia, New Zealand and Japan, January–June 2002*, 2 September.

UNHCR (2002d) 'Table 4. 'Asylum applications submitted in 20, mostly industrialised, countries, January to March 2002', *Trends in Asylum Applications in Europe, North America, Australia, New Zealand and Japan, January–June 2002*, 2 September.

UNHCR (2002e) 'Table 5. 'Asylum applications submitted in 20, mostly industrialised, countries, April to June 2002', *Trends in Asylum Applications in Europe, North America, Australia, New Zealand and Japan, January–June 2002*, 2 September.

Vašečka, I. (2000) 'Profile and situation of asylum seekers and potential migrants into EU member states from the Slovak Republic', ch. 5 in Vašečka, M. *et al.*

Vašečka, M. and Džambazovič, R. (2000) 'Of the social and economic situation of potential asylum seekers from the Slovak Republic', ch. 1 in Vašečka, M. *et al.*

Vašečka, M., Džambazovič, R., Repová, I., Vašečka, I. and Pišútová, K. (2000) *Social and Economic Situation of Potential Asylum Seekers from the Slovak Republic*, Bratislava: IOM, June.

Verspaget, J. (1995) *The Situation of Gypsies (Roma and Sinti) in Europe*, Strasbourg: Council of Europe.

World Bank (2002) *Poverty and Welfare of Roma in the Slovak Republic*, Bratislava:The World Bank/Foundation S.P.A.C.E. /INEKO/OSI, April.

Young, H. (2001) 'Labour's law of ethnic punishment shames us all', *The Guardian*, 8 May.

Osteuropa: Geschichte, Wirtschaft, Politik

herausgegeben von Wolfgang Eichwede,
Frank Golczewski und Günter Trautmann †

Gabriele Clemens (Hg.)
Die Integration der mittel- und osteuropäischen Staaten in die Europäische Union
Bd. 1, 2000, 272 S., 20,90 €, br., ISBN 3-8258-4339-4

Jerzy Jaroslaw Maćków
Die Krise des Totalitarismus in Polen
Die Totalitarismus-Theorie als Analyse-Konzept des sowjetsozialistischen Staates. Eine Analyse der System- und Strukturkrise der Volksrepublik Polen in den siebziger und achtziger Jahren
Bd. 2, 1992, 344 S., 22,90 €, br., ISBN 3-89473-369-1

Jürgen Fischer; Frank Messner;
Karl Wohlmuth (Hrsg.)
Die Transformation der osteuropäischen Länder in die Marktwirtschaft
Marktentwicklung und Kooperationschancen
Bd. 3, 1992, 529 S., 30,90 €, br., ISBN 3-89473-381-0

Andreas Fraude
"Reformsozialismus" statt "Realsozialismus"?
Von der SED zur PDS
Bd. 4, 1993, 152 S., 15,90 €, br., ISBN 3-89473-906-1

Beate Eschment
Die "Große Reform"?
Die Bauernreform von 1861 in Rußland in der vorrevolutionären Geschichtsschreibung
Bd. 5, 1994, 320 S., 30,90 €, br., ISBN 3-89473-987-8

Hauke Wendler
Rußlands Presse zwischen Unabhängigkeit und Zensur
Die Rolle der Printmedien im Prozeß des politischen Systemwandels 1990 bis 1993
Bd. 6, 1995, 160 S., 17,90 €, br., ISBN 3-8258-2460-8

Kirsten Westphal
Hegemon statt Partner – Rußlands Politik gegenüber dem "nahen Ausland"
Bd. 7, 1995, 200 S., 17,90 €, br., ISBN 3-8258-2627-9

Julia von Blumenthal
Der Präsident Rußlands im Demokratisierungsprozeß
Garant der Stabilität oder Wegbereiter der Diktatur?
Bd. 8, 1996, 184 S., 17,90 €, br., ISBN 3-8258-2642-2

Claus Neukirch
Die Republik Moldau
Nations- und Staatsbildung in Osteuropa
Bd. 9, 1996, 152 S., 17,90 €, br., ISBN 3-8258-2730-5

Christian Henry Koepke
Der Untergang des SED-Regimes
Machtpathologien und Systemzusammenbruch in der DDR
Bd. 10, 1996, 184 S., 17,90 €, br., ISBN 3-8258-2740-2

Katrin Benner
Der Vielvölkerstaat Kasachstan
Ethnische Heterogenität in friedlicher Koexistenz?
Bd. 11, 1996, 152 S., 17,90 €, br., ISBN 3-8258-2863-8

Dirk-Arne Walckhoff
Der 13. August 1961 in der Traditionsarbeit der Grenztruppen der DDR
Bd. 13, 1997, 160 S., 17,90 €, br., ISBN 3-8258-2926-x

Gabriele Gorzka; Rainer Stöttner (Hrsg.)
Banken, Kreditmärkte, Projekt-Finanzierung in Osteuropa
Länderschwerpunkte Bulgarien, Polen, Rumänien, Ungarn
Bd. 14, 1996, 216 S., 19,90 €, br., ISBN 3-8258-2840-9

Anneke Hudalla
Der Beitritt der Tschechischen Republik zur Europäischen Union
Eine Fallstudie zu den Auswirkungen der EU-Osterweiterung auf die finalité politique des europäischen Integrationsprozesses
Bd. 15, 1997, 192 S., 17,90 €, br., ISBN 3-8258-2994-4

Olaf Steffen
Die Einführung des Kapitalismus in Rußland
Ursachen, Programme und Krise der Transformationspolitik
Bd. 16, 1997, 832 S., 50,90 €, br., ISBN 3-8258-3290-2

LIT Verlag Münster – Hamburg – Berlin – Wien – London
Grevener Str./Fresnostr. 2 48159 Münster
Tel.: 0251 – 23 50 91 – Fax: 0251 – 23 19 72
e-Mail: vertrieb@lit-verlag.de – http://www.lit-verlag.de

Maximilian Puchner
Černobyl'
Ein Beitrag zu den Ursachen, Auswirkungen
und politischen Implikationen der
Reaktorexplosion vom 26. April 1986
Bd. 17, 1998, 160 S., 20,90 €, br., ISBN 3-8258-3621-5

Andreas Wittkowsky
Fünf Jahre ohne Plan: Die Ukraine
1991 – 96
Nationalstaatsbildung, Wirtschaft und Eliten
Bd. 18, 1998, 240 S., 19,90 €, br., ISBN 3-8258-3622-3

Markus Soldner
Russlands Čečnja-Politik seit 1993
Der Weg in den Krieg vor dem Hintergrund
innenpolitischer Machtverschiebungen
Bd. 19, 1999, 272 S., 22,90 €, br., ISBN 3-8258-3637-1

Regina Heller
Russische Interessen im Balkankonflikt
Rußland und die internationale Staatenwelt
seit 1992
Bd. 20, 1998, 192 S., 20,90 €, br., ISBN 3-8258-3696-7

Eva Maria Hinterhuber
Die Soldatenmütter Sankt Petersburg
Zwischen Neotraditionalismus und neuer
Widerständigkeit
Bd. 21, 1999, 160 S., 20,90 €, br., ISBN 3-8258-3932-x

Lars Jockheck
Der "Völkische Beobachter" über Polen
1932 – 1934
Eine Fallstudie zum Übergang vom
"Kampfblatt" zur "Regierungszeitung"
Bd. 22, 1999, 152 S., 20,90 €, br., ISBN 3-8258-4359-9

Elke Fein
Geschichtspolitik in Rußland
Chancen und Schwierigkeiten einer
demokratisierenden Aufarbeitung der
sowjetischen Vergangenheit am Beispiel der
Tätigkeit der Gesellschaft MEMORIAL
Bd. 23, 2000, 288 S., 20,90 €, br., ISBN 3-8258-4416-1

Katja Tamchina
Die Europäische Union und Ungarn
Fortschritte und Hindernisse auf dem Weg zur
Osterweiterung
Bd. 24, 2000, 144 S., 17,90 €, br., ISBN 3-8258-4541-9

Anne Sunder-Plaßmann
Rettung oder Massenmord?
Die Repressionen der Stalin-Ära in der
öffentlichen Diskussion seit dem Beginn der
Perestrojka
Bd. 25, 2000, 176 S., 17,90 €, br., ISBN 3-8258-4619-9

Heiko Schrader; Manfred Glagow;
Dmitri Gavra; Michael Kleineberg (Hg.)
Russland auf dem Weg zur
Zivilgesellschaft?
Studien zur gesellschaftlichen
Selbstorganisation in St. Petersburg
Bd. 26, 2000, 192 S., 19,90 €, br., ISBN 3-8258-4735-7

Gerrit Stratmann
Donor Coordination of Economic
Assistance to Eastern Europe
Mechanisms and Origins of Sectoral
Governance in International Relations. With a
preface by Hartmut Elsenhans
Bd. 27, 2000, 288 S., 20,90 €, br., ISBN 3-8258-4550-8

Karl-Heinz Schlarp
Zwischen Konfrontation und Kooperation
Die Anfangsjahre der deutsch-sowjetischen
Wirtschaftsbeziehungen in der Ära Adenauer
Bd. 28, 2000, 416 S., 45,90 €, gb., ISBN 3-8258-5055-2

Esther Meier
Eine Theorie für "Entwicklungsländer"
Sowjetische Agitation und Afghanistan
1978 – 1982
Bd. 29, 2001, 152 S., 17,90 €, br., ISBN 3-8258-5298-9

Michaela Tzankoff
Der Transformationsprozess in
Bulgarien und die Entwicklung der
postsozialistischen Medienlandschaft
Bulgarien gehört zu den Transformationslän-
dern Osteuropas, deren Entwicklung bislang
vergleichsweise wenig Beachtung gefunden hat.
Das vorliegende Buch zeichnet den Transformationsprozess Bulgariens seit 1989 nach, die
politische und wirtschaftliche Entwicklung und
besonders die neu entstandene Medienlandschaft.
Zudem wird ein theoretischer Zugang zum Zu-
sammenhang von Medien und Transformation
eröffnet.
Bd. 30, 2002, 200 S., 20,90 €, br., ISBN 3-8258-5948-7

LIT Verlag Münster – Hamburg – Berlin – Wien – London
Grevener Str./Fresnostr. 2 48159 Münster
Tel.: 0251 – 23 50 91 – Fax: 0251 – 23 19 72
e-Mail: vertrieb@lit-verlag.de – http://www.lit-verlag.de

Ingrid Oswald; Eckhard Dittrich;
Viktor Voronkov (Hg.)
Wandel alltäglicher Lebensführung in Russland
Besichtigungen des ersten
Transformationsjahrzents in St. Petersburg
„… und überhaupt ist alles viel viel schneller geworden", so faßt eine Wissenschaftlerin aus St. Petersburg den Wandel im Alltags- und Arbeitsleben zusammen. Wer sich den neuen Anforderungen nicht fügt und seine Lebensführung rationalisiert, dem droht der soziale Absturz, könnte man annehmen. Doch dagegen werden alle verfügbaren Ressourcen mobilisiert: Familie, Freunde und Bekannte, Beziehungen, Zweit- und Drittbeschäftigungen. Letztlich verändert sich alles, doch die früheren Gewohnheiten sind unverkennbar. In welche Richtung sich die post-sowjetische Gesellschaft entwickelt ist dabei noch offen: hin zu apolitischer Improvisation auf Dauer oder hin zu einem „kooperativen Individualismus", der durchaus auch ein Handlungsmuster für westliche Gesellschaften sein könnte.
Bd. 31, 2002, 240 S., 17,90 €, br., ISBN 3-8258-5805-7

Jakob Fruchtmann; Heiko Pleines
Wirtschaftskulturelle Faktoren in der russischen Steuergesetzgebung und Steuerpraxis
Das vorliegende Buch untersucht das russische Steuersystem in seinem wirtschaftskulturellen und gesellschaftlichen Kontext. Die politische Motivation hinter der Steuerreform 2000/01, ihre Auswirkungen auf Föderalstaat und Sozialsystem sowie die Reaktionen zentraler gesellschaftlicher Gruppen werden im ersten Teil analysiert. Der zweite Teil des Buches beschreibt dann Probleme der Steuerpraxis, die von Steuerzahlungen in Güterform über Verhandelbarkeit von Steuerzahlungen und Korruption bis zur Steuerhinterziehung reichen.
Bd. 32, 2002, 208 S., 20,90 €, br., ISBN 3-8258-6257-7

Heiko Pleines
Wirtschaftseliten und Politik im Russland der Jelzin-Ära (1994 – 99)
Das vorliegende Buch untersucht die politische Rolle von Wirtschaftseliten in Russland unter Präsident Jelzin. Einleitend wird der politische Entscheidungsprozess beschrieben und die relevanten Akteure auf Seiten von Staat und Wirtschaft werden vorgestellt. Neben den „Oligarchen", einflussreichen Unternehmerpersönlichkeiten, die durch politische Korruption und Medienschlachten Beachtung gefunden haben, werden dabei auch alternative Akteure, etwa die Agrarlobby und der Kohlebergbau berücksichtigt. Die konkreten Interaktionen zwischen Wirtschaftseliten und staatlichen Akteuren werden abschließend anhand einer Fallstudie zur Unternehmensbesteuerung illustriert.
Bd. 33, 2003, 448 S., 30,90 €, br., ISBN 3-8258-6561-4

Henrike Anders
Ukrainisch-katholische Gemeinden in Norddeutschland nach 1945
Die Ukrainische Katholische Kirche (UKK) in Deutschland hat ihren zentralen Sitz seit 1945 in München. Henrike Anders untersucht die Entstehung der drei norddeutschen Gemeinden Berlin, Hamburg und Hannover nach 1945. Die Anwesenheit ukrainischer Displaced Persons (DPs) in Westdeutschland ermöglichte die Einrichtung dieser kirchlichen Zentren. Besonders interessiert der Einfluß der UKK auf das Selbstverständnis der „Heimatlosen Ausländer" in ihrer religiösen und nationalen Identität unter den unterschiedlichen politischen Bedingungen vor 1945, danach und seit der Selbständigkeit der Ukraine 1991.
Bd. 35, 2003, 176 S., 17,90 €, br., ISBN 3-8258-6606-8

Osteuropa-Studien
herausgegeben von Prof. Dr. Margareta Mommsen und PD Dr. Ellen Bos (Universität München)

Silvia von Steinsdorff
Rußland auf dem Weg zur Meinungsfreiheit
Bd. 1, 1994, 352 S., 24,90 €, br., ISBN 3-89473-907-x

Margareta Mommsen; Ellen Bos;
Silvia von Steinsdorff (Hg.)
Demokratie-Experimente im Postkommunismus
Politischer und institutioneller Wandel in Osteuropa
Bd. 2, 1995, 208 S., 17,90 €, br., ISBN 3-89473-892-8

LIT Verlag Münster – Hamburg – Berlin – Wien – London
Grevener Str./Fresnostr. 2 48159 Münster
Tel.: 0251 – 23 50 91 – Fax: 0251 – 23 19 72
e-Mail: vertrieb@lit-verlag.de – http://www.lit-verlag.de

Lydia Klötzel
Die Rußlanddeutschen zwischen
Autonomie und Auswanderung
Die Geschicke einer nationalen Minderheit
vor dem Hintergrund des wechselhaften
deutsch-sowjetischen/russischen Verhältnisses
Bd. 3, 1999, 360 S., 30,90 €, br., ISBN 3-8258-3665-7

Margarete Wiest
Russlands schwacher Föderalismus und
Parlamentarismus
Der Föderationsrat
Seit Dezember 1993 existiert in Russland eine
Zweite Kammer, die die 89 Regionen vertritt:
der Föderationsrat. Er steht vor besonderen
Herausforderungen. Vor dem Hintergrund eines
schwachen Föderalismus und Parlamentarismus
muss er sich gegen eine übermächtige Exekuti-
ve und eine feindselige Staatsduma behaupten.
Erschwerend kommt hinzu, dass sein Rekrutie-
rungsmodus bereits zwei Mal geändert wurde.
Bildete der Föderationsrat dennoch eine eigen-
ständige „Kammer der Regionen"? Wer waren
bzw. sind die Senatoren? Wie wirkten sich die
Neuformierungen aus? Und welchen Beitrag
leistete er zur demokratischen Entwicklung
Russlands? Diese wechselvolle Geschichte zu
analysieren, ist Ziel der Arbeit.
Bd. 4, 2003, 384 S., 30,90 €, br., ISBN 3-8258-6595-9

Studien zu Konflikt und Kooperation
im Osten
herausgegeben von Egbert Jahn

Astrid Sahm
Die weißrussische Nationalbewegung nach
der Katastrophe von Tschernobyl
(1986 – 1991)
Bd. 1, 1993, 168 S., 19,90 €, br., ISBN 3-89473-831-6

Manfred Sapper
Die Auswirkungen des Afghanistan-
Krieges auf die Sowjetgesellschaft
Eine Studie zum Legitimitätsverlust des
Militärischen in der Perestrojka
Bd. 2, 1994, 479 S., 30,90 €, br., ISBN 3-8258-2053-x

Heribert Seubert
Zum Legitimitätsverfall des militarisierten
Sozialismus in der DDR
Bd. 3, 1995, 352 S., 30,90 €, br., ISBN 3-8258-2325-3

Ninel Danos
Wirtschaft und Verteidigung:
Bestandsaufnahme des Umbruchs in
Osteuropa
Bd. 4, 1995, 152 S., 24,90 €, br., ISBN 3-8258-2037-8

Frank Wilhelmy
Der Zerfall der SED-Herrschaft
Zur Erosion des marxistisch-leninistischen
Legitimitätsanspruches in der DDR
Bd. 5, 1995, 350 S., 30,90 €, br., ISBN 3-8258-2456-X

Egbert Jahn
Friedensforschung in und nach dem Ost-
West-Konflikt
Aufsätze aus zwanzig Jahren (In russischer
Sprache)
Bd. 6, 1997, 352 S., 24,90 €, br., ISBN 3-8258-3042-x

Astrid Sahm
Transformation im Schatten von
Tschernobyl
Umwelt- und Energiepolitik im
gesellschaftlichen Wandel von Belarus und
der Ukraine
Bd. 7, 2000, 472 S., 24,90 €, br., ISBN 3-8258-4549 4

Claudia Wagner
Rußlands Kriege in Tschetschenien
Politische Transformation und militärische
Gewalt
Bd. 8, 2000, 224 S., 20,90 €, br., ISBN 3-8258-4670-9

Volker Weichsel
Westintegration und Rußlandpolitik der
Tschechischen Republik
Bd. 9, 2000, 136 S., 17,90 €, br., ISBN 3-8258-4833-7

Bernd Rosenbusch
Die Bedeutung inner- und
zwischenstaatlicher Konflikte für
die Kooperation und Integration der
ASEAN-Staaten
Bd. 10, 2003, 296 S., 24,90 €, br., ISBN 3-8258-6583-5

LIT Verlag Münster – Hamburg – Berlin – Wien – London
Grevener Str./Fresnostr. 2 48159 Münster
Tel.: 0251 – 23 50 91 – Fax: 0251 – 23 19 72
e-Mail: vertrieb@lit-verlag.de – http://www.lit-verlag.de